Primary Understanding

Critical Social Thought

Series editor: Michael W. Apple
Professor of Curriculum and Instruction and of Educational Policy
Studies, University of Wisconsin-Madison

Already published

Primary Understanding

Education in Early Childhood
KIERAN EGAN

Routledge
New York   London

Paperback published in 1991 by
Routledge
an imprint of Routledge, Chapman & Hall, Inc.
29 West 35th Street
New York NY 10001

Published in Great Britain by
Routledge
11 New Fetter Lane
London EC4P 4EE

© *Kieran Egan 1988*

Published in 1988

Printed in the United States of America

Library of Congress Cataloguing in Publication Data

Egan, Kieran.
  Primary understanding.

  (Critical social thought)
  Bibliography: p.
  Includes index
  1. Early childhood education. I. Title.
LB1117.E38 1988   372'.21   88–4368
ISBN 0–415–90003–4   0-415-90339-4 (pb)

British Library CIP also available

To
David William Egan
with love

Contents

Series editor's introduction

In his analysis of the political and educational dilemmas we face in deciding what we should teach, Fred Inglis wisely notes that the school curriculum has a significance that extends well beyond itself. The curriculum "is no less than the knowledge system of a society." It contains "not only the ontology, but also the metaphysics and ideology which that society has agreed to recognize as legitimate and truthful. . . . [It] is the reference point and acknowledged definition of what knowledge, culture, belief, morality, really *are*."[1] Our ideas about education, then, tell us an immense amount about ourselves. They are statements about our values, about the kind of society we live in, about truth, justice, equality, and human caring. As such, these ideas are by their very nature political and ethical, and intensely valuative.

Thus, any attempt to portray education as a technical enterprise in which we are only concerned with how to get children to efficiently learn *x* is doomed to failure. It founders on the kinds of questions that naturally arise when one recognizes the power of Inglis's points. Whose knowledge is legitimate? What and whose values should guide its selection?[2] What should education be for? The fact that we ignore these kinds of questions at our own risk is made even clearer when we place them within the shifts that are now occurring in educational policy in a number of Western nations.

We are currently living in a time when what education is *for* is being reconstructed. The idea that education is for children, both for exploration and criticism of accepted wisdom and values, and for understanding the entire range of knowledge and struggles that has characterized the human condition is rapidly disappearing. In its place is a view of education as part of a strategy of economic development, of national and international competition, and of socialization into the beliefs of a limited segment of the population. As curricula and teaching methods become more and more standardized and rationalized, and as decisionmaking in education becomes increasingly driven by an accountant's profit and loss sheet, we are in danger of losing our wider visions of what education can and should be.

These bureaucratic tendencies have had a number of important results besides the withering of our vision. As I have argued elsewhere, they have led to the deskilling of teachers and have redefined important knowledge and values in a strikingly conservative way.[3] They have also led to a situation in which both teachers and students are finding it increasingly difficult to have their voices, their meanings and needs, become significant in classroom life. Thus, for instance, it is now official policy in some school districts in the United States that no teacher may deviate from the approved textbook. Anything that goes beyond such already approved material is simply illegitimate and is a "waste of time". Obviously, there will be teachers whose classrooms are alive with creative activity and who reject the reduction of education to being simply an element of reindustrialization. Yet current conditions in a number of countries are making it that much more difficult for educators at all levels to retain and expand a more substantive set of educational visions and practices.

This can be especially problematic in early childhood education, in that time period when children have their first experience of schooling. In many ways, the current processes of deskilling and standardization are robbing children of any organic sense of the relationship between curricula and their own cultural pasts and presents. As Kieran Egan puts it, the curriculum becomes trivial "when it should be intellectually at its richest." This trivialization is exactly what Egan sets out to counter. He wants to provide us with an alternative reading of what education can and should be like. The current volume is the first of a series of books in which the author plans to elaborate an education that "recapitulates" a sequence of four forms of knowing—Mythic, Romantic, Philosophic, and Ironic. Each form builds on the others and the totality enables us to prevent the reduction of education to the trivial.

Many others have raised objections to the dominant ways education is carried out in classrooms. Such criticism is essential. Yet few have linked these criticisms to the development of coherent alternatives. This sets *Primary Understanding* apart from most other literature for it articulates a vision of difference and provides a model of curriculum organization and teaching to put those ideas into practice.

The vision of education that lies behind *Primary Understanding* is not simply one of maximizing gains, which in the current social context all too often merely means getting children to compete over achievement test scores. It also stresses a process of schooling that minimizes losses. It seeks to preserve the poetic and imaginative in our children in a time when so many forces seem to conspire to purge them from our collective memory.

In Egan's argument: "The foundations of education are poetic. We begin as poets." Any education of young children that does not recognize this is, for Egan, less insightful than it should be. Given the utter import of "poetic understanding," and given the significance of fantasy in children's lives, we must develop educational theories and practices that not only encourage fantasy but are based directly on its principles and devoted to its exploration.[4] As he puts it:

> The neglect of children's fantasy in writings and research in education during this century has meant the exclusion of an influence on curriculum and learning that . . . has led to impoverishment and imbalance in schooling. . . . Children's fantasy raises some considerable challenges to the principles on which typical early childhood curriculum is based. Those presently dominant principles seem to exclude much content that might well be included to enrich children's early years of schooling; they tend overall towards the prosaic and dull and exclude much intellectual excitement, and they fail to appreciate that fantasy is not an opposite of rationality but reflects the element that gives rationality life and energy.

The author recognizes that all subjects tell stories, These are narratives about the human condition. Yet because they are narratives, they can be constantly reinterpreted. They might have ended differently. "The human mind in virtue of possessing an imagination can experiment with different endings."[5] Egan's own focus on stories, on the free yet still disciplined reign of imagination, fantasy, and myth and their importance in providing alternate readings of one's cultural past and present illuminates the intricate connections between the stories our subjects tell and the sense of possibility our children see. Just as importantly, these stories enable a connectedness between children and the past that is much richer than what is currently available in school settings. Such a sense of connectedness is absolutely essential in a society in which our ideas of continuity and community are withering. For people to care about "the common goods,"[6] it is just this sense of the collective nature of our stories that is needed.

In elaborating his model, the author is sensitive to the ideological issues that might be raised concerning his proposal. His concrete suggestions document this, for example, his argument that one should organize young children's initial study of history around the telling of the dramatic stories of human struggles against oppression. He enables us to ask the question of whose stories should be told in new and interesting ways.

In its development of a new theory of primary education, *Primary Understanding* also challenges our taken-for-granted perspectives on a number of educational issues. Egan argues expressly against the dominance of psychology in education, claiming that it cannot provide a thorough understanding of children's lives and cannot fully give us the principles under which educational activity can or should go on. In the process, he raises important questions not only about the accepted models of psychological research in education, but about figures who have offered alternatives, such as Dewey and Piaget. This is coupled with impressive criticisms of our accepted notions of literacy as well.

Some readers will recognize the influence of Vygotsky on the conceptual underpinnings of parts of this work. Yet it also shows its debt to Ong and others who have demonstrated the utter importance of language and tradition in constructing our social reality. This synthetic quality is another of the reasons many readers will find Egan's position so attractive. The breadth of its scope, its challenge to widely accepted educational theories and practices, the central place it gives to the poetic, and the provocative nature of its claims all combine to make *Primary Understanding* a significant contribution to the debate over what education should be for.

Michael W. Apple
The University of Wisconsin, Madison

Acknowledgments

I have been working quite a long time on this book and a number of people have generously given time, patience, heroic charity, intelligence, and a range of other virtues in commenting on various drafts. Some people have read the whole of one or another draft, making many helpful suggestions that have led to greater clarity and to eradicating various errors or sillinesses. Richard Angelo (University of Kentucky), Robin Barrow (late of Leicester, now at Simon Fraser University), Barbara Cowell (University of Oxford), Dan Nadaner (Palo Alto), June Sturrock (Simon Fraser University), and John Wilson (University of Oxford), all have persuaded me to reconsider and revise sections of the book. Indeed, Robin Barrow has even read considerable chunks more than once, though they were changed so much after earlier criticisms that I think he assumed it was a different book. Some people have read parts of the ms and have been most kind in providing criticisms and suggestions. Dianne Common (University of Manitoba), Cedric Cullingford (Brighton Polytechnic), Cornel Hamm (Simon Fraser University), Carolyn Mamchur (Simon Fraser University), David Nyberg (State University of New York at Buffalo), Antoinette Oberg (University of Victoria), David Olson (Ontario Institute for Studies in Education), Walter Ong (St Louis University), Louis Rubin (University of Illinois), Jonas Soltis (Teachers College, Columbia University), Robert Walker (Simon Fraser University), and Meguido Zola (Simon Fraser University) have generously given valuable criticisms or advice. Carl Bereiter (Ontario Institute for Studies in Education) and Michael Scriven (University of Western Australia) kindly gave incisive criticism of related papers which enabled me to improve this ms considerably. Similarly

Acknowledgments

Suzanne de Castell (Simon Fraser University) has criticized some of this ms and related papers in a most constructive way. I have been particularly fortunate to have had critical comments from a number of teachers: Arlene Birch, Sandra Boulanger, Daphne Morris, Sandy Oldfield, and Marlene and John Palmer in British Columbia, Di Fleming in Melbourne, and Tim Watson in Worcester, England have each read a draft and made most useful suggestions. John Tryneski at University of Chicago Press was kind and supportive beyond the call of duty, and provided most helpful criticisms. Stratford Caldecott, of Routledge & Kegan Paul, has been perhaps even more so. I should also thank Jack Cresswell – I'm not sure for what, but I have this odd feeling that I should. Last and most I thank Susanna Egan. She has read and edited two drafts of the ms and made numerous valuable suggestions. The faults that remain in the ms, despite all this help, are – you guessed it – mine alone.

I have two other kinds of debt to acknowledge. During a part of the writing and revising I was the grateful recipient of a Social Sciences and Humanities Research Council of Canada Leave Fellowship and also of the Simon Fraser University Molson Research Prize. These made possible conditions that considerably facilitated my work. And, yet again, Eileen Mallory has "processed" the ms and revisions with supernatural accuracy and speed. For that, and the unfailing good cheer with which she works, I am most grateful.

I am grateful to Harvard University Press for permission to use the extensive quotation on pages 12, 13 from Vivian Paley's *Wally's Stories*. And also to the *Harvard Educational Review* for permission to reprint parts of Chapter Two, which appeared as "Literacy and the oral foundations of education" in the November 1987 issue, and to Polly Steele for her suggestions and editing of that article.

Kieran Egan
Walnut Tree House
Oxford
1987

Introduction

"The beginning, as you know, is always the most important part" (Plato, *Republic*, II.377 (Cornford, 1941, p. 68)). Only if we get the first steps right, Plato argued, can we set the child on the proper path to educated adulthood. In order to succeed we must know clearly, to use his terms, the direction in which the eyes of the soul must be turned. So the beginning, and each step of the journey, is governed by our understanding of the proper aim of education.

"Leave childhood to ripen in your children" (Rousseau, 1911, p. 58). Rousseau, in *Émile* (1762), complemented Plato's conception of education as an intellectual journey towards clarity of vision, accumulated knowledge, and civic responsibility, by arguing that each of the stages on the journey had a quality of its own that merited attention in its own right. Childhood and adolescence are not merely imperfect forms of adulthood, they have their own perfections, and a proper education must attend to their cultivation.

These arguments for the importance of the end as the determiner of the beginning of the educational process in childhood, and for the importance of the distinctive quality of childhood in its own right, have not come easily together. Often enough they have been seen less as complementary insights than as incompatible. Plato's and Rousseau's arguments have so profoundly influenced Western thinking about education that they have provided the terms, perhaps also the polarities, of the major educational debates of this century. The trouble is that it *is* difficult to think of primary education as fulfilling children's potentials according to natural predispositions and at the same time as the accumulation of knowledge from a starting point of ignorance. In the one case our eyes are on nature to guide us in designing our curriculum ("Fix your eyes on nature, follow the path traced by her," Rousseau tells us in *Émile* (Rousseau, 1911, p. 14)), in the other they are fixed on an ideal end of accumulated knowledge and social and vocational skills to be transmitted to the child.

This polarization results, of course, from something of a caricature of Plato's and Rousseau's positions. It suppresses Plato's sensitivity to developmental stages and Rousseau's aim to make a conventional eighteenth-century cultured gentleman out of Émile (and perhaps the less said these days about his ideal for Sophie the better). It does, however, bring vividly to the fore a genuine difference of focus and emphasis that has been at the heart of educational conflicts – theoretical and practical – throughout this century. Each of their conceptions of education embodies an important general insight, with neither of which we can sensibly dispense. An aim of educational theory during this century has been to provide a coherent conception of education that gives due weight to each. The need for this has proven easier to identify than to satisfy, however. The attempts to bring the two together have been somewhat hindered by the louder part of the educational debate being taken over by proponents of the greater value of one insight over the other. So we have had "traditionalists" vs. "progressivists," "child centered" vs. "subject-centered," "experience" vs. "basic skills," and so on.

One value of these debates has been to expose the inadequacy of each insight by itself. On the one hand, the very metaphor of early education as the first stage on a journey has been shown to be misleading. Childhood is not something we leave behind. The achievements and experiences of childhood are *constituents* of our later selves – "the child is father to the man," in Wordsworth's compact phrase. "Progessivists" have established the importance of not sacrificing the distinctive qualities of childhood experience to the insistent shaping required to fit children to a given culture, society, and economy. Beyond these, beneath these, we must recognize that we have a nature to whose patterns of development, learning, motivation, and so on, our educational practices must accommodate. On the other hand, "traditionalists" have made clear that nature gives us no particular guidance. We have infinite, indeterminate potentials, and we need to describe precise ends which will provide criteria to guide our choices of which potentials to stimulate and develop. Our fulfilment comes precisely through our initiation into a particular culture and our fitting into a particular society and its economy: our nature is cultural.

Throughout this century we have seen a somewhat unsteady veering in the educational systems of the Western democracies from valuing the Platonic insight more highly to valuing the Rousseauian more highly. In times of relative peace, prosperity, and confidence there has tended to be more readiness to implement "child-centered," progressive ideas and to stimulate development of the imagination and of individual differences. In times of relative insecurity and economic depression "basic skills," "the 3-Rs," and uniform achievement of academic mastery tend to be preferred. At least, this is the broad historical generalization one sees commonly accepted, and it certainly seems to fit some of our recent educational experience.

Also during this century we have seen quite a number of attempts to articulate conceptions of education that do not give up on "high culture" and social utility or on the distinctive experience of childhood. And here is another. The challenge is not simply to recognize that, say, nature, culture, and society each makes claims on the educational process and that we need to balance them or ensure they interact harmoniously. That leads to flaccid compromises. Dewey put the challenge more clearly:

> It is the business of an intelligent theory of education to
> ascertain the causes for the conflicts that exist and then,
> instead of taking one side or the other, to indicate a plan
> of operations proceeding from a level deeper and more
> inclusive than is represented by the practices and ideas of the
> contending parties. (Dewey, 1963, p. 5)

The task, then, is to see the educational process in such a way that the Platonic and Rousseauian insights are no longer distinct but are fused. Any conception of education that succeeds in this will necessarily look a bit odd in the currently dominant traditions of educational thinking. So I will not apologize for the oddity of some of the categories I will be using in this attempt. I should also warn you now that this book does not contain the whole story. That runs beyond this volume, through three others that I will mention briefly below. What this volume does contain, though, is the working out of this conception in terms of children's learning, a new curriculum, and principles for teaching during the primary school years. This book, then, is designed to be complete in itself for those who are interested in a somewhat new approach to primary education – one that tries to integrate Plato's and Rousseau's major insights – while also serving as the first part of a more comprehensive discussion of the educational process through adulthood.

This book begins with children's fantasy. This prominent feature of children's mental lives has been somewhat neglected in the dominant educational research traditions. Fantasy, after all, is difficult stuff to get any firm grasp on and, so, difficult to do research on. Anyone who has spent much time with young children, however, knows that fantasy is a prominent part of their mental lives. This does not mean, of course, that they cannot tell the difference between their pretend worlds and reality, though it seems fair to say that the line separating one from the other is not always clear or does not particularly interest them for much of the time. Some aspects of fantasy may be due simply to children not having grasped the conditions of reality that exclude the possibility of Jack Frost and Santa Claus but include IBM executives and desk-bound admirals. But there is also a generative aspect to fantasy that seems constantly to transfigure the everyday business of their lives. It seems commonly to be one of the more energetic aspects of young children's thinking.

Fantasy, then, will be a beginning point for my sketch of primary understanding. In Chapter One I will discuss its neglect in theory and research, though not in the practice of good teachers. I will try to show that we can infer a number of things of educational importance from young children's fantasy and from the ways children move from fantasy to more realistic ways of thinking. This is not exactly a case of taking the stone discarded by the builders and making it the cornerstone of a new edifice – but there is something of that to it. Fantasy, I will argue, is not properly something we leave behind in developing more rational forms of thinking; features of fantasy, I will try to show, must become constituents of a rich rationality.

The second chapter will continue to focus on children's intellectual lives and on some of the more evident things they use to think with. I will explore some of the educational implications of the fact that young children early inhabit an oral culture. The things they have to think with do not include some of the things writing makes possible. I will cautiously consider similarities between some forms of thinking evident in adult oral cultures and in children's thinking. Among the typical strategies people use to make sense of the world and experience in oral cultures are some which, I will argue, have important uses in education.

A theme I will bring forward in this chapter, and one that will recur throughout this essay, and one that seems to me much neglected in educational writing generally, is the losses that seem inevitably a part of educating. The usual conceptions of education see it, or define it, as a straightforward progressive process; it is a process of pure gain; it is "hierarchical integrative," encompassing and adding to its previous stages; it is a gradual accumulation of worthwhile knowledge and skill. The danger of accepting such a view is that we can become insensitive to the losses that seem to be tied to each gain. Literacy – an example I will discuss in some detail in Chapter Two – is normally considered a pure gain; two parts of the foundational 3-Rs of education. Becoming literate, however, tends to undermine certain valuable cognitive and affective capacities that are commonly well-developed in oral cultures and which are evident in young children's fantasy and imaginative activities. Education, I will argue, is properly a process of important gains certainly, but also, and perhaps inevitably, a process of losses sacrificed for those gains. In the conception of education to be developed here, at least, education will be seen not simply as maximizing gains but, equally importantly, as minimizing losses. To minimize them, one first has to be aware of them, and I will try to sketch in Chapter Two some of the losses that come with literacy. In case this seems like excessively refined and idle theorizing I should perhaps add, and will try to show in the later chapters, that a clear sense of the losses that come with, say, literacy enables one to teach literacy more effectively and more richly, minimizing cognitive and affective losses. Children, after all, do not move simply from an oral to a literate culture, but rather from an oral to a literate-and-oral culture.

In Chapter Three I will focus on the story form. There is, of course, much educational writing about stories and research on children's comprehension using stories, but there is less about why stories work so powerfully to engage children's interest and even less about how the *formal* characteristics of stories can be used in teaching any kind of curriculum content, and about their implications for the early childhood curriculum as a whole.

Stories are among the few cultural universals: everyone everywhere, as far as we know, has used and been engaged by stories. Why? What are stories? Why do they work? What do they do for us? Analysis of story plots in general, and of those which most engage young children in particular, provides us with some new ways of thinking about an aspect of young children's learning, and provides us with some new principles for selecting and organizing curriculum content that will engage children's interest and encourage their exploration of their world and their experience. In this chapter I will argue for a much wider appreciation of the story form as fundamental to our thinking – a conclusion increasingly supported by psychological research – and as meriting much greater prominence in educational thinking and practice.

In Chapter Four I will discuss a number of more detailed features of children's understanding, rounding out the characterization I have been trying to build through the previous three chapters.

Rather than move on directly to discussing the curriculum and teaching, I will pause for a chapter and reflect on – to use a rather grand term for it – my methodology. Chapter Five will be given over to defending the soundness of the approach so far, showing the firmness of its empirical base, and clarifying how it begins to bring together the Platonic and Rousseauian insights. The overall approach is a new kind of recapitulation scheme, which I will introduce briefly below.

In Chapter Six I will outline an early childhood curriculum which embodies the principles developed in the earlier chapters. It looks somewhat unlike the curricula we are familiar with in the dominant traditions of education, but it makes, I think, more educational sense. Many educationalists have tended increasingly to see the curriculum as sets of more or less discrete objectives to be attained sequentially. There have been some important technical advances made in this movement for the organization and control of the content and practice of teaching. A significant part of my argument in this chapter will be towards reemphasizing some organic aspects of the curriculum that have tended to be neglected. I will represent the curriculum also as a set of great stories to be told, not simply as objectives to be attained. In Chapter Seven I will discuss further the implications of the principles developed in the earlier chapters for methods of teaching and for the planning and design of lessons and units of study. Analogously to the theme of the previous chapter, I will represent an important part of the teacher's role as the principal story-teller of our culture. The stories the teacher tells are not simply fictional; they are also the great true stories of our history, science, mathematics, and so on.

This, then, is the first of four volumes that describe a program for educating people from about the age of four or five to maturity. Each volume deals with how people at particular ages can best make sense of the world and of experience, what things are educationally most valuable to learn, and how one can most meaningfully and engagingly teach those things at the appropriate ages. Each volume can be read separately as an essay on the practice of education during the particular age range it deals with, and the set can be read as an attempt to articulate a new and coherent conception of education and of the individual's development to educated maturity.

The conception of education I will elaborate in these volumes might best be seen as layered. I will describe the educational program as made up from four somewhat distinct layers, in each of which we develop a somewhat distinct form of understanding. The educational program prescribes how these forms of understanding can be acquired sequentially during an individual's formative years, yielding in their coalescence a modern educated consciousness.

In the first part of each volume I will characterize the particular form of understanding. In this volume I will characterize the primary form, which I will call Mythic understanding, and I will try to show that this constituent of mature understanding is most readily accessible during our early years. In the second volume I will similarly deal with Romantic understanding, in the third with Philosophic understanding, and in the final volume with that mature coalescence of the previous forms which I am calling Ironic understanding.

Choosing labels is often a risky business. I hope you will accept these simply as attempts to suggest some central feature of each constituent layer of the educational process, allowing the characterizations of the layers to give meaning to the labels, rather than allowing other associations of the labels to color their meanings.

Having chosen to call this overall scheme recapitulationist, I should perhaps take a few introductory paragraphs explaining what might seem the perverse move of associating this essay with one of the few traditions in the history of educational inquiry that is generally assumed to have been convincingly undermined and repudiated. Even so, this essay outlines a recapitulation scheme; it argues that the individual's path to a modern educated consciousness follows in some significant ways the path of our culture's forging of that consciousness.

The plausibility of nineteenth- and early twentieth-century recapitulation schemes rested on the superficial similarities between the ways we can generally describe the historical development of a culture and individuals' initiation into that culture during their youth. The individual in becoming educated follows a path – recapitulates a process – which the culture itself forged. In a trivial sense, of course, all educational programs are recapitulationist. The term serves to distinguish a particular tradition when the historical description of the culture's development becomes a significant guide to the structuring of the curriculum.

The movement to develop distinctive recapitulationist curricula began in the latter part of the nineteenth century, as another expression of the immense influence of evolutionary theory. The movement, which had been prominent mainly in Germany and the USA, though influential throughout the Western world, collapsed as a result of a number of problems. The initial formulations of recapitulation theory in education referred for support to the "ontogeny-recapitulates-phylogeny" doctrines of mid-century biology. The undermining of the simplistic version of that doctrine in biology was one blow to recapitulation schemes in education (Gould, 1977). They also tied themselves into a somewhat primitive developmental psychology, expounded in North America by G. S. Hall among others, and as the foundations of that recapitulationist psychology came into disrepute so educational schemes based on it lost favor. Perhaps most important in their demise was their fundamental conflict with progressivism in North America and the modern education movement in Great Britain and Europe. The commonest form of recapitulation curriculum was the "culture-epoch" type. In this, children began by studying the primitive periods of human history and development, because children were taken to be psychological savages themselves. In such curricula the modern world did not appear until the end of schooling. A basic tenet of progressivism and modern education was that children must begin their exploration of the world with what is at hand and around them. By the mid-1920s the tide of progressivism and modernism had swept recapitulationist curricula away.

The recapitulationist dimension of my program will be developed through the first three volumes. It will be discussed in Chapter Five of this volume and more fully in Volume 4. It differs from the recapitulationist schemes that were common at the beginning of this century in a number of ways. I make no attempt here to base the program on biology or psychology, though my argument does have a psychological dimension. It is different perhaps most significantly in what it claims is recapitulated. "Culture-epoch" theorists were imprisoned in the assumption that it was the knowledge or content of cultural history that had to be recapitulated through the curriculum. What is recapitulated, I will argue, are the forms of understanding.

The analysis of modern educated consciousness that undergirds this essay concludes that it is composed of four major, somewhat distinct, constituents. These were developed historically in the making of modern consciousness, in a complex but roughly distinguishable sequence. Mythic, Romantic, Philosophic, and Ironic layers of modern consciousness may seem odd categories for characterizing an educational program. Certainly we are familiar with more technical sounding terms. But I will argue that education can be better grasped in terms of such forms of understanding. The Romantic capacity to feel wonder at the particularity of the world, or the Philosophic capacity to search for general patterns or recurrence in phenomena, and the extensive set of such sense-making capacities that I will outline in these volumes, seem to me the kind of terms from which we can construct a clear and coherent conception of the process of education. Any four-layer model, of course, must be simplistic and too schematic to catch the complexity of education adequately, but it can perhaps provide a general map and sense of direction.

Perhaps a note of elaboration of this point is worth a further paragraph. In the early chapters of this book our subject is in small part cultural history – features of mythic thinking and the development of rationality – and in larger part children's intellectual lives. The forms and contents of thinking, the nature of ideas, are more complex than any language we have developed to refer to them. Ideas are protean things, sliding and changing constantly. The ways we normally refer to them are a little like the clear primary-colored diagrams one sees in expensive biology texts, indicating the distinct elements of an organism. The neat pictures are so unlike the largely monochrome mess we encounter on first seeing the organism under a microscope. But the neat clear diagram helps the eye to discriminate the discriminable parts of the real thing. So too, though much less reliably, the ways we represent ideas and children's thinking are terribly crude simplifications that strive after the shifting shapes of mental life. The theories and models we compose to represent some features of this immense complexity need to be seen as like the crudest of diagrams. There is evidence occasionally in education that some tentative finding from research or some hesitant theory is taken as the whole truth about large areas of children's thinking, so this *caveat* is worth making here, and is intended to be borne in mind while reading what follows here as much as anywhere else. No doubt this is not a warning you need, but it serves the defensive purpose of clarifying a little my sense of what this scheme can offer.

My aim, then, is to describe as well as I can an ideal of education and a program for realizing it. This essay prescribes practical steps for educating children within the normal contexts of schools and homes in modern Western societies, and it is coherent with what is logically and psychologically the case. The analysis of each layer of understanding yields principles from which I will compose a new curriculum and describe ways of planning teaching that will lead to more meaningful and engaging learning.

1

Some Educational Implications of Children's Fantasy

Introduction

In some senses fantasy seems the opposite of rationality and, as education is preeminently the process in which rationality is prized and developed, children's fantasy has usually been neglected as having no educational value or interest. When it is noticed, it is often considered an enemy of education. Rationality and reality are closely entwined in our mental lexicon: rationality is the tool we use to discover reality. Education is the process in which we use rationality to show and discover what is real and true, and so fantasy, which ignores the boundaries of reality, is seen as the enemy which slips out of the constructive constraints of reason and runs mentally amok in unreal and impossible worlds. Fantasy asserts the impossible, the unverifiable, the unfalsifiable; it is casually hospitable to contradiction, irrelevance, and inconsistency. In rational activity the mind is awake, about constructive work, in accord with reality, attuned to the logics whereby things operate; in fantasy there is mind-wandering, illogic, dream-like indulgence of the flittering shapes of the idle mind, disregard of hard empirical reality.

This, anyway, is how fantasy is sometimes represented as at odds with constructive rational thought. And certainly these characteristics of fantasy are common elements of young children's talk. What was once so often dismissed as the mindless babble of children, or considered quaintly charming, has increasingly of late been recorded and carefully transcribed. We can see fantastic elements constantly transform discussions that adults might like to shape otherwise:

Wally: I know all about Jonas. He got swallowed by the whale.

Fred: How?

Wally: God sent him. But the whale was asleep so he just walked out.

Fred: How did he fly up to God? I mean how did he get back to shore if it was so deep?

Wally: He didn't come from the sky. But he could have because there's an ocean in the sky. For the rain to come down.

Fred: Oh yeah. That's for the gods. When they go deep they never drown, do they?

Wally: Of course not. They're just going nearer to Earth.

Jill: How does the ocean stay up?

Fred: They patch it up. They –

Wally: They take a big, big, big bag and put it around the ocean.

Eddie: Which reminds me. Do you know how many Christmas trees God gets? Infinity.

Teacher: Who gives Him Christmas trees?

Eddie: He makes them.

Wally: When people burn them. . . . You see he's invisible. He takes up the burned parts and puts them together.

Rose: Are there decorations?

Wally: Invisible decorations. He can see them because He's invisible. If you tell Him there's an invisible person here, He believes it.

Eddie: You can't fool God.

Wally: Sure you can. It's a good trick. You can say, "I'm here," and you're really not, but He can't see you. He can only see invisible things. You can fool Him.

Eddie   But He hears you.

Wally: Right. He hears you talk. He talks, too. But you have to ask Him. He talks very soft. I heard Him.

Eddie: You know, 353 years ago everyone could see God. He wasn't invisible then. He was young so He could stay down on Earth. He's so old now He floats up in the sky. He lived in Uganda and Egypt.

Fred: That's good, because everyone in Egypt keeps. They turn into mummies.

(This is taken, with thanks, from Vivian Paley's *Wally's Stories*, pp. 30, 31. In that book she shows what can result from sensitively encouraging children's fantasy rather than trying constantly to correct it or suppress it in favour of more logically acceptable forms of thought.)

Anyone who has spent much time with children knows that a prominent part of their mental life is fantasy, and that much of this fantasy is playful, energetic, and, one cannot help but feel, an important and wholesome activity. But this is not, of course, how it has always been viewed. We have inherited the idea that fantasy and reason are in opposition. This comes most powerfully from the ancient Greeks. In Greek psychology, expressed in their myths, there is a clear contrast between Apollo, representing order, harmony, and reason, and Dionysus, representing frenzy, fantasy, and passion. Our inheritance of this ancient contrast has come through the Victorians, many of whom used their somewhat perverted view of ancient Greece as a social and educational model. In their image of ancient Greece they, unlike the Greeks, greatly emphasized Apollonian reason and creative order and depreciated the wild element contributed by Dionyian religion (Dodds, 1951; Jenkyns, 1981; Turner, 1981). The educational job of a civilized society, to the rational Victorians, was to teach the young to tame, control, or suppress fantasy and to order their lives on rational principles. So in the myths, the growth of civil order is reflected in Apollo's taming of Dionysus, suppressing the orgiastic and fantastic aspects of his cult, and leading him into the civilized sanctuary at Delphi.

Plato, who has so profoundly affected our ways of making sense of the world and experience, also saw reason and passion as opposed principles. The Plato who wrote poems and tragedies was in conflict internally with Plato the philosopher; and so "he struggled within himself and proclaimed one part of himself the enemy of the other. He knew his inner war had to end with the victory of reason and the grudging surrender of passion, the victory of philosophy over poetry" (Simon, 1978, p. 157). As reason must rule the appetites, the senses, and the will, so those with most reason must rule those with less. And so Plato wanted philosophers to be kings and wanted to banish poets from his reasonable and realistic Republic and, as we shall see below, wanted to exclude fantasy from the education of children.

This image of rationality and fantasy as conflicting opposites, then, is very ancient and profoundly ingrained in our common-sense psychology and in our language. ("Ignore him; he lives in a fantasy world.") It is only relatively recently that some people have tried to show that fantasy is not reasonless, and that those expressions of fantasy in dreams, myths, and "primitive mentality" also have their order and reason, and uses, if one only looks at them properly. Fantasy, dreams, and myths also have their logics, but the matrix of their logic has to be sought, to use another old metaphor, in the heart as well as in the head.

This newer image of fantasy is akin to the product of what Lévi-Strauss calls in his pun-laden way *La Pensée Sauvage.* The leaden English translation, *The Savage Mind,* misses the French associations of *sauvage* with freedom, unbridled playfulness, the touch of Dionysus. *Pensée* also carries the punning associated of "thought" and "pansies" and so the echo of Ophelia's mind-wandering "and here is pansies, that's for thoughts." Children's fantastic narratives, the stories that most engage children, have this quality of freedom, this mind-wandering lack of apparent logic.

One of the major contributors to our developing image of fantasy as something other than an opposite of reason is Freud. He has taught us, though we may sensibly dispute much of the framework in which he has embodied his insights, that our fantasy is not mad and reasonless, but has its logic. In his distinction between primary and secondary processes he echoes an older distinction between *mythoi* and *logoi*; the latter in each case representing the reality principle which seeks to overcome the undiscriminating preference for constructing mental worlds that conform with our desires. One of Freud's disciples, Bruno Bettelheim, has recently argued with some force and ingenuity that fantasy not only has its enchanting uses but also, especially as it is embodied in folk-tales, provides a vital educational and psychological benefit to children. I will consider some of his arguments below.

My purpose here, however, is not to praise children's fantasy, nor, obviously, to bury it, and there seems to survive an equally regrettable tendency in some to sentimentalize it and try to preserve it in children and even offer it as a model for adult thought. Nor do I want to seem to be suggesting that the kinds of fantasy stories and characters common in Western middle-class children's literature and talk are *natural* engagements for the young mind. I have little knowledge of how widespread such thinking is in other times and places. As Bettelheim notes, however: "Through most of man's history, a child's intellectual life, apart from immediate experiences within the family, depended on mythical and religious stories and on fairy tales. This traditional literature fed the child's imagination and stimulated his fantasizing" (Bettelheim, 1976, p. 24). Emphasis may usefully be put on "stimulated" here. For whatever reasons – natural, cultural, developmental, some mix – it seems clear that a diet of fantasy stories either generates or gives form to, or some mix, pullulating intellectual activity in young children. My initial purpose is to explore what may be inferred from the form and content of this fantastic activity for education. And while we may not establish anything firmly to begin with, this slightly odd perspective will enable us to see a number of important educational issues in a new light; it will allow us to approach them from the side, as it were, and it will perhaps enable us to see ways past some long-standing educational *impasses*.

The Neglect of Fantasy

It seems worthwhile to begin this brief inquiry by considering why something so obvious in children's intellectual lives, and in all our experience, should have been so neglected or depreciated in educational literature. That it has been seen as an opposite of rationality is obviously a large part of the answer, but it is worth looking at how some of the most influential educational thinkers have dealt with it. It is perhaps an overstatement to head this section the way I have, but not much of an overstatement, I think, given the prominence and persistence of fantasy in children's mental lives. There is a long tradition of hostility to, or irritation with, children's fantasy in works that have profoundly affected thinking about education.

Plato's arguments for barring from his state the makers of "phantoms far removed from reality" (*Republic*, X. 604) are at the beginning of this tradition. These "poor things by the standard of truth and reality" (*Republic*, X. 604) appeal to an inferior part of the soul and undermine reason. Whatever stories are available must be censored because even in stories "a high value must be set upon truthfulness" (*Republic*, II. 388) for their purpose is to express what we can discover of "how the truth is to be told about human life" (*Republic*, III. 392). Plato's concerns are moral and his reasons for these conclusions are too well known, if still matters of dispute, to need sketching here. But this great story-teller and myth-user nevertheless seems to want to exclude fantasy: "Mothers . . . are not to . . . scare young children with mischievous stories of spirits that go about by night in all sorts of outlandish shapes"

(*Republic*, II. 380) because such stories lead to "the presence of falsehood in the soul concerning reality" (*Republic*, II. 381) (Cornford, 1941).

In the Christian tradition the typical fantastic features of children's thinking received no greater attention and no higher valuation. We have to wait for Blake and Wordsworth before we hear again echoes of Christ's wonder at the distinctive qualities of childhood: "Suffer the little children to come unto me . . . for of such is the Kingdom of God." St Paul's message to the early Christians was to put off childish things as irrelevancies in face of the serious tasks of adulthood. The doctrine of original sin also discouraged attention to young children's "natural" expressions. Our nature is corrupt from the beginning and our natural condition is enmity with God and with our fellow man. The Church and its sacraments provided the means of restoring amity – charity – between oneself and God and between oneself and one's fellows (Bossy, 1985). St Augustine in *The Confessions* influentially represented childhood as a time of monstrous egotism, evil temper, violence, and the range of vices: "I am loth, indeed, to count it as part of the life I lead in this world" (St Augustine, 1944, p. 8). In the Christian view, which prevailed through many centuries, childhood was a time of unreason during which adults began the work of controlling the evils and weaknesses of human nature. Childhood was rarely and at best dimly perceived as exemplifying anything of distinctive value.

Childhood, as a subject of concerned attention, fared little better from the Enlightenment. The philosophic insight that concluded Descartes' search for a bedrock of knowledge was "I think, therefore, I am." Rational thought was what distinguished humanity, and rational thought emerged slowly through an arduous process of education. The fantasy of childhood was a confusing froth to be blown away from the infancy of mind in order that rationality can begin to be formed. "Only in its *promise* of humanity – that is, its potential of rationality, its eventual educability – was [childhood] in any way a subject worthy of interest, study, and attention" (Coe, 1984, p. 11).

The most powerful Romantic reaction to this view of childhood might have been expected to draw respectful attention to children's fantasy. But at the fountainhead of "progressive" educational ideas we find Rousseau quoting Plato with approval. Rousseau's most startling and influential idea for early childhood education is that the child "should be taught by experience alone" (Rousseau, 1911, p. 56). The ruin of young children is the

> apparent ease with which they learn . . . you fail to see that this very facility proves that they are not learning. Their shining, polished, brain reflects, as in a mirror, the things you show them, but nothing sinks in. The child remembers the words and the ideas are reflected back; his hearers understand them, but to him they are meaningless. (Rousseau, 1911, p. 71)

Early education, as it had been generally conceived by traditionalists, was merely "Words! Words! Words!" The aim for Rousseau is to keep the young child uninfected by knowledge, reading, and words, words, words. These only create confusion which cannot later be completely sorted out. Let the child experience nature and see how it runs. "His ideas, if indeed he has any ideas at all, have neither order nor connection; there is nothing sure, nothing certain, in his thoughts" (Rousseau, 1911, p. 70).

In this context Rousseau considers fairy-tales and fantasy generally as more words which will convey intellectual confusion and moral chaos. Like Plato he objects to fairy-tales, even the very best of them, on moral grounds. Because of their impressionability young children will indeed gather moral messages from fairy tales, but because of their simplicity and lack of experience they "will reverse the order and imitate the villain instead of taking warning from his dupes" (Rousseau, 1911, p. 80). And even worse:

> How can people be so blind as to call fables the child's system of morals, without considering that the child is not only amused by the apologue but misled by it? He is attracted by what is false and he misses the truth. . . . Men may be taught by fables; children require the naked truth. (Rousseau, 1911, p. 77).

Rousseau then takes his readers through La Fontaine's "The Fox and the Crow", showing line by line the confusions and perversions that it would induce in the child's mind. His point is that most of the tale is utterly meaningless, a part of it is totally confusing, and the remainder perverts the truth of nature which should be the child's sole mentor. ("So foxes talk, do they!")

It is hard to take Rousseau's alarmingly literal readings of La Fontaine seriously. Tied to this is our slowly developing understanding of children's thinking. Rousseau's opening observation – "We know nothing of childhood" (Rousseau, 1911, p. 1) – is one that would be even more of an exaggeration today than it was in his day. We do know some things, and they challenge Rousseau's premise about children's invincible ignorance or confusion.

I need hardly mention the immense influence of evolutionary ideas in education, and their support for a view of children's thinking as "primitive" and of interest only in providing methodological guidance for how most effectively to "civilize" it. I have already touched on the early evolutionary recapitulation schemes, and will return to that topic in Chapter Five.

Dewey's relationship to his self-appointed progressivist followers is a contentious one whose intricacies are not my concern here. But Dewey's sensitivity to children's thinking and his sophisticated social philosophy have certainly tended to be debased and perverted in substantial parts of the progressivist tradition. What I want to focus on here are some phrases of Dewey's that I will take out of context much as they have been taken out of context in progressivism at large. Progressivists' preoccupations with certain aspects of social initiation allowed them to color Dewey's words and use them in a more impoverished sense than Dewey intended. The net effect, however, has been that such sentiments of Dewey's as I shall quote below have also led to a depreciation of fantasy in progressivism. A fundamental principle of Dewey's educational thinking is expressed in his observation that "It is a cardinal precept of the newer school of education that the beginning of instruction shall be made with the experience learners already have," and that there should be "orderly development towards expansion and organization of subject matter through growth of experience" (Dewey, 1963, p. 74). "Experience," however, came to be seen in significant sections of progressivism largely in terms of the everyday practical world of children's lives. In addition,

Dewey's claim that "The knowledge which comes first to persons, and that remains mostly deeply ingrained, is knowledge of *how to do*; how to walk, talk, read, write, skate, ride a bicycle, and so on idefinitely" (Dewey, 1966, p. 184) has tended to focus progressivist attention on the mundane and practical world in which children live. What has been lost is the ability to see that world as the child sees it, transfigured by fantasy.

Most adults hardly notice the cracks in a sidewalk or between paving stones. For most children, however, such cracks are fraught with fantastic meaning. Watch a child negotiate his or her way along a pavement or sidewalk, occasionally skipping a beat to ensure that no crack is stepped on, or making sure that a crack touched by the left foot is balanced by one touched by the right. A part of the lore and language of school children that is rich and energetic, and largely hidden from adults, concerns such details of daily life. As the Opies note: "One of the inexplicables is the amount of lore which has become associated with flagstones, and apparently all children, when the fever is upon them, are punctilious about the way they walk along an ordinary pavement" (Opie and Opie, 1959, p. 240). I recall the common rhyme reported by the Opies:

> If you tread on a nick
> You'll marry a brick
> And a beetle will come to your wedding

Throughout North America we find just a few variants on the theme of

> Step on a crack
> You'll break your mother's back

(For anyone who doubts, or has forgotten, that children's fantasy transforms much of their dealings with their everyday environment, the Opies' *The Lore and Language of Schoolchildren* is a huge compilation of fascinating evidence. See also Knapp and Knapp (1976) and Sutton-Smith (1981).)

Despite his invaluable observations about the importance of children's present experience, Dewey's profound distrust of any form of thought not rooted in social experience and practical doing led him, too, to disapprove of "the tendency . . . of the imagination to run loose" (Dewey, 1966, p. 348). Thus he notes:

> Unfortunately, it is too customary to identify the imaginative with the imaginary, rather than with a warm and intimate taking in of the full scope of a situation. This leads to an exaggerated estimate of fairy-tales, myths, fanciful symbols, verse, and something labeled "Fine Art," as agencies for developing imagination and appreciation . . . The result is an unwholesome exaggeration of the "phantastic." (Dewey, 1966, p. 236).

Dewey's purpose here is not to depreciate imagination, of course, but rather to dissociate it from activities which are cut off from practical, socially meaningful action, and to inject it into *all* teaching and *all* areas of worthwhile activity. What has been picked up more prominently in the progressivist tradition is Dewey's occasional discounting of children's fantasy: "mind-wandering and wayward fancy are nothing but the unsuppressible imagination cut loose from concern with what is done" (Dewey, 1966, p. 236). Given this depreciation of fairy-tales, myths, and the "phantastic," and the constant focus on the practical and on the social experience of the child, one can see why the progressivists no less than the traditionalists they reacted against have seen children's fantasy merely as something to be suppressed or prevented by wholesome, realistic, and practical enterprises.

In Britain, Susan Isaacs, for yet different reasons, also depreciated the kind of thinking evident in fantasy. Indeed, she seems to see such fantasy as not really a result of thinking at all. It is a kind of chaotic fog from which real thought, sensibly ordered or structured, emerges:

> I consider it very important that we should not blur the distinction between thought and fantasy in our theories of intellectual growth. . . . The egocentrism of the little child is strictly an affair or feeling and fantasy, not of thought. He is egocentric insofar as he has not yet learned to think. . . . But the essential characteristic of egocentric ways of dealing with reality is surely that they *have* no structure. (Isaacs, 1930, p. 107).

I have sketched these ideas not as historical curiosities that have yielded to modern enlightenment, but because they are still in various combinations very much alive, influencing images of children's thinking, educational practice, and curricula. Bantock, for example, expresses his distaste for children's attraction to the "extraordinary." He disapproves of their wanting "to explore the pathological or the odd or the distant, the remote and the fantastic. . . . Why not try to explore and transmute the ordinary, the everyday?" (Bantock, 1981, p. 93). There is a powerful tradition of educational research that tends, very much in the Platonic and Christian manners, to consider children's interests as largely irrelevant to the task of education: "Their interests, too, at an early age tend to be sporadic and evanescent" (Hirst and Peters, 1970, p. 37); "The interests of children . . . will never, in many cases, produce the educational objectives we want. . . . But interests can be created, and it is surely a basic function of education to create interests in what is worthwhile" (Hirst, 1974, p. 17). This is all very well as far as it goes, but where it is pointed is away from children's interests, far away from their fantasy, and in the direction of inserting the kinds of academic "interests" some adults think children ought to have. These arguments are tied to a Platonic conception of education, in which the mind is formed by mastery of various "forms of knowledge." In this view young children clearly do not have much in the way of "mind," and as "mind" is what makes us distinctively human, this view leads to assertions such as "nobody is born a human being" (Oakeshott, 1971, p. 46). Children are "postulants to the human condition" and they achieve humanity, and mind, by being "initiated" into the "inheritance of human understandings" (Oakeshott, 1971, p. 46, 47). Before this deliberate initiation, "in the morning twilight of childhood, where there is nothing that, at a given moment, a clever child may be said exactly to know or not to know," there is only "inclination . . . casual encounters provoked by the contingencies of moods . . . fleeting wants and sudden enthusiasms tied to circumstances . . . current wants and 'interests' " (Oakeshott, 1971, pp. 47, 48).

Most empirical research programs into children's cognition and development have also tended to ignore children's fantasy – despite its prominence. Clearly, given the dominant methods of empirical research used in education, fantasy is difficult to deal with in any reliable way. Even the most imaginative program of research on children's development, which began with Piaget's observation of the importance of children's consistent errors on Binet's intelligence tests, initially focused almost exclusively on a narrow set of logico-mathematical operations. It is not to depreciate the significance of these operations in young children's thinking to note that this narrow focus did block out from view the wild energy of what might be its dominant mode. In the frequently delightful interviews with children which Piaget published in support of various of his claims, one finds children's "fantastic" answers dealt with rather sternly and the question posed again to insist on a realistic answer that exposes the appropriate developmental stage of logico-mathematical operations.

Gareth Matthews (1980) also points this out. He argues the limitations of Piaget's method, in which the "only valid criteria . . . are based on multiplicity of results and on the comparison of individual reactions" (Piaget, 1951, p. 7). This immediately rules out the *sauvage* responses of each child. Such responses are sternly to be disregarded as "mere romancing." Piaget adds: "One would like to be able to rule out romancing with the same severity as [those answers designed to please the questioner]" (Piaget, 1951, p. 10). Matthews's concerns are to show that Piaget, ironically, discourages philosophical puzzles in his pursuit of logico-mathematical developments, and to suggest that Piaget is one of those people who "are immune to philosophical puzzlement. For them there is, perhaps, much to learn about the world but nothing to puzzle over" (Matthews, 1980, p. 54). One might add that this early focus of Piaget's work discouraged other energetic and evident features of young children's thinking. Their romance and fantasy were considered merely contaminants to his attempt to chart the growth of what he calls intelligence. The child who cannot, on the one side, conserve liquid quantity may, on the other, lead a vivid intellectual life brimming with knights, dragons, witches, and star warriors. It would be needlessly bold to prejudge which is more important to future intellectual growth. (More recent work in the Piagetian tradition, I should add, has considerably enlarged the range of children's thinking that it deals with.)

Now this picture of universal hostility to children's fantasy is clearly overwrought. It is achieved by ignoring much, and taking a one-sided view of much else. But it is not entirely – dare I say – fanciful. The dual effects of seeing human distinctiveness in rationality and of the diffused notion of original sin have discouraged close attention to the characteristics of children's fantasy. That there may be something of permanent value in children's fantasy, something to be built on rather than displaced, is an idea which arrived in our tradition through poetry – Blake's and Wordsworth's in particular – but in a form which did not lead to any systematic educational theory. Rather it has served as an inspiration to particular educators but has had only small influence on the dominant traditions of theory and research. My aim is to incorporate it into the educational scheme to be elaborated here.

The image of unanimous depreciation of fantasy presented in this section will also, more accurately, appear in conflict with the real world of classrooms in which children's imaginative writing and reading are encouraged and rewarded. I do not want to suggest that I am attempting to rescue fantasy from total neglect. That would obviously be pretentious and silly. Many good teachers in schools around the world are encouraging children's fantasy, despite what the major educational theorists say, and regardless of the fact that educational researchers add very little. They do this because their common sense and experience tell them that such activities are intellectually stimulating in various ways. So I am not arguing that there is a unanimous *practical* neglect of fantasy.

One sensible job for the educational theorist is to analyse and refine common sense and experience, and to seek more general implications either from research findings or from common observations. Teachers who encourage fantasy activity tend not to pursue more general implications of what they observe and experience daily: they lack the time and physical resources to do so in most cases. The point of this section has been to argue that those who are the most influential theorists, who might have encouraged research and analysis of this kind on children's fantasy, have tended, for the various reasons given, to discourage it instead. What is new in what follows, then, is not the accepting attitude towards fantasy – this is quite common in schools, in homes, and also in courses on early childhood and children's literature in colleges and universities. Rather it is the more general pursuit of the implications of some common observations about children's fantasy for the curriculum and for teaching methods.

Well, this is going to be quite a long chapter, mainly somewhat theoretical, and it may seem distant from educational issues. I want to add a few observations about fantasy and make some connections between children's fantasy and mythic thinking, in order to begin sketching characteristics of mythic understanding. It might be useful to take a break here for a section and consider how attention to some very obvious features of children's fantasy enables us to reconsider some common beliefs that have enormous practical influence on early childhood education and the primary curriculum.

Abstract Concepts and Concrete Contents

Let us begin by considering two striking features of children's fantasy. First, the settings and characters tend to be exotic, distant, and unlike anything in children's everyday experience. Why should this be so? What is it about smurfs, witches, and dragons that is more intellectually engaging and apparently meaningful than the stuff of their daily experience? Children who have built a smurf village with blocks and played in it with little smurf figures all morning will break for lunch only with reluctance and after terrible threats. Second, the characters, and the narratives in which they interact, seem to be built on simply binary opposites. We see the unrelenting conflicts between the good and the bad, the big and the little, the brave and the cowardly, the oppressors and the oppressed; we see the embodiments of struggles between security and fear, love and hate; and underlying them all we see the basic rhythms of expectation and satisfaction, of hope and disappointment. The narrative seem to be made up from clothing the abstractions in endlessly varied contents and the characters in endlessly varied interactions and combinations.

It seems to follow from this that the claim in the previous paragraph that children find their fantasies more engaging than their everyday experience is at least in part false, because based on an improper distinction. Indeed, smurfs are not a part of their everyday reality, but the conflicts between good and bad, fear and security, big and little, are. So it seems fair to say that, when engaged by their fantasies, children are also in some sense dealing with the stuff of their daily experience. (A general point that I assume, and take to be now generally accepted, is the somewhat paradoxical one that fantasy is constantly reflecting on and reflected from reality. Often it perverts some feature of reality in order better to reflect on it or on other features of reality. "Fantasy is a literature of paradox. It is the discovery of the real within the unreal, the credible within the incredible, the believable within the unbelievable" (Egoff, 1981, p. 80).)

So dealing with children's fantasies, which in turn deal with good and bad, love and hate, fear and security, and so on, we are not dealing with intellectual froth, but with the early forms and early developments of the most profound and fundamental concepts that we use to make sense of the world and of experience.

If this might be conceded about the abstract substratum of children's fantasy, what can we say of the content? What of smurfs and talking bears and dragons? Is not that perhaps merely froth? In Chapter Four I will suggest a part of an answer which has implications for teaching. Here we might note that "a child's familiarity with such characters (as witches and fairies, Santa Claus and Cinderella) represents a widening view of the world, an extension of the boundaries away from the self toward an unknown horizon" (Applebee, 1978, p. 74). But we can note, also, underneath such fantastic characters the interplay of a conceptual world that can carry us towards some challenging conclusions about curriculum.

Clearly the content of narratives about Gargamel and smurfs, Luke Skywalker and Darth Vadar, the good fairy and the wicked giant is not within children's everyday experience. That is, they don't have to have seen a real smurf to understand what smurfs are. Indeed what makes them a part of fantasy is that there are no real smurfs. Yet equally clearly children have no problem inventing stories for such characters and they easily understand those which are written by adults who have a feeling for children's fantasy. What *is* within their experience, of course, is the set of abstract concepts on which the contents are articulated. It is because children understand in some degree concepts of good and bad that the conflicts between Gargamel and the smurfs, or Luke Skywalker and Darth Vadar make sense. What makes any particular content meaningful, then, is not that children have experience of that particular content in their daily lives, but that the content can be articulated in terms of those underlying abstract concepts that children know most profoundly. The abstract concepts, it seems, provide the means of access to understanding particular content.

This simple observation challenges a couple of very influential, largely taken-for-granted, assumptions. First, we may radically reinterpret the truism that when teaching and designing curricula we must move gradually from the known to the unknown. The current and past assumption has involved interpreting this triusm very largely in terms of content. In that progressive "expansion and organization of subject matter through growth of experience," children's experience is seen as of the everyday world with which they interact. The dominant form of the Social Studies curriculum is the concrete epitome of this principle. It assumes that what children know when they come to school are things about families, homes, neighborhoods, and so on. Thus the curriculum is filled with these things and, having learned yet more about them, children's concepts of homes, families, and so on may be expanded towards the "unknown." The anti-educational effects of this interpretation of the truism about moving from the known to the unknown will be considered below; here it is enough to note that if we interpret what children know in terms of the abstract concepts we have seen giving life and energy to their fantasy worlds, then the content we may consider appropriate for the primary curriculum is not restricted to the *content* of children's experience.

Even in Arthur N. Applebee's interesting *The Child's Concept of Story* (1978), where there is evident sensitivity to some kinds of form/content distinctions, "fantasy" is treated within the rather prosaic tradition of progressivism, "not so much as the 'fantastical' as it is part of a continuum that begins in the world of immediate experience, passes outward to distant lands, and outward again into purely imaginative realms" (p. 74). But this is surely only partially true, and if we are to insist on the continuum necessarily passing through distant lands, most commonly not true at all. Applebee does not so much reflect on this expanding horizons scheme as use it as a presupposition which then serves to organize his observations. So, he observes, "The sort of familiarity which a child demands in a story is often a social one, a doing of things which the child expects to have done. Thus *Peter Rabbit* is a manageable story for Carol at two years eight months because of its familiar family setting" (p. 75). But this covers over a number of reasons why the story is manageable and engaging to very young children. If surface familiarity is the key, what are we to make of the fact that Peter is a rabbit? And what about the wild wood, which is safe, and the cultivated garden, which is dangerous, and the closeness of death, and so on? That is, the means of access to such stories cannot simply be through their familiar settings. If this were so, the genre of fantasy would not exist. If we want to understand young children's intellectual access to knowledge, the first and clearest observation we can make from their engagement with fantasy is that familiar settings account for very little. A more obvious and engaging means of access is through the powerful abstract concepts that we see providing the underlying structure of fantasy stories.

Second, the above observation leads us to reconsider the importance of "active doing" in children's early learning. This challenge does not lead us to favor passivity in young children, but should increase respect for children's abilities to deal with the world intellectually. The progressivists' interpretation of what activity should involve is taken in part from their interpretation of Dewey's claim, quoted above, that the first and most deeply ingrained knowledge is knowledge of *how to do*. If we pause for a moment and consider the abstract substratum whose understanding at the most basic level provides meaning to children's fantasy, we may conclude simply that Dewey's claim is inadequate. Before children can walk or talk, before they can skate or ride a bicycle, they know joy and fear, love and hate, power and powerlessness, and the rhythms of expectation and satisfaction, of hope and disappointment. Children who never learn to walk of talk or read know love and fear, expectation and satisfaction, hope and disappointment. So the knowledge which comes first to people and which remains most deeply ingrained is not knowledge of "how to do"; it is of the fundamental categories upon which we learn increasingly to make sense of anything in the universe and in human experience. If our concern in education is with understanding the world and experience and the growth of knowledge about these, our beginning focus might better be on what children know of the most basic concepts whereby these can be made meaningful. Their ability to walk or skate as typical of what children know first and best is a poor foundation for a process of conscious understanding of the world and human experience.

Perhaps there is a touch of "straw-manning" here – setting Dewey up improperly as the fall-guy. In an epistemological treatise one would want to pause here and disentangle different senses of "know," and probably conclude that there is no necessary conflict between Dewey's argument and my observation. The problem with such precision here is that it engages the wrong point. The point is less with epistemological sophistication than with the educational practices that have followed from the common, unsophisticated, interpretation of Dewey's words. Similarly, the theoretical sophistication behind Piaget's support for "active doing" in primary schools is very largely diluted in the interpretations that guide practices purportedly based on it.

Anyway, reinterpreting the slogan "from the known to the unknown," we might see "the known" in terms of fundamental abstract concepts and "the unknown" as *any* content we might wish to teach. The educational problem then becomes how we can organize the content we want children to learn in a form that makes it accessible given the abstract concepts which children already have. Put this way, we are encouraged to conceive of planning lessons and units, say, not just as organizing objectives in logical sequences of content associations, but as plotting on the powerful abstract concepts children already possess.

If we consider children's lives before they come to school and we interpret what they know in terms of contents, we will be led to a principle of "expanding environments," in which our early curriculum will focus on themselves and their immediate surrounding and gradually move out from their daily experience. If we interpret what they know in terms of the kind of fundamental abstract concepts mentioned above, we may assume that they come to school knowing about power and weakness, for example, oppression, resentment, and revolt, courage and fear. (To say that they have a concept of oppression does not of course mean that they can articulate the word "oppression" and provide a definition of it. Rather I mean simply that they *use* such concepts in making sense of certain experiences or stories. If they did not have concepts of oppression, resentment, and revolt – whatever actual terms they might use – they literally could make no sense of the *Star Wars* stories.) They may have learned about such things painfully or within the protection of a loving family. But however learned, such concepts enable them to understand the basic story of Robin Hood and the Sheriff of Nottingham, for instance. Children seem to have direct access to the meaning of such stories through those fundamental abstract concepts learned from their daily experience. G. K. Chesterton makes the point nicely;

Some day, if I ransack whole libraries, I may know the outermost aspects of King Stephen, and almost see him in his habit as he lived; but the inmost I know already. The symbols are mouldered and the manner of the oath forgotten; the secret society may even be dissolved; but we all know the secret. (1953, p. 174).

In the process of making sense of the story of Robin Hood, children not only have to *use* those basic concepts but they also have to *expand* them. The intellectual act of embodying a concept in different content would seem the most important step that leads to conceptual elaboration. For children to use concepts with which they are already familiar in order to make sense of a medieval adventure the concepts must, to use Piaget's term, in Piaget's sense, accommodate to the new content.

So a value in learning about the distant, the remote, and the fantastic, is that such knowledge can serve to expand, enrich, elaborate, refine those underlying abstract concepts that are the main tools that children have with which to make sense of the world and of experience. If, for whatever reasons, we encourage children to explore the ordinary and the everyday, we are discouraging such conceptual elaboration. In such cases, not only is the content familiar, but the substratum of underlying concepts is even more so; children are thus required to make only minimal accommodations.

Bertrand Russell has a nice line about the first task of education being to destroy the tyranny of the local over the imagination. The progressivist or "modern" position that has become almost a presupposition in the organizing of curricula, particularly in North America, seems to entail two beliefs, both of which seem to me false, and both of which tend towards tyrannizing children's imaginations with the local and the provincial. The first belief is that children cannot engage or understand content that is remote from their experience. The second is the complement of that; the belief that children can most readily engage conceptually the content of their daily experience. I have argued above that the first belief is false. Now we might note in addition that the everyday world around us is surely among the last things that we come to grasp intellectually. Our parents are the last people we come to know. Caught fish discover water only as they leave it.

Young children seem to take their immediate surroundings too much for granted to be able to deal intellectually with them. It is, as T. S. Eliot says, only at the end of all our exploring that we arrive where we started and know the place for the first time. The simple binary organizers that young children use to make sense of the world cannot easily get a hold on the prosaic complexity of everyday experience. This is also perhaps connected with Anna Freud's discovery that their earlier years were less accessible to children than to adult patients.

Furthermore, a slightly paradoxical aspect of human development, but one that is fundamental to this scheme, is that we do not, cannot, make sense of ourselves and of our experience except within the context of our world and our society. The "expanding horizons" form of curriculum begins with the self and immediate experience. I will argue throughout that we might more sensibly see our discovery of ourselves and the meanings of our experience as proceeding along a "contracting environments" scheme; we begin outside reality, in fantasy, we then make contact with the extremes of reality – what I will discuss as romance – then we fix the main coordinates within which we locate ourselves and our experience – "philosophic" ideologies and metaphysical schemes – and at the end of all our exploring perhaps we may come to a proportionate sense of ourselves. A part of the educationally dysfunctional tyranny of the local over the imagination is the tyranny of the self. An important element of fantasy is that it carries the imagination beyond the self; as Wordworth put it;

> Oh! give us once again the wishing-cup
> Of Fortunatus, and the invisible coat
> Of Jack the Giant-killer, Robin Hood,
> And Sabra in the forest with St. George!
> The child, whose love is here, at least, doth reap
> One precious gain, that he forgets himself.
>
> (*Prelude*, Bk V, 340–5)

The other related point that should be made, I suppose, is that we do not have isolated "selves" that we can discover. We are social, historical, cultural, etc., beings and our "selves" are constituted within these contexts and are knowable as we understand these contexts. To imagine that exploring ourselves –

"Who you are" – can serve as a meaningful starting point for our exploration of the world and of human experience seems to follow a superficial logical connection and to ignore common sense and everyday experience.

A curriculum that is reluctant to leave the everyday world, which children inhabit as fish inhabit water and to which they have no easy intellectual access, can neither compete with children's fantasy nor attract the engagement in fantasy towards reality. The educational task is to begin the process of attaching those basic concepts, which make children's fantasy so engaging and meaningful, to the real world. The kind of curriculum that is based on the principles that have been disputed above offers children a most difficult path to reality. It begins with what only adults can easily manage in a meaningful way, and moves gradually towards more distant content that students are then conceptually unprepared to deal with. That is, some of the most prominent and widely accepted principles that shape particularly the primary and elementary school curriculum at present seem to be not just wrong but something close to the opposite of what might promote children's educational development.

It might be added that the confusion between underlying concepts and surface content is also encouraged, again ironically, by those developmental psychologists who try to infer principles for the curriculum from experimental findings. David Elkind (1976), for example, as a result of his empirical studies observes that the formal operational concept of "belief" only "develops" during teen years, and from this he infers that it is pointless teaching young children about different religions. Other research based on Piaget's theory has indicated that children do not typically "develop" some of the concepts basic to historical understanding until well into the teens (Hallam, 1969), and on such results some educationalists infer that it is hopeless to try to teach history to young children.

If we stay with history for the sake of example, we may accept that young children typically do not have a concept of historical causality. But we may at the same time observe that they clearly do have a concept of the causality that holds stories together and moves them along. While they may lack concepts adequate for a proper sense of historical chronology, they clearly understand "before" and "after," and "long, long, ago," and "just a little while later." While they may lack a sophisticated concept of kingship, or of interacting elements within political structures, they clearly do understand power and weakness, oppression, resentment, and revolt, ambition and punishment. And while they may lack concepts of politically constructive or destructive behavior, they clearly do have concepts of good and bad. If we conduct a simple inventory of the concepts children must have in order to engage in their fantasy narratives and understand the stories they most enjoy, then we have available a set of concepts that may be used to begin teaching history. In addition we might reasonably conclude that the sophisticated adult concepts do not simply "develop." The adequacy of our more sophisticated adult concepts will turn on our having learned the simpler concepts earlier and gradually elaborated them in appropriate ways. (Again, I should add that this follows from a criticism not so much of Piagetian theory and research but of the uses it is sometimes put to in education.)

What seems to follow from this consideration of one aspect of children's fantasy is that some of the principles that have a dominant place in present thinking about curriculum organization are misconceived. In misconceiving what children know best when they arrive at school and how they can proceed to learn new knowledge, these principles lead to a curriculum that hinders rather than helps children to engage reality during primary and middle school years, and includes in secondary school years material that students are then unprepared to deal with. The general shape of the curriculum that would follow if the observations in this section are anywhere near accurate will be sketched in Chapter Six.

So taking fantasy seriously is intended to raise fundamental questions both about teaching and about curricula. The presently dominant assumptions about both have been formed under the influence of ideas that have depreciated fantasy, and thereby depreciated significant features of young children's thinking and learning. Obviously I am not just advocating the practical value of using fantasy stories in the Language Arts curriculum nor simply recommending that children write and read (in however elementary a form) their own fantasy narratives as a means to stimulating improvements in literacy. More generally I think that a serious consideration of even superficial features of fantasy as in this section, draws us to look for more adequate principles on which to build a curriculum and to reassess some of our pervasive assumptions about children's learning and our teaching.

If we go a little deeper, and then wider, in our consideration of children's fantasy we might begin even to affect our very concept of early education.

Children's Fantasy and Myth

In this section I want to explain why I have chosen to call this first layer of understanding "mythic," and why I think we should bother with myth at all in a book about young children's education. To do this I will make some simple connections between children's fantasy and myth, and in the process consider some of the related difficulties that have stood in the way of the study of both of them. The major difficulty became apparent in the first section: the assumption that rational forms of thought are somehow natural and that myth and fantasy are therefore abberations that need to be accounted for as resulting from ignorance, "primitiveness," infirmities of mind or available language, or whatever. Even interpreters of myths who have admitted an unfashionable "reverance for the primitive time" tried to discover "hidden and involved meanings beneath the "absurd and stupid" narratives; indeed, the absurdity of the stories was such that it was assumed they could only be parables of some mysterious kind, encoding a hidden rational message. Francis Bacon (1609) asks us to consider any myth story and we will see how no one could possibly have made up or dreamed such fantasies:

> Jupiter took Metis to wife; as soon as he saw she was
> with child, he ate her up; whereupon he grew to be with
> child himself; and so brought forth out of his head Pallas in
> armour! Surely I think no man had ever a dream so monstrous
> and extravagant, and out of all natural ways of thinking.
> (Bacon, 1905, p. 823)

The final phrase here is significant. It is the assumption of the naturalness of rationality that has made myth such a puzzle.

In this section, then, I will briefly discuss the study of myth, and sketch some recent work that indicates the sensibleness of using the term "mythic understanding" for the foundational layer of modern education. I will mention six similarities between mythic and young children's thinking. In the following three chapters I will explore these similarities in some detail, showing how the foundational layer of eduction can be built firmly on some features of our mental activity that have tended to be somewhat neglected.

Now I need to tread here as circumspectly as do children along cracked paving stones. The subject of myth is riven with disputes and enormous diversity of interpretation, and so is fantasy. "Myth," after all, is most commonly used to mean something that is false. Myths are those alien and often bizzare stories collected from "primitive" peoples, full of half-human, half-animal creatures and crazy, dream-like incidents. What am I suggesting about young children's thinking by the choice of such a term? And, given that this is a layered scheme, what am I suggesting about the foundational layer of educated adult thinking? And what does fantasy have to do with myth anyway?

This last question at least can be answered fairly directly, if somewhat superficially. Myth stories nearly always contain creatures or events that are impossible in the real world. When we invent stories with these characteristics we call them fantasies. We accept as fantasy any imaginative creation of impossibilities, extending from the pretend games with the dress-up box to the elaboration of impossible worlds in sophisticated "fantasy" literature. A fantasy may be entirely realistic, except for one element. Fantasy exists as a literary genre when the readers accept the cancellation of a particular aspect or aspects of reality. It is a genre where the suspension of disbelief takes on an added dimension to that required for any fiction to work. But fantasy can also be seen as a pervasive element in Western literature, beyond the obvious departures from reality in the minor genre of "fantasy" (Hume, 1985).

Fantasy stories can be modelled closely on myth stories, and clearly the huge corpora of myth stories discovered during the nineteenth and twentieth centuries have given a stimulus, and elements of form and content, to the composition of fantasy stories. Myths and fantasies are now a central element in children's literature. Collections of folk-tales and myth stories from around the world are abundantly available. These are usually rewritten to suit the conventions of the story form in our culture and also to suit the intellectual abilities of children. Authors in our culture can copy the forms of folk-tales, writing new stories in a similar genre. There is some awkwardness about copying the form of myth stories, however, and it is generally considered laudable when a collection of myth stories can claim to be "authentic." We cannot write new myth stories – such inventions are simply fantasy stories. Clearly myth stories "belong" to people in some way that makes us feel uncomfortable about appropriating them to our culture. They call for respect in a way that other kinds of stories do not. (Though we recognize that folk-tales are somewhere on the continuum between our conscious fictions and myths.)

A crucial difference between fantasy and myth, then, is not necessarily evident in any overt elements of the stories, but lies rather in the hearers' or readers' beliefs about them. Myths for us are literary fantasies, but we call them myths to acknowledge that they have or have had an important public role in some other culture, and in that culture they were believed to express profound truths.

What we see in children's fantasy, then, is something akin to what we see in myth stories – imaginative impossibilities carried forward on a narrative. But we expect our children to know, or to learn, the difference between their fantasy and what is real. Now this way of putting it suggests that myth-users who claimed their myths were true could not distinguish between their fantasies and reality. This is precisely how myths were judged: as false claims about what is real. Much of the problem lay in the rational criteria that were built into the meanings of "belief" and "true" – criteria that were not appropriate for distinguishing the functions of myths in alien cultures.

Both in ancient Greece and in nineteenth-century Britain and America the rational evaluators of "primitive" myths concluded that they were false attempts to describe the beginnings of the world and the early history of their "primitive" societies. Hecateus of Miletus began his *Genealogies* with the observation that the (myth) stories of the Greeks "are many, and in my opinion, ridiculous." The early Greek *logographoi* (writers of rational prose) concluded that their grandparents who told the old myths told lies. Similar evaluations in the nineteenth century have given us as a popular meaning for "myth" – that which is false. What is false in all this, however, is the assumption that myths represent some failed attempt to tell rational truths, and that when people claimed to believe a myth this was the same as claiming to believe a rational proposition.

The study of myth in this century has taken us beyond these early misconceptions. But myths continue to present puzzles to rational people. One puzzle has been due to our considering rationality such an obvious and effective way of thinking about the world. Given this obviousness, it is bewildering that systematic rational thinking should be so rare and so late an achievement in the long human story. Why have all cultures everywhere either evolved from mythic forms of thinking or remained mythic? Myth seems so peculiar a way of thinking that it is hard for us to understand why it appears historically to be much more "natural" and pervasive than rationality.

Such problems raise more of those questions that I cannot answer here, or anywhere. What I want to do is briefly consider some interpretations of myth that take us beyond the simplistic sense of myths as false accounts, in order to indicate why it is a reasonable label for a form of understanding, especially when that form is to take a place in a recapitulatory scheme.

Now we come to one of the longest and most cracked paving stones in the scholarly path. The study of myth during this century has been pursued in widely diverse disciplines, with widely diverse interests and working with widely diverse interpretations of its nature and functions. At best the study of myth has formed a meeting ground for anthropology, psychology, classics, literary criticism, and other disciplines. At worst, the sense of myth in some branches of these disciplines seems to have little in common with the sense in others. It would be difficult, but not impossible, to chart the extensive and scattered family of meanings of "myth" used in various disciplines in this century.

Anthropologists – from the armchair cataloguing and ingenious theorizing of Frazer, to the functionalism of Malinowski, to the structuralism of Lévi-Strauss – have made clear that when myth-users claim that their myths are true they do not mean true in the sense in which we might claim a rational proposition is true. Increasingly the logic of myth has been shown to be different from that of rational forms of inquiry and expression, but different in complicated ways. Myth is a crucial feature of its users' lives, helping to make adequate sense, and determining the sense to be made, of their experience and of their social and economic roles.

The evolutionary ideas of the nineteenth century encouraged a simple story in which the newly discovered "primitives" and their myths represented a stage of cultural evolution equivalent to the archaic, or pre-archaic, Greeks. The crucial step that accounted for the immense difference felt to exist by so many nineteenth-century gentlemen between themselves and the "primitive" peoples of the world was the "Greek miracle," the birth of rationality. The clear air of ancient Greece served to lift suddenly the mythic scales from people's eyes, so that they could finally see the world and experience as they really are. From then on the story of human cultural progress to the present was thought to be clear.

Prominent among those who undermined this story was F. M. Cornford. Cornford was one of the "Cambridge classical anthropologists" who drew on the work of Durkheim, Lévi-Bruhl, and Frazer. He, along with Jane Harrison, and A. B. Cook, and Gilbert Murray at Oxford, looked at the ancient Greek myths and at ancient Greek philosophy and historiography, with minds influenced by Durkheim's revolutionary ideas about how societies work and are held together and with the massive collections of myths and the cross-cultural organization of them provided by Frazer.

In *Thucydides Mythistoricus* (1907), *From Religion to Philosophy* (1912), and *Principium Sapientiae: The Origins of Greek philosophical Thought* (published in 1951, nine years after his death) Cornford argued that our interpretation of events is always controlled in large degree "by some scheme of unchallenged and unsuspected presuppositions" (Cornford, 1907, p. viii). A key to understanding any work is to try to uncover these presuppositions. Applying this principle, he shows that works that were taken as crucial in leaving myth behind are in fact suffused with mythic thinking. The ancient Greek enlightenment, he argues, was not made by replacing myth with rationality, but by building a layer of rational thought on top of persisting mythic presuppositions. He shows these at work in Thucydides' *History* and in the early Ionian "physicists."

He shows, for example, that early rational "physicists" presupposed that their job was to answer the mythic questions, with their structuring assumptions, "How did the world come to exist out of primordial chaos?" and "What are things ultimately made of?" While it may appear simply a rational speculation to conclude as an answer to the latter question that all things are ultimately made of earth, air, fire, and water, and their combinations – and the rational Hippocratic writers could assume that the human body consisted of related "humors" - Cornford shows how these elements are derived directly from the mythic answer to the same question. The stories of Zeus in the ethereal sky (fire), Hades in the misty shadow (air), Poseidon in his watery sea, and their shared ground on earth, express in mythic terms the same divisions of elements. (Put so, the connections may seem almost arbitrary but Cornford shows in detail the connections between gods and godless speculation.)

We find, then, a strong structural continuity undergirding the move from mythic to rational thought. This continuity is disguised or hidden if our focus is on the surface level of narratives rather than on the deeper level of presuppositions and structural foundations. This insight has been elaborated in numerous areas of study, some of them showing up inadequacies in Cornford's own work and that of his fellow "classical anthropologists." What is elaborated, however, is the understanding that myth has its own complex logic and that this logic is not an opposite to rational thought. Rationality does not simply displace myth; it arises from, and is developed "on top of," mythic thinking. Historically the main marks of the development of rationality were the repudiation of supernatural agents in accounts of the world and of human experience and the quest for coherence in such accounts – a coherence based on precisely defined concepts and distinctions among the various levels of reality. In myth we find "a logic of the ambiguous, the equivocal, a logic of polarity" (Vernant, 1980, p. 239), and on top of this, rationality has elaborated its logic of non-contradiction.[3]

If one were writing a study of myth, Cornford would hardly figure so prominently – indeed, his name does not even appear in Blumenberg's *Work on Myth* (1985). He figures prominently here because of the importance of his work in undermining the simplistic distinction between mythic and rational thinking. Prominent also in this story is Lévi-Bruhl's somewhat neglected *How natives Think* (1910), and the suggestive, occasionally brilliant, but rather opaque work of Lévi-Strauss. Their work will provide some unobtrusive support for the following chapters. More obtrusive, in the next chapter at least, will be the contributions of those who have studied the techniques of thinking and expression of people who are not literate, and their studies of the move from orality to literacy. Parry (1928), Lord (1964), Havelock (1963), Ong (1982), and Goody (1977) have further helped to undermine the opposition of mythic and rational thinking. The great adumbrator of these studies is Giambattista Vico, whose *The New Science* (1744) argued with great originality that myth is a product of the human mind working in its poetic mode: the early peoples who generated myths, he argued, were

> poets who spoke in poetic characters. This discovery, which is the master key of this Science has cost us the persistent research of almost all our literary life because with our civilized natures we cannot at all imagine and can understand only by great toil the poetic nature of these first men.
> (Vico [1970] p. 5)

It seems we must say much the same of our own childhood. Vico's "discovery" was that rational prose, so much a part of our "civilized natures," was a late achievement in human thinking, and that it grew from, and on, our "poetic nature." A study of human understanding, then, required not simply close attention to the logic of rational discourse but also to metaphor and the other poetic tropes and to the functions of rhyme, rhythm, and meter. We will have to consider what "poetry" is, especially with regard to children's thinking. This will be pursued not so much as would be appropriate in a treatise on poetry and poetics but rather by drawing on such research to highlight some common and commonly observed, but in education commonly neglected, features of young children's thinking.

The sense of myth being not some curiosity of "primitive" mentalities but rather an expression of fundamental forms that persist in all human thinking but whose more bizarre surface features are held in check by rational logic has given rise to various explorations of modern forms of mythic thinking. Psychology and psychoanalysis are rich in claims about the modern forms of mythic thinking. Certain schools of literary criticism see the search for the mythic underpinnings of modern fictions as the key to their meaning. In poetics some see mythic patterns, following Aristotle's identification of the plot (*mythos*) as the soul of the work, as basic elements for analysis, and so on. A problem with this proliferating literature of course, is that "myth" has come to mean so many rather different things that it is in danger of losing any useful meaning altogether. Yet this diversity, complexity, and even vagueness is not unconnected with my reasons for choosing "mythic" as a label for this first form of understanding. It too is diverse, complex, and our understanding of it is only vague, as is our understanding of almost everything to do with human thinking. I will summarize, now, my reasons for choosing this label:

First, and most generally, is Cornford's image of mythic thinking as vivid and powerful and persisting into rationality at a fundamental level. In the recapitulationist scheme to be sketched in this essay, this first level of children's understanding persists as a foundation for educated adult thinking. The distinctive quality of young children's thinking, in this view, is to be accounted for by its lack of further layers of understanding which coalesce with it and modify it.

Second, myth-users and children compose, or learn and take advantage of, narratives which provide intellectual security by making a totalized sense of the world and of experience. In myth-using societies this totalized view is achieved in part by obliterating history. The myths tell of a sacred beginning in which things as they are now were made. This gives present social arrangements the authority of the sacred. Young children lack the experience of social change that can provide an historical sense of their present experience and they, too, very readily accept totalizing accounts of why the world is the way it is. I don't want to overdo this connection. Rather, I am pointing at the strong desire for intellectual security that myths provide and that young children seem to require from accounts that have clear mythic characteristics.

Third, and connected with the previous item, the narratives of myth and of children are commonly story-shaped. Both achieve crucial aspects of intellectual security by representing the world and experience as largely story-shaped. This is the subject of Chapter Three, so I will elaborate there.

Fourth, myth-users and children charge their environments with meaning and significance in a way not common for modern educated adults. Myth-users and children do not do this the same way, of course. For the myth-user the environment is charged with meaning by its contact with the sacred; in the case of most children it takes a form such as is detailed in the Opies' *The Lore and Language of Schoolchildren*. To take the above example of the cracks in paving stones: more or less arbitrary elements of the environment are charged with a potent significance by children's projections of an internal drama onto them. This sense of the numinous in what adults often take as purely utilitarian elements of the environment is a feature of children's thinking that will be considered in the next chapter, as will its educational implications. Oakeshott, quoted earlier, refers to the "twilight of childhood," suggesting that the child's mind perceives the world vaguely, unclearly, dimly, but those who seem best able to recall childhood unanimously do so in terms of brightness, sharpness, a sense of abundance and fullness of meaning – "Then did I dwell within a World of Light" (Thomas Traherne, in Coe, 1984, p. 255). Now clearly it will be pointed out that Oakeshott and the autobiographers of childhood are referring to different things; Oakeshott to rational thought, these others to sensations and feelings. A part of my purpose is to undermine the appropriateness of this distinction, particularly when dealing with young children's understanding, and I will be arguing that they are not referring to different things, just that some have a much better and more accurate idea of that thing than others.

Fifth, prominent among the structural features of children's and myth-users' thinking is the use of certain kinds of classification, prominent among which is the use of binary organizers. Lévi-Strauss has shown, perhaps to an exaggerated degree, the ubiquity of binary opposites in myths. We can observe in children's stories and their own narratives the ubiquity of such binary structures as love/hate, fear/security, good/bad, big/little, courage/cowardice, and perhaps less obviously but no less pervasively, nature/culture, life/death. I will consider some of these classificatory structures and their implications for teaching in Chapter Four.

Sixth, young children and myth-users employ, in varied ways, techniques of thinking that rely on the resources available within oral cultures. This comparison needs to be made with care, because young children in our culture are brought up in an environment that takes literacy largely for granted and encourages forms of thought that are entirely influenced by the techniques made possible by literacy. I will argue in the next chapter that more sensitivity to the techniques of thinking made possible by literacy, and to the techniques of thinking possible in the absence of or prior to the internalizing of literacy, can help us better to understand young children's forms of understanding, what is entailed in the achievement of literacy, and how to encourage the acquisition of literacy. Myth is a vivid and accessible expression of basic features of thinking in the absence of writing; young children's fantasy is another.

As myth can be seen, however murkily still, to provide important foundations for rational inquiries, so, I am suggesting, in children's fantasy we can see the establishment of some important foundations for educated adult understanding. We do not become educated all at once, and in the sequence of the educational process, I will argue, the particular "mythic" characteristics of educated adult understanding can be most readily acquired during early childhood. There seems to be a disposition to acquire these particular characteristics during early childhood, if they are to be acquired at all.

So I have chosen "mythic" as a label for these reasons. It is not so much that I think this view of myth is right, and that my educational program turns on this. Rather I am using the term "mythic" more as a suggestive metaphor, in order to point at certain features of myth as indicating something crucial about early childhood education that has not been adequately attended to. The value of the educational program will turn on the accuracy of the empirical observations on which it is based and on a range of other considerations to be discussed later. The variety of conclusions about myth, however, make it reasonable to talk about children's fantasy and children's thinking in general as having some prominent mythic qualities.

Conclusion

Because educational theorists and researchers have tended to focus on other aspects of children's thinking than their fantasy, and because what we focus on tends to take up a disproportionate area of what is assumed to exist, conclusions about learning and curriculum have been reached on what may reasonably be considered incomplete data. A curious aspect of psychology's influence on education concerns the way in which the particular content chosen more or less randomly for experiments on cognitive functioning has affected the curriculum. A simple example may be seen in the Piagetian conservation experiments. Despite the fact that the particular content of the experiments was chosen only to expose underlying cognitive processes, and despite Piaget's arguments that the cognitive developments exposed by the experiments could not be *taught*, one found a number of preschool programs making the teaching of conservations a part of their curriculum. More generally, Dewey's focus on early local experience and the easy, natural learning derived from it, influenced the move away from history and geography towards a Social Studies curriculum made up largely from the content of children's local experience. We find a similar move in the growth of modern education in Britain: Susan Isaacs argued that children's "native interest in things and people around them – the street, the market, the garden, the railway, the world of plants and animals – does in fact offer us all the opportunities we need for their education" (Isaacs, 1930, p. 9). So the neglect of children's fantasy in writings and research in education during this century has meant the exclusion of an influence on curriculum and learning that, I will argue further, has led to impoverishment and imbalance in schooling. Apollonian harmony and balance should perhaps, ironically, lead us to reinstate Dionysus to his proper place in our mental life and in our children's education.

A preliminary point of this book, then, is that children's fantasy raises some considerable challenges to the principles on which the typical early childhood curriculum is based. Those presently dominant principles seem to exclude much content that might well be included to enrich children's early years of schooling; they tend overall towards the prosaic and dull and exclude much intellectual excitement, and they fail to appreciate that fantasy is not an opposite of rationality but reflects the element that gives rationality life and energy. Apollo without Dionysus may indeed be a well-informed, good citizen, but he's a dull fellow. He may even be "cultured," in the sense one often gets from traditionalist writings in education – that is, an "appreciator" or consumer of culture. But without Dionysus he will never make and remake a culture.[4] However we may regret our schools' difficulties in achieving educational ideals, we need occasionally to ponder whether some of their difficulty is not due to a deficiency in the ideal. The argument of this book is that we are tending to ignore a large part of each child's mental life in the way we construct our curricula and in how we try to teach them.

Children's fantasy has been a subject of vivid argument and different conclusions, particularly in Freudian and Jungian psychologies. Some slight influences of this have seeped into education, particularly in Children's Literature and where educational and psychotherapeutic interests seem to converge. But in the mainstream theories and research there has been a general neglect of fantasy. While many teachers encourage fantasy and imaginative play, the theories and research that dominate educational thinking tend rather to suppress consideration of this very evident aspect of children's thinking. The result is that great emphasis is given to some intellectual characteristics while others, surely equally important, are very largely ignored.

Children's easy access to the meaning of typical fantasy stories suggests that meaningful content need not be that which is immediate to children's everyday experience. Indeed it seems precisely such everyday experience whose meaning becomes conceptually accessible only in adulthood. Underlying the content of daily experience is a set of abstract concepts. These are concepts of enormous power in human thinking and seem to be among the earliest intellectual tools children learn or develop. Because children's fantasy is largely ignored in educational theory and research so these powerful abstract concepts, and children's ability to make use of them in making sense of the world, has tended to be ignored. At the important beginning of formal education, then, we are tending to trivialize the curriculum precisely when it should be intellectually at its richest.

It is perhaps important to stress here that this focus on fantasy, myth, and poetry does not mean that my interest is simply on the arts in early education, or just on the role of poetry or creative writing. My argument is that we can see more clearly in these an ingredient of children's thinking that needs to be borne in mind also when considering science and mathematics. Science and mathematics, no less than poetry and drama, emerged slowly from myth, and need to be seen accurately as still requiring the use of aspects of our minds which gave them birth. In fantasy we see the imaginative elaboration of impossibilities, a creative play on the shifting abstractions which undergird the fantasy content. Fluency and ease in this kind of intellectual play is not – I will argue – removed from our ability to play with the constructed abstractions of mathematics and science. These are not simple representations of reality that we must prosaically chart, but they, no less than any of our fictions, require imaginative construction. As Niels Bohr put it: "It is wrong to think that the task of physics is to find out how nature is. Physics concerns what we can say about nature" (Bohr, in Pippard, 1986). Again, one need not get too fancy about all this high-flown theorizing, but it is important to get a proportionate sense of the nature of subjects like mathematics and the sciences so that what one asks young children to do to begin with is true to that nature and true to what they will be doing should they pursue them to their present end. In our beginning is our end; in our end is our beginning.

If we need to look further than the simple prominence of fantasy in children's thinking to justify the plausibility of an inquiry such as this, we might reflect that education is concerned with the communication of meanings, that we do not seem to do this especially successfully in schools given the time we spend at it, and that, for whatever reasons, children's fantasy seems to be one of the most meaningful and readily engaged parts of their mental lives. If our aim in education is to encourage that sense of meaningfulness and engagement with reality, we might sensibly explore why their fantasy worlds are so meaningful and engaging to them, and see whether we can use what we learn to serve educational purpose.

2

The Domestication of the *Sauvage* Mind

Introduction

So we have inherited from the ancient Greeks the notion of a deep-cutting distinction between rational and irrational thinking. The word commonly used for "reason" was *logos*, which was also the term used for "word" or "speech." For the Greeks of the Platonic tradition, then, taking a rational view enabled one to mirror the reality in words: "We have a rational grasp of something when we can *articulate* it; that means, distinguish and lay out different features of the matter in perspicious order" (Taylor, 1982, p. 90). Rationality entails trying to perceive things as they are, despite our hopes, fears, or intentions regarding them. One may achieve such a view by *theoria* (sight, speculation, contemplation): theoretical understanding results from taking a disengaged perspective. Only the knowledge that results from this kind of intellectual activity, Plato argued (*Timeus, passim*; *The Republic, passim*), is true knowledge. The manner in which Plato distinguished rational thinking and its product – true knowledge (*episteme*) – from irrational thinking and its various products – confusion, superficial plausibility, mere opinion (*doxa*) – involved setting up a number of enduring conceptual associations. Among these associated ideas, and of particular interest here was that of adulthood with the attainment of *episteme* and childhood with *doxa*. (See the parable of the line in *The Republic* (trans. Cornford, 1941, Ch. XXIV) and for discussion of the sets of associations see Simon, 1978, pp. 164ff.) This rational theoretic understanding, Plato and his pupil Aristotle argued, gives a superior view of reality. Those who violate the basic standards of the articulation of

47

this theoretic understanding are, in this view, irrational, and they fail to articulate what is real and true.

With the "rediscovery" of classical Greece by nineteenth-century European scholars, and the growing sense of Greece's cultural superiority over the classical Roman models that had dominated European intellectual and artistic life during the previous century, the distinction between rational and irrational thinking began a new career. It proved a convenient tool for dismissing from serious comparison with Western forms of thought those forms of "primitive" thought that expanding colonial empires and early anthropological studies, or travellers' tales, were bringing increasingly to the attention of European and American peoples (Jenkyns, 1980; Turner, 1981). When combined later in the century with the extensions of evolutionary theory, the distinction between "rational" and "irrational" thinking helped to generate theories about the development of human societies from irrational beginnings to the refined rationality of contemporary Western intellectual life. Frazer (1900), for example, argued that human thought always passes through a magical stage, to a religious stage, and finally to a rational scientific stage. This distinction has developed during this century into everyday language, finding varied more or less casual uses as terms of approval or disparagement. At the same time, in the scholarly world the distinction has come increasingly into question. Anthropologists such as Evans-Prichard (1936), for example, have argued the rationality of witchcraft in particular cultural settings, and classicists such as Dodds (1951) have pointed to the irrationality of significant features of Greek life and thought. Vexed and problematic though the distinction is, it remains deeply embedded in Western cultural history and habits of thought (Hollis and Lukes, 1982; Putnam, 1981; Wilson, 1970).

The mental life of children has commonly been represented in terms influenced by this distinction. Children are assumed to begin life in irrational confusion and ignorance, and education is regarded as the process of inculcating both rationality and knowledge. In his allegory of the cave in *The Republic* (trans. Cornford, 1941, Ch. XXV) Plato likens the process of education to unchaining prisoners in a dark cave; while chained, they can see on the cave wall only flickering shadows of what is happening outside, and, when released, they are led out to behold reality. The power of such allegories and metaphors lies in their providing a persuasive image that is not itself open to the kind of questioning that the surrounding explicit arguments are subjected to. Indeed many of Plato's basic epistemological arguments have lost much of their influence, but his allegories, metaphors, and myths still maintain a pervasive shaping force over Western minds. It is the developmental allegory, augmented by nineteenth-century evolutionary ideas, that I want to disturb here.

The title of this chapter is a play on Jack Goody's title *The Domestication of the Savage mind*, which is in turn a play on Lévi-Strauss's *The Savage Mind*, whose original French title, *La Pensée Sauvage*, was briefly discussed earlier. Goody's book tried to undermine the distinctions commonly held in the West, even in Lévi-Strauss's work, between the kind of thinking prominent in societies such as ours and that in "primitive" societies. Attempts have been made to capture the perceived differences in distinctions such as primitive/developed, irrational or prerational/rational, mythic/historical, simple/complex, mythopoeic/logico-empirical, "cold"/"hot", traditional/modern, and so on. Goody argues that any distinction that suggests "two different modes of thought, approaches to knowledge, or forms of science" is inadequate, not least because, as he points out, "both are present not only in the same societies but in the same individuals" (Goody, 1977, p. 148). That is, whenever we try to define precisely some distinctive feature of "our" thinking, we can always find examples of it in "their" cultures, and whenever we identify a distinctive feature of "their" thinking, we can find cases of it in "our" culture. Horton has shown that what have been accounted distinctive features of scientific thinking are common in traditional cultures in Africa (1970, 1982), and it has now, post-Freud, become a cliché that certain central features of mythic thinking are common in Western cultures (Blumenberg, 1985). (One wonders, for example, whether Malinowski's (1922) outrage at the wastefulness of piles of rotting yams in the Trobriand Islands would be equally directed at the "mountains" of dairy food and grains and "lakes" of wine that have accumulated in support of the farming policies of the European Economic Community.) "We" and "they" constantly exhibit thinking that is both rational and irrational, complex and simple, logico-mathematical and mythopoeic. We are "them" and they are "us."

What about the evident differences, then, between modes of thinking used in oral societies and those used in complex industrial ones? While we may indeed recognize common features in forms of thought that were in the past considered entirely dissimilar, we need to recognize also that Western science, history, and mathematics are hardly identical with anything found in oral cultures. One can scarcely claim that differences do not exist. How do we account for them if we reject explanations involving "primitiveness" or deficiencies of mind or of language? And how do we characterize the dramatic changes in forms of thought and methods of inquiry made during the Greek classical period – changes that involved the birth of philosophy, critical history, and modern science? Goody (1977) maintains that the evident differences are best accounted for as due to technology, and especially the technology of writing. His argument builds on, and extends, a growing body of work that is clarifying how literacy affects strategies of thinking. The economy of the mind inclines us towards particular strategies in an oral culture, where what one knows is what one remembers, and to some different strategies in a literate culture, where various mental operations can be enormously enhanced by visual access to organized bodies of knowledge.

I will begin this chapter, then, with a brief account of some of the fruitfully overlapping branches of research in classical studies and anthropology that have helped to clarify the kinds of thinking that have proven effective in cultures that do not have writing. This may seem a peculiar route to the early childhood curriculum and to methods of teaching and learning. Homeric formulae and metrical patterns in Gaelic and Anatolian heroic tales may indeed appear somewhat remote from the usual range of educational research. Yet we have become accustomed to more technically complex discussions in reports of empirical research on children's thinking, and the seeming peculiarity of this discussion of oral cultures may be mitigated by reflecting that it is simply an attempt to approach the same topic by a different route. And who knows, approaching children's education via the material of human cultural development might even come to seem at least as sensible a procedure as those presently dominant. Anyway, my aim for this chapter is to try to attach research on "oral thinking" in a fairly direct way to early education.

The path from orality to literacy is one that Westerners want all children to take as they pass through our educational systems. Better understanding of what this move entails might clarify some of our practical educational problems. It might, for example, help us find ways to reduce the rates of illiteracy in Western societies, and perhaps also to improve the quality and richness of literacy we can achieve. From the research that has so far drawn on increasing knowledge of orality and of the transition to literacy, it is clear that any adequate conception of literacy must take in much more than simple encoding and decoding "skills" and encompass significant features of rationality (Olson, 1977, 1986). That is to say, even though there is considerable difficulty in characterizing rationality with precision, it is increasingly clear that the acquisition of literacy can have cognitive effects that have traditionally been considerd features of rational thought – particularly those associated with "abstract" thinking.

The research on orality is of interest also, however, because of its potential support to my recapitulation scheme, and to more adequately characterizing "mythic understanding." This scheme does not consider early education as beginning the process of making little savages into civilized people, thereby recapitulating the progress of "the race". This nineteenth-century fallacy, encouraged by superficial notions of evolution, still persists in perhaps attenuated form, as we saw in the previous chapter. Rather, by making children literate we are recapitulating in each individual's case the internalizing of a technology that has profound and some quite precise effects on cognitive processes and modes of communication. As Walter Ong notes, "Technologies are not mere exterior aids but also interior transformations of consciousness" (Ong, 1982, p. 82); "Writing is a technology that restructures thought" (Ong, 1986, p. 23).

"Technology" is a slightly aggressive term to use for writing, and "tools" for thinking is a handy but tendentious metaphor. One is led to assume that spades and computers have similar transforming powers over our manual and cognitive functions. That they have transforming powers is without doubt, but that these are the same as or akin to what internalizing literacy produces needs further arguments and evidences, not metaphorical glossing over. I would prefer to use a less aggressive and less tendentious term than "technology" for writing – not on etymological grounds but simply because of its modern associations – but am hard put to come up with a good alternative. My preferred term suffers the disabilities of being "foreign" and perhaps a bit pretentious. It is a coinage of Lévi-Strauss, as far as I am aware: in discussing the structural categories underlying totemic classification he debunks the notion that totemic species are chosen because of their economic or culinary value. He argues that totemic species are not so much "bonnes à manger" (good things to eat) but rather "bonnes à penser" (good things to think with) (Lévi-Strauss, 1962). Literacy is a set of *bonnes à penser*, as well as having the utilitarian values which are so obvious. (It is bad enough introducing a new technical term in one's own language but pinching one from another language and then using it, as I shall, in improper grammatical forms – using it throughout as a feminine plural noun – is verging on the outrageous. But I am trying to find a term for "things to think with" that is not caught up in the language of concepts or of psychology that would bring a bulging baggage of uncontrollable associations. I hope readers, and particularly Francophone readers, will be indulgent to this stratagem.)

The main purpose of this chapter is to explore oral *bonnes à penser*. Orality, we shall see, is not a condition of deficit – to be defined simply as the lack of literacy. Thinking about orality only in terms of literacy is like, in Walter Ong's neat simile, thinking of horses as automobiles without wheels (Ong, 1982, p. 12). Orality entails a set of powerful and effective mental strategies, some of which, to our cost, have become attenuated and undervalued in significant parts of our culture and in our educational systems. I will explore some of the effective strategies of thinking used in oral cultures, and will then note some similarities between these and common features of young children's thinking. I will consider Albert B. Lord's argument that orality and literacy are "contradictory and mutually exclusive" (Lord, 1964, p. 129), and will argue in reply that they are so only in certain particular regards, and that some of the *bonnes à penser* of orality are unnecessarily lost for many children in our educational systems, or are suppressed to an unnecessary degree, and that with some small ingenuity we might find ways of conserving a number of them. Some indeed, I will argue, should be conserved as foundations for more sophisticated forms of understanding. This discussion is designed to lead into Chapter Six on the early childhood curriculum, in which the implications of this chapter will be worked out into a curriculum.

A word of caution is required here, more for me perhaps than for you. Any simple assumption about equating the thinking of adults in oral cultures with that of children in ours will be undermined in two ways. First, the one set are adults and have the accumulated experience and development children necessarily lack. Second, most children in Western cultures live in an environment that presupposes literacy and its associated forms of thought; constant adult interactions with young children assume conventions that depend on literacy, and pre-literate children are constantly encouraged to adopt forms of thinking and expression that are more easily achieved as a product of literacy. My purpose is to focus on forms of thought that are *bonnes à penser* if one is not literate. Consequently, I will be seeking comparisons between forms of thought used by members of oral cultures and those used by modern Western children. The basis of the comparison, however, is neither knowledge content nor psychological development but techniques that are required by orality. Keeping this idea to the fore will, I hope, allow us to avoid the kind of deprecatory ethnocentrism criticized above.

A related caution: I will not be trying to establish an exhaustive inventory of the intellectual strategies common in oral cultures. Nor do I see the purpose of education in Western cultures as uncritically preserving and developing such strategies. We are not in the business of preparing children to live in an oral culture – though it may be worth reiterating that we are preparing them for a literate-and-oral culture. Indeed, we see fast developing around us features of what Ong has called "secondary orality." The electronic media are its most energetic promoters, but even newspapers and journals are explicitly, and somewhat paradoxically, relying more and more on strategies of communication that draw increasingly little on the skills of "high literacy" and their associated forms of thought (Ong, 1977). So, we need to remember that orality is not the end of our educational development, but it is a constituent of it, and its study might provide some *bonnes à penser* for constructing a richer primary school curriculum and a richer sense of how children might effectively learn the contents of that curriculum.

A central theme of this chapter, then, might be summed up in Lévi-Strauss's observation:

> I think there are some things we have lost, and we should perhaps try to regain them, but I am not sure that in the kind of world in which we are living and with the kind of

scientific thinking we are bound to follow, we can regain these things exactly as if they had never been lost; but we can try to become aware of their existence and their importance. (Lévi-Strauss, 1978,p. 5)

Rediscovering Orality

I noted earlier that the language and thought of children and of inhabitants of oral cultures have been neglected and then studied at about the same time and with much the same underlying assumptions. Their neglect coincided with the general assumption that the prevailing conventions of literate (male) adult language and thought were natural, rational, proper. With the gradual decay of confidence in this assumption we have seen other forms of thought and language increasingly taken seriously as rational adaptations to particular environments and circumstances. With the recent gathering conviction that even more of our knowledge than we had suspected is "fictive" – is compounded of elements contributed by the mind's ways of making sense as well as by empirical observation – we have seen the "languages" of apes, dolphins and broccoli taken seriously and carefully investigated.

A preliminary to rediscovering orality might be the rediscovery of the strangeness of this literacy which for most of the time we take so much for granted. Here goes my BIC PF-49 Fine across the paper and your eyes can scan the printed page at ten times the speed it takes to write. My writing is being done now and your reading is being done now, though they are perhaps years apart. Time is obliterated. In an oral culture words are sounds that, once spoken, pass away for ever. They can be repeated, but each repetition will be new and slightly different. There are no fixed criteria or models for oral words – nowhere to look them up and check their proper meaning, nowhere where they can continue. Once you close this book the words will wait patiently in their lines for another eye to seek them out. When words are not used constantly in an oral culture, or stories not told, they exist only as long as they are remembered by some individuals.

What are words made up from? Letters, we tend to assume. But words are made up of sounds. We conventionally say that we write things down. But what we write down are symbols designed to represent the sounds of words which signify things. The transmutations from things to letters involve remarkably complex processes which we only hazily understand, and originally required a series of remarkable inventions which we can only hazily chart. The early beginnings of letters seem to lie in pictorial representations of things; the symbols come then to represent the sound of the words for things; then by great creative intelligence symbols were invented to represent the syllables of language – and so one need have many fewer symbols than words and things – leading to the enormous achievement of the Semitic alphabet, which used symbols to represent the limited set of consonants of language. The "Greek miracle" seems tied in with the separation of vowels and consonants and so the invention of an alphabet that could much more adequately and unambiguously represent the sound of language and so could much more easily be written and read. Reading and writing were no longer complex tasks requiring long training, and even then inevitably involving difficulties and ambiguities of interpretation. Once a system of clearly representing the sound of language was invented it could be relatively easily learned and internalized, with dramatic cultural effects. This "genesis of symbolic forms," of which we have only hints and guesses, "is the odyssey of the mind" (Langer, 1946, p. ix).

The relatively recent rediscovery of orality by Western scholars is connected with some problems presented by Homer's epic poems. The influential evolutionary paradigm of late Victorian times seemed to work fine if one focused on the development of science: from myth to rationality to empirical science was an entirely plausible progressive story. The more general applicability of this paradigm to human culture, however, ran up against the anomaly of Homer. Classically educated Victorians were more familiar with those far battles on the windy plains of Troy, with the wooden horse and how the topless towers of Ilium were finally brought down, with the long journey of the wily Odysseus to his home in Ithaca twenty years later, with the tragedy of noble Hector, and with the anger of the mighty Achilles than with much of the Victorian society around them. How could such vividly powerful epics and their richness of human insight, their technical sophistication and emotional force, their overwhelming, engaging reality be composed by and for what were in all other regards considered primitive people? "Primitive" mentality – supposedly a mess of irrationality and confusion – must, it would seem, have had the resources to create some of the greatest cultural achievements.

Two other complications arose. First, the story of the *Iliad*, long regarded as straightforward fiction, came to be seen as about actual events that occurred in the thirteenth century BCE. This historicity began to be established by Heinrich Schliemann's excavations at Troy and Mycenae during the latter part of the nineteenth century, and has gradually become fuller and clearer, allowing Michael Wood to gather the pieces together in the persuasive picture presented in the popular television series, and book, *In Search of the Trojan War* (Wood, 1985).

The second complication was the growing evidence that Homer and the other poets in the tradition of which he was a part were illiterate. As Berkley Peabody puts it, "Despite the implications of its name, literature does not seem to have been the invention of literate people" (Peabody, 1975, p. 1). Homer, the master poet, lived about five hundred years after the events of which he sang, at a time when the kingdoms whose ships sailed for Troy were themselves long destroyed. Increasing knowledge of the spread of literacy in Greece made it increasingly difficult for scholars to imagine Homer, traditionally blind anyway, sitting at a table *writing* his poems.

But how could such technically complex poems, many thousands of lines in length, be composed without writing? Surely no illiterate bard could make up those supple hexameters as he sang, and then recall them word for word? Virgil, the other great epic poet of the ancient world, labored for years writing his *Aeneid*. We know that he constantly revised it and on his death-bed asked that it be destroyed. Surely no illiterate bard could toss off a book an hour on the hoof, as it were, of a power, vividness and quality that the great Virgil struggled for years to match, and couldn't.

The story of the rediscovery of the Homeric method of composition is itself an epic of scholarly ingenuity, and one which I will sketch only most briefly. Our focus must turn away from Patroclus on the walls of Troy and the academic battles to uncover the historical reality behind the poems to the techniques of oral composition that were first exposed through the study of Homer's texts and then elaborated through anthropological studies. It is a different kind of story, but not without its own interest.

This story begins with an American in Paris. Having completed an M.A. at Berkeley in California, Milman Parry wrote his Ph.D. thesis in Paris. He argued that the structure of the Homeric poems and their every distinctive feature are due to the requirements of oral methods of composition. Parry supplemented his arguments during the early 1930s by studying the methods of oral composition still being used by Yugoslavian singers of heroic tales. After Parry's early death his work was continued by Alfred B. Lord.

Parry's analyses of the *Iliad* and *Odyssey* showed that they were largely made up of formulae – repeated morphemic clusters – whose composition was dictated by the metrical requirements of the hexameter line. For example, Homer has a large number of adjectival epithets for most of the recurring nouns in the poem – for wine, the sea, ships, the major characters, and so on. The epithet chosen at any point is not necessarily the most apposite for the meaning of the line but is dictated rather by its fit into the meter of the line. In many cases the epithet is almost meaningless, but it allows the hexameter to ride along (Kirk, 1965, Ch. 1). One fifth of Homer's lines are repeated more or less entirely elsewhere in his epic poems, and in about 28,000 lines there are about 25,000 repeated phrases (Parry, 1928). (The belief that Homer's poems were oral compositions was not new with Parry, of course. It was suggested by Vico in 1744, and more emphatically by Wolf in 1795. But Parry was the first to show in detail how the poems would have been composed orally and show the distinctive marks of their oral composition (see also Burke, 1985 and Griffin, 1980).

The oral poet did not memorize the poems he performed, as we would have to do. Rather the singer learned through a long apprenticeship – a long non-literate apprenticeship – the particular metrical form of his tradition, until it was like a somatic rhythm, in which he could think. The content of the song was held together first by a clear grasp of the overall story and within that the meter determined the patterns of sound. As Albert B. Lord puts it, "Man without writing thinks in terms of sound groups and not in words" (Lord, 1964, p. 25). The oral performance, then, does not involve repetition of a memorized poem or recitation as we know it – the idea of a fixed text is a product of literacy – but rather each performance is a new composition. It may be very like others, and

57

certain patterns will recur from performance to performance, but the singer is composing, not repeating something fixed in memory. We see, in Lord's words, "the preservation of tradition by the constant re-creation of it" (Lord, 1964, p. 29). Or as Jack Goody puts it, referring to modern performances of myths in oral cultures, what we see is not repetition of a fixed model but a "continuous creation" of the basic story at each telling.

Chunks of sound, then, are arranged metrically in the Homeric poems, and agglomerate line by line to repeat the heroic story. The poet "stitches" the chunks together as he goes, the formulae to fit the metrical line, and the episodes to fit the story. The Greeks called such trained singers "rhapsodes," literally "song-stitchers" – though the rhapsodes of the classical period were trained rather like modern actors, literate learners and repeaters of a fixed text. Homer and his illiterate fellows were composing stitchers. The oral singer had in mind a story, an absolutely overwhelming metrical pattern in which the story was to be told, and a wide array of formulae that made fitting the elements of the story to the meter of the line *relatively* easy. It seems likely that Homer came as a culmination of his tradition, and recited his poems to trained scribes.

Perhaps we can see some features of this skill at work in the gifted musical improvisor. A Beethoven or Mozart at the piano had so internalized the process of composition and their instrument that they could take a theme and elaborate and develop it endlessly, delighting their audience with their disciplined spontaneity.

In the early 1930s, Parry supplemented his arguments by studying methods of oral composition being used by contemporary singers of heroic tales in Yugoslavia. After his death, his work was supported and extended by Albert B. Lord's studies (1964) of comparable singers in the Balkans. Lord has described in some detail the conditions of their intensive, and almost invariably nonliterate, training, which cannot be very unlike Homer's (Lord, 1964, esp. ch. 2). This work has been further elaborated by Berkley Peabody's ingenious analysis of Hesiod's *Works and Days* (1975). Peabody showed in still greater depth how the oral poet uses the techniques developed over uncountable generations to realize for the audience a kind of alternate reality. That is, the techniques of oral poetry are designed to discourage critical reflection on the stories and their contents, and instead to "enchant" the hearers, drawing them into the world of the story. I will describe some of these techniques below.

This process of catching up the audience, of enthralling it, and impressing the reality of the story on it, is a central feature of education in an oral culture. The social institutions of oral cultures are sustained in large part by sound, by the spoken or sung word, and whatever it can achieve in the way of committing individuals to particular beliefs, expectations, roles, and behaviors. In sustaining social institutions the techniques of fixing the crucial patterns of beliefs in the memory – rhyme, rhythm, formula, story, and so on – are vitally important. Education in such cultures is largely a matter of constantly immersing the young in the enchanting patterns of sound until they resound to them, until they become "musically" in tune, harmonious, with the institutions of their culture.

The Homeric poems were called the educators of the pre-classical Greeks because they performed this social role. They were not learned by every Greek because of their aesthetic value; that was instrumental to their general social value as "a massive repository of useful knowledge, a sort of encyclopaedia of ethics, politics, history, and technology which the effective citizen was required to learn as the core of his education equipment" (Havelock, 1963, p. 29). In such an education a very large proportion of mental energy has to go into ensuring memorization of the main messages of the culture, because they can exist and survive only in people's memories. Little mental energy is left for reflection on those messages, or analysis of them, because such activity would interfere with the need to sink them unquestioningly into every mind.

A further extension of Parry's and Lord's work was undertaken by Eric Havelock. His *Preface to Plato* (1963) and *Origins of Western Literacy* (1976), and *The Muse Learns to Write* (1986), show that the principles of poetic composition that Parry and Lord rediscovered help to make clearer the achievements of early Greek philosophy, and help in particular to clarify why Plato wished to exclude poets from his ideal state. Plato's *Republic* is re-read, so to speak, as a program for educating people to discard the residues of oral culture and to embrace the forms of thinking that full literacy makes possible. In Havelock's interpretation, Plato says that the mind need no longer be immersed into the oral tradition, memorizing and copying the paradigmatic structures and patterns of the Homeric poems, but can be freed to engage its proper objects – which we might call abstract concepts, and what Plato called Forms or Ideas. Plato characterized this mode of thinking as opposed to the Homeric tradition; Plato's scheme of education, as he represents it, brought the mind to reality, while Homer's crippled the intellect by its seductive illusions and distortions of reality.

So the new forms of thinking made possible by literacy, near their beginning in educational discourse, were represented as enemies of the oral *bonnes à penser*: "Plato's target was indeed an educational procedure and a whole way of life" (Havelock, 1963, p. 45). There are clear ambivalences in Plato's reflections on the oral tradition (see the *Phaedrus* and the possibly apocryphal *VIIth Letter)* and on Homer, but in the end those forms of thinking, education, and society which were geared "to retain tenaciously a precious hoard of exemplars" (Havelock, 1963, p. 199) had to be destroyed to make place for the new abstract forms of thought and whatever world they brought with them. Plato did not conceive his educational scheme as building on the oral tradition, but as a replacement for it. His work, in Havelock's words, "announced the arrival of a completely new level of discourse which as it became perfected was to create in turn a new kind of experience of the world – the reflective, the scientific, the technological, the theological, the analytic. We can give it a dozen names" (Havelock, 1963, p. 267). Plato's influence is so strong in Western thought that it is extremely difficult for us now to imagine the kind of consciousness created in the oral tradition, and the kind of experience created for listeners by a singer of tales or teller of myths.

Havelock's description of the techniques of oral recitation by singers of heroic tales in the ancient world shows that audiences received poems rather differently from the way we read the text of those poems today. The accumulated purpose of those techniques was to ensure "a state of total personal involvement and therefore of emotional identification with the substance of the poetized statement that you are required to retain" (Havelock, 1963, p. 44). A youth in an oral culture, whether Greek or aboriginal Australian, needed to expend considerable mental resources to learn the oral foundations of his or her cultural institutions. The professional singers – in whom the rhythms and stories of the culture profoundly in-dwell – are central figures in such cultures, but the messages are repeated constantly and everywhere. Proverbs and maxims and clichés and formulae uttered at the table, on rising or going to sleep, in the market or the field, are constantly repeated bits and pieces of the great myths or epic poems of the culture. African children, for example, traditionally learn the practices and mores of their ethnic groups through riddles asked by their grandparents. In religious school throughout the Muslim world, young students commit to memory phenomenally long passages of Koranic literature and law. It is likely that biblical stories were first repeated and handed on by singers and storytellers, as are the tales of African griots in many places today.

Learning the sustaining messages of an oral culture is different from the constant effort at accumulation of knowledge with which we are familiar. In an oral culture memorization is central, but it is not performed in the way that we might try to learn something by heart. For us memorizing is usually an attempt to copy a text in such a manner that we can repeat it on command – our techniques are typically impoverished, involving largely repetition, some mnemonics perhaps, saying it aloud with our eyes closed, and so, rather ineffectually, on. In an oral culture, learning proceeds more at a somatic level, using the whole body to support the memorizing process. The Homeric singer, and singers throughout the world, usually use a simple stringed instrument, sometimes a drum, whose beat reinforces the rhythm of the telling and draws the hearer into the enchantment of the song. The audience does not so much listen to it, as we might listen to a play, but they are invited to live it. The acoustical rhythm created by the singer and his instrument is supported by the repetitive meter, by rhythmic movements of the body, by the pattern of formulae and of the story, to set up conditions of enchantment that impress the message into the minds of the hearers. "The entire nervous system, in short, is geared to the task of memorization" (Havelock, 1963, p. 151). The techniques of the skilled performer generate a relaxed, half-hypnotized, pleasure in the audience; "rhythmic patterns, vocal, verbal, instrumental, and physical, all set in motion together and all consonant in their effect" (Havelock, 1963, p. 152). (For a fuller account, see Havelock, 1963, Ch. IX: "The psychology of the poetic performance.")

This semi-hypnotized state is similar to that described often by anthropologists as the condition in which audiences receive the foundational messages of their culture. Lévi-Strauss rather dramatically claims that his study of mythology aims "to show, not how men think in myths, but how myths operate in men's minds without their being aware of the fact" (Lévi-Strauss, 1969, p. 12). He preferred to compare this process to a musical performance rather than to linguistic forms or texts: "Thus the myth and the musical work are like conductors of an orchestra, whose audience becomes the silent performers" (Lévi-Strauss, 1969, p. 17). While no Western educator would wish to replicate all aspects of this phenomenon in schools (!), it seems important to understand the nature of this receptive state. Anyone familiar with children's rapt attention to television broadcasts may recognize some aspects of the condition described here.

Similarly Edmund Leach argues that the structural patterns of myths and their underlying messages are communicated powerfully and unambiguously despite considerable variations in the surface stories and performances.

> Whenever a corpus of mythology is recited in its religious setting, such structures are "felt" to be present, and convey meaning much as poetry conveys meaning. Even though the ordinary listener is not fully conscious of what has been communicated, the "message" is there in a quite objective sense. (Leach, 1967, p. 12)

In Lévi-Bruhl's words, when a sacred myth is recited in ritual or other settings of heightened emotion, "what they hear in it awakens a whole gamut of harmonics which do not exist for us" (1985, p. 369). The written form of the myth which we can study "is but the inanimate corpse which remains after the vital spark has fled" (Lévi-Bruhl, 1985, p. 369).

In his re-examination of orality Jack Goody (1977, 1986, 1987) has not only undermined traditional notions of the move from "primitive" to rational thought, and instead shown that the differences typically educed as evidence for such a shift are better understood as epiphenomena of the move from orality to literacy; he has also clarified some particular steps that accompanied the move from orality to literacy – which I will draw on later – and he has detailed, with Ian Watt, various consequences of literacy against the background of orality (Goody and Watt, 1968).

(For the best current survey of this field see Ong's *Orality and Literacy* (1982).)

I want to turn now from the story of the rediscovery of orality to simply listing some of the main *bonnes à penser* common in oral cultures. This will not be a systematic survey, but one motivated rather by my educational interests. I will begin with those features of orality exposed by this brief discussion of Parry, Lord, Havelock, Goody, and Ong, and try to elaborate these by drawing on some other works.

Oral *Bonnes à Penser*

In listing certain features of oral cultures I do not mean to imply that such cultures are all alike; nor do I imply that they all use much the same set of techniques for preserving their cultural institutions. Clearly there are enormous differences among the oral cultures of pre-classical Greeks and early twentieth century Trobrian islanders, of aboriginal Australians and the indigenous peoples of the northwest coast of America before extensive contacts with European peoples. Clearly oral cultures throughout the world have invented different *bonnes à penser* effectively to give form to and preserve their particular institutions. Myth comprises a range of techniques that differ significantly from place to place. And myth itself, according to Lévi-Bruhl, is a cultural invention designed in part to recreate or recapture the sense of participation in nature from which the great neolithic inventions of animal taming, agriculture, tool and pottery making, weaving, and who knows what linguistic inventions (tenses? the subjunctive?!) had long alienated its developers. So it is not at all to deny the ungraspable diversity of oral cultural institutions that I will gather hereunder three sub-headings an "ensemble of characteristics" of orality–to use Lévi-Bruhl's translator's term (Lévi-Bruhl, 1985, p. 29).

It is inevitably difficult for us to think of orality simply as a positive set of bonnes à penser. What intrudes on our attempts to understand orally sustained forms of thought is the intellectual capacities and forms of communication that have been stimulated by literacy. But we need to make the effort to see orality as an energetic and somewhat distinct set of ways of learning and communicating, not simply as an incomplete and imperfect use of the mind waiting only for the invention of literacy. Orality, then, is not at all the same as what we usually mean by illiteracy. Illiteracy is perhaps best understood as a condition in which one has not acquired the positive capacities orality can provide without gaining those of literacy either. Let us then consider what goods these oral *bonnes à penser* seem to serve, so that we might more explicitly be "aware of their existence and their importance," and then consider which among them might be good also for us and which might be worth our efforts to preserve or to stimulate.

Poetics of memory

Let us begin considering orality by focusing on what seems to be the central reason it involves some different tactics of thinking from literacy; it needs to rely on memory. If the institutions of one's culture rely on the living memories of its members then the techniques that seem best able to impress the appropriate messages into their minds and maintain them there in as stable a form as possible are vitally important. The common Victorian sense of the "mental incapacity" of people in oral cultures, as assessed by their distaste for or inability to perform mental functions that were commonplace in literate Western cultures, kept running into odd anomalies. Lévi-Bruhl, writing in 1910, summed up one such. He described various prodigious, but to the natives commonplace, feats of memory:

> This extraordinary development of memory, and a memory which faithfully reproduces the minutest details of sense-impressions in the correct order of their appearance, is shown moreover by the wealth of vocabulary and the grammatical complexity of the languages. Now the very men who speak these languages and possess this power of memory are (in Australia or Northern Brazil, for instance) incapable of counting beyond two and three. The slightest mental effort involving abstract reasoning, however rudimentary it may be, is so distasteful to them that they immediately declare themselves tired and give it up. (Lévi-Bruhl, 1985, p. 115)

64

Now there are some difficulties in Lévi-Bruhl's way of putting this, due in part to his assumptions about the "prelogical" and "mystic" nature of "primitive mentality." It is not, for example, a matter of his subjects having a "power of memory" so much as a highly developed set of techniques for learning and remembering. Also I will argue below that the problem for his subjects does not lie in "abstraction" as such – a common assumption also applied to children's thinking – but rather in the dissociation of thought from matters embedded in one's lifeworld. Goody, for example, describes his innocent request of some LoDagaa to count for him. "Count what?" was their, to them, obvious question. They had a number of sophisticated forms of counting, and an abstract numerical system, but their methods of counting cows and cowrie shells differ. Nor, as we shall see, is "abstract reasoning" beyond anyone with a human mind; it is just that certain particular mental capacities involving abstraction that are very heavily dependent on writing are not available to people who do not write or read.

Nevertheless Lévi-Bruhl describes the apparent anomaly of mental prodigies among the supposedly mentally deficient. He perceived that there were no differences on any simple scale of mental superiority/inferiority, but that the conditions of life in oral cultures stimulated different mental developments to deal with those conditions. And he was precise in locating a wide range of these differences. The uses of memory in oral cultures, he concluded, "are quite different because its contents are of a different character. It is both very accurate and very emotional" (Lévi-Bruhl, 1985, p. 110).

Oral cultures engage the emotions of their members by making the culturally important messages event-laden, by presenting characters and their emotions in conflict in developing narratives – in short, by building the messages into stories. "All myths tell a story," Lévi Strauss points out (Lévi-Strauss, 1962, p. 26), and we have already seen Albert B. Lord's conclusion about the role of the story in providing the firm structure for the constant reconstruction of heroic songs. The formulae and groupings and meter in the end "serve only one purpose. They provide a means for telling a story . . . . The tale's the thing" (Lord, 1964, p. 68). The story form is one of the few cultural universals – everyone, everywhere has told and enjoyed stories. They are one of the greatest cultural inventions for catching and fixing meaning. Perhaps my use of "invention" here is a bit tendentious, in the way in which I criticized "technology" above. Perhaps "discovery" is more appropriate; some enormously creative person or people discovered that messages shaped into the distinctive form of the story were better remembered and carried a charge of emotional identification that greatly enhanced social cohesion and control.

Myth stories also, of course, have what we would consider aesthetic values. But while we distingish aesthetic from utilitarian values, for members of oral cultures these are bound up together. The aesthetic force of myths or heroic tales is a part of what makes them memorable. The story form through most of human experience has been one of the most powerful and effective sustainers of cultures across the world. Its great power lies in its ability to fix affective responses to the messages it contains and to bind what is to be remembered in emotional associations. Our emotions, to put it simply, are more effective at sustaining, and helping recall of, memories of events (Bartlett, 1932), (though literate memory-training can also produce prodigies, as Matteo Ricci demonstrated (Spence, 1984); see also Frances Yates, 1966). This connection between emotions and memory should not be a surprise if we reflect on the events of our lives that are most memorable. Almost invariably we find that they are accompanied by vivid emotional associations, and retain quite clearly a particular emotional tone. Most of the world's cultures and its great religions have at their sacred core a story, and we indeed have difficulty keeping our rational history from being constantly shaped into stories. Certainly the simplified histories sanctioned in the schools of most nation states have at least as much in common with the origin myths or oral cultures as they do with the austere ideals of rational historiography (Ravitch, 1983).

So one of the techniques developed in oral cultures long ago whose importance for education we have of late tended to forget or neglect or perhaps even repress is the story form. I think there are a number of ways we might use this most powerful of communicative media in education today, especially in the primary school. Indeed, I think the story has so many and such important uses that I will give over the next chapter to exploring its nature and potential educational uses.

In the previous section I noted some of the other techniques that are used in oral cultures to create conditions for effective reception and memorization of the most important cultural messages. The condition of emotional enchantment that Havelock describes owes much to the story form, but also a lot to those other techniques with which the story is embellished – we have seen the functions of rhyme, rhythm, meter, repetition of formulae, redundancy, and we should add the constant use of highly vivid or visual images conveyed through their sensory qualities. These techniques we can find used in oral cultures throughout the world to establish faith in various social institutions. The techniques Havelock describes at work enchanting archaic Greeks are much the same as E. E. Evans-Pritchard shows being wielded among the contemporary Azende to instil faith in the witch-doctor (E. E. Evans-Pritchard, 1936).

These have been, of course, prominent among the techniques of Western poetry, and the condition of mind that Havelock describes is close to what we would readily describe as poetic. As with the singers of heroic tales, or the reciters of myths, the poet is the shaper of sound to create particular emotional effects and to fix particular meanings. The shaping of sound finds one outlet in poetry and another, to be considered in the next two volumes, in rhetoric. These two, along with music, are perhaps the most evident and direct manifestations of the oral tradition that have survived in the literate world.

Prominent among the *bonnes à penser* of poetic thinking is metaphor, and its sub-set of poetic tropes. Mythic understanding moves fluidly according to the complex logic of metaphor, more readily than it follows the systematic logics of rational inquiry. As Cassirer notes, "It is a familiar fact that all mythic thinking is governed and permeated by the principle [of metaphor]" (Cassirer, 1946, p. 92). This metaphoric power should be easily appreciated and easily accessible to us, as it suffuses our language at every turn. "Every turn" and "accessible" and "power," and so on, all involve casual uses of metaphor. It is clearly one of the foundations of all our mental activity, a foundation upon which our systematic logics of rational inquiry also rest, or – a better metaphor – a ground out of which they grow. Myth and our everyday language, then, are permeated with metaphor; as Ernst Cassirer concluded: "The same form of mental conception is operative in both. It is the form which one may denote as *metaphorical thinking*" (Cassirer, 1946, p. 84). Or, as Lévi-Strauss observes, "metaphor . . . is not a later embellishment of language but is one of its fundamental modes –

a primary form of discursive thought" (Lévi-Strauss, 1962, p. 102; see also Cooper, 1986).

These, then, are a few characteristics of orality for our ensemble, generated by the need to memorize and be committed to one's cultural institutions. We find these techniques, these *bonnes à penser*, in greater or lesser degree in all oral cultures:

> At different periods and in different cultures there are close links between the techniques for mental recall, the inner organization of the faculty (of memory), the place it occupies in the system of ego, and the ways that men picture memory to themselves. (Vernant, 1983, p. 75; see also Finnegan, 1970, 1977)

We are familiar with these *bonnes à penser* still, but usually in a much attenuated or altered form. Rhyme, for example, seems little more than fun for us now, a part of children's games, anachronistic and therefore ironic in modern poetry. We would hardly consider its systematic use a matter of vital social importance. We can write, so do not need rhyme to sustain the memory of our institutions. These survivors of orality – rhyme, rhythm, meter, story, metaphor – serve largely – I am tempted to write "merely" – aesthetic purposes for us. While metaphor and story may still seem to us culturally important in some imprecise way, we tend to think of rhyme and rhythm as merely casual cultural survivors, hangovers able to find a precarious new purpose entertaining the literate – like the lords and ladies of a defeated civilization made into clowns and dancers to entertain their conquerors. But art has a utilitarian purpose when it supports faith – whether in gods, in the validity of one's cultural institutions, in one's society, in one's sense of oneself. So as we go on we might stir up a bit of unease in thinking about any of the *bonnes à penser* invented to create and sustain memory as mere entertainments. Their origins lie in the remarkable human ambition "to liberate the soul from time and open up a path to immortality" (Vernant, 1983, p. 95). All the world's amazing cultural and technological achievements since the development of literacy have been built on their efficacy and the intellectual space they once did and can still generate. We would do well, therefore, to consider carefully their actual and potential roles in early childhood.

Participation and conservation

An Ojibwa Indian observed: "The white man writes everything down in a book so that it will not be forgotten; but our ancestors married the animals, learned their ways, and passed on the knowledge from one generation to another" (Jenness, in Lévi-Strauss, 1966a, p. 37). This expresses a sense of participation in the natural world, a sense of having knowledge that is different from the kinds of propositions that are a staple of rational inquiries. It reflects a mental condition anthropologists have tried often to describe as a kind of oneness with nature, compared with which our normal relationship with the natural world seems alienated. "The mainspring of the acts, thoughts, and feelings of early man was the conviction that the divine was immanent in nature, and nature intimately connected with society" (Frankfort, *et al.* 1949, p. 237). All attempts to pin-point the causes and character of this sense of participation in nature suggest that although myths and consciousness in oral cultures are inadequate when it comes to pragmatic control *over* the world, they somehow do an admirable job of enabling people to participate comfortably *in* their lifeworld. But it is not a simple condition, obviously, nor one we can feel unequivocally regretful of having largely lost. Ong describes it this way:

> The psyche of a culture innocent of writing knows by a kind of empathetic identification of knower and known, in which the object of knowledge and the total being of the knower enter into a kind of fusion, in a way which literate cultures would typically find unsatisfyingly vague and garbled and somehow too intense and participatory (Ong, 1977, p. 18).

One of the corner-stones of Western rationality is knowing, as it were, where we end and the world begins; distinguishing the world from our feelings, hopes, fears, and so on. This form of thinking seems to be very largely a product of literacy. As Ong puts it, "Writing fosters abstractions that disengage knowledge from the arena where human beings struggle with one another" (Ong, 1982, pp. 43, 44), or, in Peabody's words: "The shift in medium from utterance to record affects the way such an institution works and tends to change what was an immediate, living, active agent into an increasingly distant, timeless, passive, authority" (Peabody, 1975, pp. 1, 2). In an oral culture the ear is most highly attuned to picking up cultural messages, supplemented by the eye. In our case, it is usually the other way around.

Sound is alive and participatory. It is effective within only a short physical range. The hearer must be in the presence of the speaker – there are no carefully crafted memos from the president or manager. "The living word," as Socrates put it, ". . . has a soul . . . , of which the written word is properly no more than an image" (Plato, *Phaedrus*, trans. Jowett, 1953, p. 279). The living word is the word in the arena of human interactions and conflicts. It is not the distanced and "cooled" word of the written text. Language use in an oral culture, then, tends to be, in Ong's phrase, "agonistically toned" (1977, p. 113); it is charged with the direct energy of the speaker's body, and so the speaker's hopes, fears, wants, needs, intentions, and so on. Oral heroic tales are full of bragging, elaborate abuse of adversaries, and exuberant praise of leaders or those from whom the speaker wants a favor. The tensions of daily struggles are face-to-face in an oral culture. These facts of oral life lead to a highly polarized world, of good and evil, friends and enemies, fear and security, and so on.

Ong points out that the mental life of oral cultures "is sure to carry a heavy load of praise and vituperation" (1977, p. 112), because "if one does not think formulary, mnemonically structured thoughts, how can one really know them, that is, be able to retrieve them, if the thoughts are even of moderate complexity?" (p. 104). Thus, because oral cultures "necessarily store knowledge largely in narrative concerned with interacting human or quasi-human figures," (1977, p. 112) there is a powerful pressure to polarize. The Batomba of Subsaharan Africa for instance, have two typically polarized paraphrastic names for White foreigners: "The white man, honored by all, companion of our chiefs" or, as occasion may demand, the pointed expression "You do not touch the poisonous caterpillar" (Ong, 1977, p. 112). In such societies the forms of verbal play also tend to be "agonistically toned" – riddles, tricks, and jokes are often characterized by a playful competitiveness or even aggressiveness.

A symptom perhaps of our moving towards Ong's "secondary orality" is the increasingly common use of "I hear what you're saying" for what used to be the commoner "I see what you mean". Literacy is a distancing medium, relying on the eye and its ability to pan back and forth over a text. The forms of thought it has stimulated bear the etymological mark of the eye's increasing dominance. "Idea" has the same root as "video," and theory – *theoria* – is a spectacle, something observed. The eye cannot as easily perceive the emotion in words as can the ear, and so in writing we learn to make our language more objective. This has led to some of the quainter excesses of high literacy, as when writers abhor suggesting that they are actually the producers of a text by using "I," at worst conceding that "it is the opinion of the author . . ."

In an oral culture, "the meaning of each word is ratified in a succession of concrete situations, accompanied by vocal inflections and physical gestures, all of which combine to particularize both its specific denotation and its accepted connative uses" (Goody and Watt, 1968, p. 306). This embeddedness in the lifeworld means that words are not themselves objects of reflection in any systematic way, and consequently oral cultures have no epistemology in our sense. While words are tied into their context of reference philosophical problems do not arise. In oral cultures people do not dissociate words from things to the point where they might wonder how short the legs of a small table have to be for it to be considered a tray. This feature of their thinking has nothing to do with "defects" or "inadequacies of the primitive mind," but is rather a function of the uselessness of many of our forms of thought and techniques of thinking in the conditions of most oral cultures. "In an...unlettered society the memory is loaded with nothing that is either useless or unintelligible" (A. Parry, in M. Parry, 1971, p. xiii). In nearly all oral cultures, for example, time is reckoned in terms of the significant daily activities of the social group. An "abstract" or, better, a dissociated or disembedded system for measuring time, such as we employ, is useful only when it is necessary to coordinate a large number of quite diverse kinds of activities. Such diversity does not exist in most oral cultures, where time measurement reflects the sequence of activities that constitute the rhythms of daily life.

Luria (1979, ch. 4) describes studies he performed with illiterate peasants in remote areas of the Soviet union. He posed to them apparently simple problems, such as: In the far north, where there is snow, all bears are white. Novaya Zemlya is in the far north and there is always snow there. What colors are the bears around Novaya Zemlya? His subjects would, no doubt politely wishing to play their part in the conversation, reply that they had never been to Novaya Zemlya so didn't know or that they had seen a black bear **but never a white one, and so on. That is, the kind of conversation in which Luria tried to engage these peasants was a kind whose rules and underlying forms of thought are familiar to us, but which** could only appear bizarre to non-literate peasants. The point is not a concern with mental capacity, but with social utility, and the influence of the latter over cognition. Pragmatic thought in oral cultures participates more intimately in the lifeworld; it does not have any need to treat the world and experience as objects distanced from their emotional, aesthetic, and utilitarian needs. As such, it makes "no clear-cut distinction between subjective states and the properties of the cosmos" (Lévi-Strauss, 1969, p. 240).

Oral cultures have been described as inclined towards homeostasis, conservatism and stability in ways that our modern literate cultures are not. Such cultures, of course, undergo changes of many kinds - migration, disaster, invasion, merging with others - but the mental forms dominant in oral cultures strive to maintain verbal accounts of the culture's life that assert continuity and stability. One striking difference between oral and literate cultures is their somewhat different attitudes to the past: we have and value accurate historical accounts whereas oral societies cultivate what J. A. Barnes has called "structural amnesia" - systematic procedures for "forgetting" or wiping out from the oral records of the culture's past (cf. Goody and Watt, 1978, p. 309). Although oral cultures often preserve the memory of particular historical events in stories or in memorized genealogies of leading families, it usually turns out that the record kept does not accurately reflect past reality but is faithful rather to present social conditions and statuses. As conditions and status change, so do the accounts or **genealogy. Malinowski (1954) shows this process at work among the Trobriand islanders. As changes occurred in the structure and power relationships of the society, so the myths of origin changed** to reflect the current social structure. The historical changes, that is, were gradually effaced, or, as Malinowski concluded, "myths serve to cover certain inconsistencies created by historical events" (Malinowski, 1954, p. 125). The oral record of the past, then, ensures that "the individual has little perception of the past except in terms of the present" (Goody and Watt, 1968, p. 310).

We find it hard to think of this structural amnesia as anything other than an unawareness of history, another incapacity due to the lack of literacy. It seems merely a way of making the best of a bad job, or the only strategy one can manage if one cannot keep written records. But the positive value of such structural amnesia is that it tends to preserve a sense of stability and clarity. The social structure and its prevailing institutions are constantly supported by whatever sanction is contained in the myths, whether of sacred ancestors or gods, and are constantly renewed; "time is recorded only biologically without being allowed to become 'history' – that is, without its corrosive action being able to exert itself upon consciousness by revealing the irreversibility of events" (Eliade, 1959, pp. 74, 75). One technique constantly used to achieve this end is the assertion of continual rebirth–rebeginning as the first beginning. We preserve a vague shadow of this in our New Year festivals. Although Malinowski suggests that myth is simply a pragmatic charter determining social roles and tasks, nevertheless the sense of intellectual security it seems commonly to give is not to be casually depreciated. This is indeed another of those *bonnes à penser*; sloughing off the memory of events that are no longer relevant or useful to present life.

This emphasis on preserving stability through selective memory of events relevant to recent social conditions leads to what is often characterized as a conservative frame of mind. It is indeed conservative, but in a radical sense. The pressure to preserve in memory the institutions of one's culture does not invite playful innovation of experimentation. While no doubt some oral cultures are more resilient in this regard than others, on the whole anthropologists attest to the powerful sanctions against change: "The most apparently trifling innovation may lead to danger, liberate hostile forces, and finally bring about the ruin of its instigator and all dependent upon him" (Lévi-Bruhl, 1985, p. 42). The cultural institutions support a limited stock of archetypal forms of appropriate behaviour for each member of the society, and the repetition of these alone is sanctioned and validated by the myths. These are the behaviors of sacred ancestors or gods, which it is the human task to imitate: "The inhibition against new invention, to avoid placing any possible strain on the memory, continually encouraged contemporary decisions to be framed as though they were the acts and words of the ancestors" (Havelock, 1963, p. 121) or, we might add, gods. Or, as Eliade puts it, the individual in oral cultures "acknowledges no act which has not been previously posited and lived by someone else, some other being who was not a man. What he does has been done before. His life is a ceaseless repetition of gestures initiated by others" (Eliade, 1959, p. 5). In such a culture "only the changeless is ultimately significant" (Frankfort, 1961, p. viii).

While no doubt there are oral cultures for which these generalizations are somewhat less appropriate than for others, they do point to further common *bonnes à penser* of such societies. The pressure against change and innovation serve stability, order, and intellectual security. One's familiar territory is intellectually mapped out, is categorized and under secure control – its dangers are known. Alien territory, outsiders, the new, threaten one's categories; the taboos are casually broken by those with different beliefs and habits (Douglas, 1966). The resources of orality considered in this section help to provide intellectual security and a sense of persisting order in a society despite historical changes. They also help to preserve a sense of participation in nature which users of literate forms of thought find somewhat alien. Not entirely alien, of course; attempts to recapture this sense of participation in nature find their most common literate expression in poetry. It is in the work of poets such as Wordsworth that the sense of participation in nature is most plausibly recaptured, and, significantly for my general argument about the cognitive effects of orality, it is in preliterate childhood that he most vividly locates it:

> No outcast he, bewildered and depressed.
> Along his infant veins are interfused
> The gratification and the filial bond
> Of nature that connect him with the world.
> (*The Prelude*, Bk. II, 241-244).

Classification and explanation

Inhabitants of oral cultures often have remarkably detailed knowledge of the flora and fauna of their environments; but their systems for classifying this knowledge tend to be very different from ours. Many anthropologist have commented on members of oral cultures who could give remarkably detailed inventories of kinds of plants, trees, or weather conditions but had no words for "plant," "trees," or "weather." This further supported their conclusions about such people's inability to "abstract" - a defect they were supposed to share with children (and women). And many educationalists still assume that children are deficient in this way. Yet we find in many oral cultures, and in children, the constant use of enormously abstract concepts – such as "good" and "bad." Indeed there are some purely oral languages which use abstractions where we would prefer concrete terms (see Boas, 1911). It is not, to repeat it yet again, abstraction that is the problem, but dissociation from the lifeworld. Literacy enables and encourages this kind of dissociation; it is a product of the techniques of writing not a property that some human minds have and others lack. For example, the proposition "The bad man killed the poor child" is rendered in Chinook: "The man's badness killed the child's poverty" (Lévi-Strauss, 1966a, p.1). A major difference between oral cultures and our own lies not in their incapacity for abstraction, but in our dissociation from the life world. This kind of dissociation is a product of the techniques of writing, not some property that some human minds possess and others lack: "Writing, and more especially alphabetic literacy, make it possible to scrutinise discourse in a different kind of way . . . this scrutiny favoured the increase in scope of critical activity, and hence of rationality, scepticism, and logic" (Goody, 1977, p. 37).

Common among the basic techniques of classification in oral cultures is the use of what Lévi-Strauss calls "binary opposites." "All classification," he wrote, "proceeds by pairs of contrasts" (Lévi-Strauss, 1966a, p. 139). These are not necessarily opposites in any precise logical or empirical sense, but become used as such by serving as the basis for further discriminations: "The substance of contradictions is much less important than the fact that they exist" (Lévi-Strauss, 1966a, p. 95).

It is notorious that Lévi-Strauss's analyses of myths turn on his first identifying sets of binary opposites on which the myth is built. To many of his critics this has often seemed a rather arbitrary business, but after the volumes of his *Introduction to a Science of Mythology*, even the most skeptical reader has to concede, at least, the surprising prevalence of such oppositions giving structure to the contents of myths.

I will return to this briefly in the following section and in more detail in Chapter Four. The generality of Lévi-Strauss's claim makes this a particularly contentious point, but it is one of some importance I think, and one with significant implications for teaching and learning in primary schools. Lévi-Strauss claims to show something of how in oral cultures people generate the significant discriminations on which thought can run, of how the mind "passed from empirical diversity to conceptual simplicity and then from conceptual simplicity to meaningful synthesis" (Lévi-Strauss, 1966a, p. 131). This echoes some features of the process of educating young children, and we might profitably attend to the echoes.

The more simple and general observation to make about classification in oral cultures is that any attempt at classifying is clearly basic to rational thought. It makes little sense to consider people who develop sophisticated classificatory schemes "irrational." The differences between classificatory schemes in oral cultures and those in our scientific culture commonly rest on the qualities of phenomena used as the basis for classification. Lévi-Strauss's *Introduction to a Science of Mythology* is, as he puts it, an attempt "to prove that there is a kind of logic in [the] tangible qualities" of the concrete phenomena of everyday life – of the raw and the cooked, honey and ashes, and so on (1969, p. 1). While our children's constant classifications of their universe are necessarily less sophisticated, an understanding of the logic they use in forming them may help us understand their development of literacy and other forms of knowledge.

The kinds of explanations offered in oral cultures about natural and cosmological phenomena often seemed to Victorian intellectuals perverse or crazy, and were taken as clear evidence of oral peoples' infirmities of mind. Unfamiliar medical practices were considered bizarre (although today a growing body of anthropology literature elucidates the physical or psychological efficacy of many traditional practices). Lévi-Strauss, however, pointed out that the mistake of earlier interpreters of such explanations "was to think that natural phenomena are *what* myths seek to explain, when they are rather the *medium through which* myths try to explain facts which are themselves not of a natural but a logical order" (1966a, p. 95). We must, he said, attend to the form as well as the content of such explanations if we are to understand them.

For us explanation is a central part of our project to understand and control nature, to have practical effects. But its main purpose in oral cultures "is not a practical one. It meets intellectual require-ments rather than or instead of satisfying needs" (Lévi-Strauss, 1966a, p. 9). In serving such intellectual purposes it does not, like our logics, tie itself to the ways the world in fact works, indeed the *sauvage* mind, "does not bind itself down, as our thought does, to avoiding contradictions" (Lévi-Bruhl, 1985, p. 78). This perhaps overstates the matter - certainly casual self-contradiction is not a typical feature of the daily conversation of inhabitants of oral cultures any more, nor probably any less, than of an average group of professors. But in the myths of various oral cultures, and in their medical lore, our concern with non-contradiction is not a prominent structuring feature. Underlying the surface of explanations that may seem bizarre to Western observers, however, is a quest for order in diversity whose motive should be familiar to us from the similar motive that drives our science (Horton, 1970, pp. 131-171).

The mode of thought that directs oral cultures' approaches to classification and explanation is closely linked with the modes of expression discussed earlier. Malinowski observed of the Trobriand Islanders: "They never explain in any sense of the word; they always state a precedent which constitutes an ideal and a warrant for its continuance, and sometimes practical directions for the procedure" (Malinowski, 1954, p. 110). What seem like explanations in oral cultures do not focus only on the relevant relationships among content features, but they mix in the whole equipment of the psyche – the explanation, that is, is cast in the form of a narrative in which characters, events, motives, and emotions carry the ideas forward – leading to what Goody calls the "personalization of theory" (Goody, 1977, p. 42).

Such explanations tend to look more like, and commonly take the form of, a story. They are stories wrapped up in, or gathering up, the psychic life, the emotions, hopes, and fears, and the prominent contents of their lifeworld. This world of story-shaped explanations echoes Bacon's observation: "For as hieroglyphics came before letters, so parables came before arguments" (Bacon, 1905, p. 824).

From our point of view this kind of thinking is ineffective. What we mean by "effective," however, is caught up in our conception of a diverse, ever-changing, and, we hope, improving society. Thought in oral societies is and has been generally effective in preserving stability and order in their cultural institutions.

Children's *Bonnes à Penser*

The research on orality sketched above has a number of implications for early childhood education; here I will consider just a few. The implications turn on the validity of the connections that can be established between characteristics of orality and the thinking of young children in modern literate cultures. I started by noting the need for caution in making such connections. Psychological developmental connections seem particularly inappropriate. For example, the fact that adults in oral cultures commonly cannot perform intellectual tasks such as properly concluding "disembedded" syllogisms or successfully achieving Piagetian conservations (Ashton, 1975; Buck Morss, 1982), does not mean that they are psychologically or developmentally equivalent to children in Western literate cultures. Nor does the fact that adults in Western literate cultures can commonly perform such tasks make them psychologically superior or intellectually more fully developed. It means only that Western adults have adapted to a cultural environment shaped by centuries of elaboration of the thinking techniques made possible by literacy. Second, it is inappropriate to seek connections in the *content* of thoughts between adults in oral cultures and children in Western cultures; the concern here is, rather, what they think *with*. The connections I am focusing on are in certain formal characteristics of thought, in the strategies and resources the human mind has available and has developed over countless centuries, in oral cultures. As young children in Western literate cultures themselves inhabit an oral culture, they have access to the intellectual resources of early orality until such a time as literacy is internalized.

There are two ways in which we might hope to establish relationships between the resources available to thought in oral cultures and those deployed by modern Western children. The first is analytic. This focuses on the necessary requirements of thought in oral conditions, and on what is entailed by the need to memorize when written recording is not available. Such analytic work obviously goes forward most securely and fruitfully when combined with the second method, which is empirical. We can observe characteristic features of language and thought in oral cultures around the world, and see whether we find similar features in the language and thought of preliterate children in Western cultures; we can, then, suggests some research issues that are worthy of further attention. The empirical observations alone can tie those correlations together causally.

The body of this chapter has outlined a variety of formal characteristics of thought inferred from observations in oral cultures. acteristics of thought inferred from observations in oral cultures. One obvious source of equivalent material about modern Western children is in ethnographic studies of their lore and language. Fortunately, there are a number of quite substantial studies of children's oral cultures, notably those made by the Opies (1959, 1969, 1985) in Britain, and the Knapps (1976) and Sutton-Smith (1981) in the United States.

It is possible to take each of the characteristics of orality indicated above and find clear analogies in the oral culture of modern Western children. The implausibility of such empirical connections being merely coincidental is underlined by the analysis of orality and what it implies for linguistic forms and techniques of thinking – an analysis owed largely to the main authorities cited above, in particular, Goody, Havelock, and Ong. Let us provisionally assume that this kind of study of oral cultures throughout the world can yield a better understanding of orality and that an understanding of orality can help us better understand young children's minds in literate cultures.

Too often, I think, our perception of young children is clouded when we consider them illiterate and lacking in the skills of Western rationality. It is far better, I would argue, to regard them as positively oral: they have a distinctive culture of their own. While the image of young children as *tabulae rasae*, waiting only to be written on, or empty vessels to be filled with knowledge, is no longer prominent in educational discourse, we persist in characterizing young children in terms of the absence of the development and knowledge that constitute the mature condition. Even otherwise liberating theories such as Piaget's, for example, represent the developmental process as the gradual accumulation of increasingly sophisticated capacities and their hierarchical integration. Such theories, when used to reflect on education, focus attention on the sequence of capacities to be developed, **helping further to define young children in terms of what they lack. In Piaget's scheme, for example, they are *pre*-operational. Developmental schemes focused on the acquisition of the forms** of thought characteristic of literate cultures, such as Piaget's focus on logico-mathematical structures, show a gradually rising scale of achievement to adulthood. It we were to focus instead on the thinking techniques of oral peoples, we would surely produce a quite different "developmental" profile. It would likely be one in which achievement peaks very early in Western children's lives and then in very many cases begins a long and inexorable decline after about age seven. If the techniques of orality are, as I suggested earlier, conducive to formation of the imagination, we might have cause to be very concerned about this.

My general point is that the *bonnes à penser* available to people who do not read and write, and who consequently lack the capacities that literacy provides, condition the mental life and the forms of expression of such people, whether they be modern children or members of oral cultures. What such people think *about* is no doubt endlessly varied, and conditioned by all kinds of other social, environmental, and developmental facts. What *resources* they have to think with, however, and the effects of these resources on how they learn and make sense of their world and experience, is the focus of concern here. I will leave aside entirely any question of the historical continuity of these *bonnes à penser* from immeasurably ancient oral cultures to present day inner city streets and school yards. The apparent absurdity of such a thesis needs serious attention in light of the work of Peter and Iona Opie (Opie and Opie, 1959, 1985). What is clear from their work is that wherever numbers of children of various ages can spontaneously interact, as in school yards or in town and city streets, there is a continuing oral culture of childhood, parts of which are more ancient and persistent than anyone thought possible. It was known that certain nursery rhymes and folk tales, usually read by parents, went back for centuries. But even in cases whose content betrays a seventeenth century origin, the rhyme or tale or singing game or verbal trick may be much older, having simply been refashioned in the seventeenth century by a process the Opies describe as operating constantly. Rather like the reshaping of myth stories to modern conditions, so the Opies record old rhymes and games incorporating the names of modern cartoon characters or film stars, these new forms spreading with astonishing rapidity across their widespread field of research in Britain. The singing games played today in city streets and school yards are passed from generation to generation of children, with barely any contact with the cultural life of adults. The Opies identify games similar to some of today's in pre-Renaissance times, and it seems not unlikely that the child from a modern city might well recognize the chants of a circle song game which referred not to the Grand Old Duke of York or London Bridge falling down but perhaps to grand old Hector and those topless towers of Ilium tumbling long ago.

So, while we can ignore for now the historical transmission of oral *bonnes à penser*, clearly children respond spontaneously to particular long-persisting oral cultural institutions of their own, such as the singing games. This has something to do with fundamental structure of the human mind (which will also remain ineffable as far as this inquiry is concerned) but also, and more accessibly, it has something to do with learning some of the *bonnes à penser* of orality.

One purpose for exploring these here is to try to offer a somewhat different way of viewing young children's intellectual capacities than is common at present. In the same way that anthropologists have exposed that "primitive thinking" is not necessarily any less sophisticated or less complex than scientific thinking, merely dealing with different things for different social and intellectual purpose and in particular using techniques that allow "accumulation", so we might develop an equivalent sense of the intellectual sophistication of young children if we stop considering their mentality and ability to learn almost exclusively in terms of the mastery of the techniques of rationality. The commonest primary curriculum today is designed as though aware only of young children's primitive literacy-generated *bonnes à penser* and as though almost entirely unaware of the highly developed, rich and agile oral capacities and *bonnes à penser* children bring with them to school. Well, enough of the sermonizing; let us consider under the same headings used in the previous section some oral *bonnes à penser* available to young children.

Poetics of memory

No doubt due to the influence of computers, and to models of thinking in Artificial Intelligence research and Cognitive Science which build on analogies with computer functions, we tend even more now to think of the memory as a kind of static store which has been put in place by learning and can be accessed by a process of recall. This way of conceiving the human memory is hardly intuitively obvious. Indeed, without literacy and the ability to store coded information outside of the mind, one could hardly think of the memory as a store-house. In early Greek psychology, as expressed in myths, Mnemosyne is the goddess of memory and is also the mother of the poetic muses. In the oral tradition in particular the memory is an active force and in the long tradition of rhetoric "reason" and "memory" are considered nearly synonymous (Ong, 1958). The active memory is not confined to oral cultures, of course. The computer storage called "memory" is clearly unlike the human memory in all kinds of significant ways. The analogy holds only because of the element of factual recall. But what is "recalled" from the human memory is rarely the same as what went in. By focusing, as we have, on the importance of emotional coloring and affective impressing of cultural messages, analogies we make with computers become hopelessly inappropriate. The human memory is an ever-active, emotionally charged, organizing, classifying, reorganizing, and reclassifying faculty, whose separation from "reason" or, indeed, "emotion" makes only limited sense for limited purposes. Indeed "memory" might be likened to the notion of "consciousness." If our concern is with young children learning the bases of their cultural lives, then we are more appropriately concerned with emotion and the active "poetic" memory than with lodging discrete information and skills for later recall. Our memory is more like a place of creative ferment that transforms the character of its contents than a set of library shelves where things can be looked up and taken out on call.

The set of *bonnes à penser* discussed under this sub-heading in the previous section are all in some form evident in the games, songs, and expressions common among children today. Rhyme, rhythm, meter, and the story form are ubiquitous. The prominence of rhyme in everyday speech will in all English-speaking countries elicit the response, "You're a poet and didn't know it" (Opie and Opie, 1959, p. 73). The strength of rhythm and meter is such that many children's songs are made up of parodies of well-known, usually solemn or sacred, songs carried on echoes of the same rhythms and meters. The Opies report variants of this practice all over Britain (1959, p. 108). A children's taunting rhyme recalls the lively competitiveness and moral core of many verbal games observed in oral cultures:

> Liar, liar, pants on fire!
> Nose as long as a telephone wire.
> (Knapp and Knapp, 1966, p. 11)

Children's easy use of metaphoric thinking is evident in their ability to understand the kinds of metaphors that fill all languages – "It's bitter cold," "He feels bouncy today" – and their easy perception of the distinction between literal and metaphoric usage – "Mom killed that plan!" In what might be expected to be the constraining circumstances of constructed tasks, Gardner et al. (1975) report that nursery school children are much more likely than older children to complete with a metaphor a sentence of the form "He looks as gigantic as   ." This ready grasp of metaphor and punning is prerequisite to an understanding of the jokes that are common in children's oral culture: "What did the quarter say when it got stuck in the slot?" "Money's very tight these days"; "Why does Fred work in the bakery?" "I guess he kneads the dough"; "Bad luck," said the egg in the monastery, "Out of the frying pan into the friar", and so endlessly on.

It seems to me important to emphasize the centrality of metaphor in children's intellectual lives, in part because it is commonly neglected, and in part because it seems crucial to what ought to be the active, generative, imaginative core of human intellectual life. There is evident in metaphor a logic that eludes our analytic grasp. Metaphor does not reflect the world but generates novelty. In Max Black's words "it would be more illuminating . . . to say that metaphor creates the similarity than to say it formulates some similarity antecedently existing" (Black, 1962, p. 83).

Children's sense of the story form seems to exist very early in life; it is clearly evident in the language of many children by age two (Applebee, 1978; Pitcher and Prelinger, 1963). Binary opposites, too, are evident as the most prominent structuring elements in the classic folktales (Bettelheim, 1976) and in children's invented stories (Paley, 1981). The stories are particularized versions of the struggles between such moral concepts as good and evil, bravery and cowardice, fear and security, hope and despair, and so on.

Rhyme, metaphor, and stories are, of course, found in adult cultures as well. This in no way undermines their identification as prominent features of orality. In literate Western cultures we do not move from orality to literacy, but rather from orality to a combination of literacy and orality. The *bonnes à penser* of oral peoples do not disappear with the acquisition of literacy; they may be attenuated, but even the most highly literate people are also dependent in many circumstances of their lives on some aspects of orality. In addition, literate adults use techniques of thinking encouraged specifically by literacy; the Western forms of rational inquiry and the standard written forms for reporting their results have developed in part by their exclusion of the techniques of orality. Attempts were made in the past to reach accommodation between the two in the field of rhetoric (see Ong, 1971; Todorov, 1982, ch. 3), but their clear separation, institutionalized by the dominance of positivistic science, is evident in the still common use of the dismissive phrase "mere rhetoric." Prior to that institutionalizing in the West, it was not considered odd to mingle features of orality and literacy. Alexander Pope, for example, might compose his *Essay on Man* in rhyming couplets – something that might be considered unusual today in a work of anthropology, sociology, or psychology. Orality tends to survive, however, in the daily lives of literate peoples; it is attenuated to the point of near invisibility only in the cultures of positivistic science and technology, and in the realms of the most refinedly "literate" scholarship.

The techniques used to impress the institutions of oral cultures into the minds of their members were successful because they created powerful images. These were not simply imagined events or characters but were events or characters charged with binding ties of emotional attachment. These techniques stimulate – in a sense bring into being – the imagination; that ability to be

[handwritten marginal note: If goal of oral cult. to create vivid int. world, what wld be corresponding goal of lit? To think wt. that vivid world "interfering"]

moved by, to behave as though one perceives and is affected by, what is actually not present or real. We live in a world of nature, but have invented techniques, developed over uncounted millennia, for stimulating a vivid mental life that draws members of a society together by strong affective bonds. For children in our society, too, these techniques create mental worlds distinct from the natural world around us, mental worlds charged with vividness and emotional intensity. These are worlds that generally give delight and hurt not and that can enrich our interactions with the world of nature. In their spontaneous play and in their games children use these techniques to create what Huizinga has called "a second, poetic world alongside the world of nature" (Huizinga, 1949, p. 23).

So the techniques for memorization stimulate and develop the imagination and the emotions. They create a poetic world which is parasitic on the world of nature but which is also distinct from it, in that things impossible in nature can be imagined to happen. This emotional, imaginative world, generated by the need to remember, is the location from which our culture starts. Becoming a human person, then, we may say in distinction from Oakeshott's claim, is more intimately or fundamentally tied up with the development of an imagination than with the development of those features of rationality which he identifies. Influenced by psychoanalysis, Ruth Griffiths concludes her studies of imagination in early childhood with the observation: "It appears evident that phantasy or imagination provides the normal means for the solution of problems of development in early childhood" (Griffiths, 1935, p. 187). She saw clearly that "Imagination may be called the reflection of the emotional life" in the sense that the conceptual fluidity and flexibility of the imagination allows expression, and development, of the emotional life in ways that action or behavior could not. But she adds that "the function of imagination in childhood involves much more than a mere expression of emotion, and may be shown indeed to be necessary to intellectual as well as to emotional development" (Griffiths, 1935, p. 119).

This is a point to be developed throughout this essay; as rationality is rooted in and emerged gradually from myth in our cultural history, so its development in individuals today can be better understood if seen as rooted in and developed from the *bonnes à penser* that are the main intellectual resources of our first oral culture of childhood – what I am calling mythic understanding. The superficial similarities between the *bonnes à penser* of oral cultures and children's spontaneous play and fantasizing, then, are more profoundly similar in their main intellectual function – they create, stimulate, and develop the imagination. The imagination is the general concept we use for the *bonnes à penser* that generate the poetic world apart from nature. In developing a rich and flexible poetic or imaginative world we elaborate the *bonnes à penser* which enable us to deal more adequately with the world of nature and to establish meaning in our experience. This, I will argue, is the foundation of education. It is not something to be *replaced* by logico-mathematical, more rational, more realistic forms of thinking. These forms grow out of it and ideally grow along with it; it is what gives rationality life, color, and meaning.

The *bonnes à penser* of the culture of young children, then, strikingly resemble those common in preserving the institutions of oral cultures. The lore and language, play and games, fantasy and stories, of young children constitute an oral culture which persists from generation to generation, sustained by techniques now familiar to us, and changing gradually in response to present needs. That culture is largely invisible to most adults, as we tend to focus on our interactions with children as determiners of their cultural lives. In those interactions, of course, it is the *bonnes à penser* of rationality that predominate. But, even so, we should not underestimate the amount of support we give to the development of oral *bonnes à penser*. We supply a reliable source of memory storage for children, so remove the pressure to master the techniques of orality that in oral cultures come from the adult world – though the need to "know the words" before they can enter certain games provides some of this pressure in their own oral culture. But we also use endless formulae to impress an array of behavior patterns on children, for road safety, cutlery and utensil use, care of toys and furniture, etc. We recite proverbs, tell stories, teach rhymes, play verbal games, tell jokes, etc. These all help to build the mental structures that systematize memory and poeticize the prosaic world, creating imaginative space and the power to be enchanted by magic and ecstasy. If we begin to think of the objectives of our early childhood curriculum as tied up with magic and ecstasy, with imagination and the *bonnes à penser* of oral cultures, we might see our way to making literacy, numeracy, and rationality richer and more meaningful attainments.

Participation and conservation

Autobiographers of childhood all describe the mysterious sense of participation in nature that characterizes earliest experience, achingly unrecapturable once the prosaic demands of the pragmatic world carry us away from our first world. The powerful image used again and again in our culture for leaving that early participatory consciousness is the loss of Eden (S. Egan, 1984, esp. Ch. 2). Catching the flavor of that early consciousness requires the powers of the poet because the "experience of childhood . . . is something vastly, *qualitatively* different from adult experience, and therefore cannot be reconstituted simply by accurate narration" (Coe, 1984, p. 1).

It is no wonder that the Garden of Eden is placed at the beginning of human experience. That place of security in nature is an image, an echo, of our early childhood: "Few childhoods, even among the most sordid and the most degrading, are entirely without *some* experience of paradise" (Coe, 1984, p. 67). The – one would like to write "invariable" but so many children have to deal with much horror – ideal for normal childhood is a sense of being at home in the world, experiencing a oneness, an immersion and participation that absolutely takes the world for granted, about which there may be endless questions but no doubts.

This in-dwelling in our first world is characterized also by a sense of the luminosity, vividness, brightness of those particulars which catch children's attention. This magical wonder can be engaged by the mysterious heart of a glass marble or the perfection of a soap bubble or, more commonly, by parts of the natural world. (Oddly perhaps, almost all autobiographies of childhood are silent about toys; they seem to make no lodgment in the mind.) Panstovsky reminds us that "everything was different. Everything was more vivid – the sun brighter, the smell of the fields sharper, the thunder was louder, the rain more abundant and the grass taller" (In Coe, 1984, p. 285). This sense of abundance and brightness suffuses the autobiographies of childhood. Thomas Traherne, whose memory of earliest childhood seems more vivid and powerful than most, summed it up long ago: "Then did I dwell within a world of light" (*Divine Reflections in the Native Objects of an Infant-Ey,* c. 1670, in Coe, 1984, p. 255).

In part no doubt some of this memory of vividness is purely a physiological matter, supported by research that indicates the decay of our senses of taste and smell in particular. But the source of so many sensations and perceptions in early childhood being remembered as particularly powerful and vivid is a note echoed again and again. In the middle of a Liberian jungle Graham Greene plays the same note:

> I had got somewhere new, by way of memories I hadn't known I possessed. I had taken up the thread of life from very far back, from so far back as innocence. . . . One doesn't believe, of course in 'the visionary gleam', in the trailing glory, but there was something in that early terror and bareness of one's needs. . . . The sense of taste was finer, the sense of pleasure keener, the sense of terror deeper and purer. (Greene, 1936, pp. 120, 127)

The sense of participation in nature seems to owe something to a consciousness that, to put it clumsily, is not yet conscious that it is conscious. One of the distinctive features of thought in oral cultures is a general lack of systematic reflection on thought itself. When we develop the *bonnes à penser* that enable us to be conscious of our consciousness we bite the apple of the tree of knowledge and leave Eden. Our educational purpose is not to preserve this sense of participation in nature that relies on being unreflective about one's thinking, but we will want to explore whether some of its vividness, its intellectual security, and its sense of wonder cannot be in significant part taken with us when we leave Eden.

The "agonostic tone" which Ong described as characteristic of much daily interaction in oral cultures finds echoes in the culture of childhood today. And before seven or eight there seems little difference between boys and girls in this regard, though the particular forms might differ somewhat. Bragging, exaggerating the extent of one's achievements or those of one's friends of parents, are common, as is the polarized world of good and bad, friends and enemies, love and hate, fear and security. The high pitch of vocal force is characteristic too.

A significant feature of living in Eden is that things do not change. Children are notoriously conservative with regard to pragmatic elements of their lives. They become immersed in the particulars of their lifeworld and cannot weigh the possible benefits of change against the fixed supports of their known world. As Coe puts it: " 'Whatever is, is right' – necessarily so, since there is no known alternative" (Coe, 1984, p. 239). They have not yet developed the conceptual capacities which are our agents of dealing with change – the set of *bonnes à penser* we may sum up as historical consciousness. Thomas Traherne catches the sense of immortality and permanence that is a feature of Eden and of early childhood describing a view over a field of "immortal wheat which never should be reaped nor ever was sown" (in Coe, 1984, p. 25).

Childhood is the secure haven from which we start our journeys through the vicissitudes of life. It is the source of our sense of home and of our sense of our true selves, and much of our wandering journey is made up of trying to recapture that security, that true self that is always with us somewhere within but so hard to keep contact with. Although our articulation of our sense of self is clearly a social construct, there is beyond that a sense of a unique consciousness that seems beyond what is socially constructed in language and the particular social forms of particular times and places (see Hanson, 1986). Matthew Arnold writes of the "unspeakable desire After the knowledge of our buried life" and the struggle to keep to "our true, original course," and to act and speak true to "Our hidden self" (Matthew Arnold, "The buried life"). Our consciousness begins in a unique, isolated identity, then through language and the shared *bonnes à penser* with which we communicate we gradually become socio-political members of a culture, but within each socio-political being there remains the memory of that isolated, unique self from very far back. An ideal education will not be happy to allow our buried selves to remain lost, providing no guidance as we negotiate

our ways through life. We will want to conserve and secure our sense
of self, and cultivate ways of being true to it.

Classification and explanation

Coe suggests that "the first intellectual preoccupation of the child
is to establish its inventory" (Coe, 1984, p. 239). One prominent
part of the inventory will usually be collections of small, easily
obtained, brightly colored items. These are often classified, but
typically in schemes that make little sense or are not satisfactory
from an adult point of view. The properties of the objects which
form the basis for classification will often vary, so no overall logical
scheme is commonly apparent (Inhelder and Piaget, 1969). This is
perhaps a somewhat negative way of looking at it. If we focus on
the degrees of progress towards logical classificatory schemes we
are likely to see young children's classification, not as a positive
thing in itself, but merely as an immature form of something that
is to develop later. It is hard sometimes to suppress a sense of
irony reading a researcher's report of a young child's inability
to coordinate more than a single feature of some object in a
classification task; it does sometimes seem that the researcher
has precisely the same difficulty coordinating more than a single
feature of what the child is about. The intellectual focus in the
one case we call science, in the other, a mental incapacity. This
returns us to the difficulties anthropologists have had with the
classificatory schemes of various oral cultures. The discoveries of
the sophistication and underlying similarities with scientific forms
of thought of some of these "primitive" forms of classification
(Horton, 1970) might alert us to be more circumspect in dealing
with young children's classification schemes. Our rational schemes
are determined by their effectiveness for some purpose; children's
schemes are not so exclusively concerned with pragmatic effects but
with intellectual order and aesthetic satisfactions.

The point made in the previous section about the use of
"abstract thought" in oral cultures might be repeated here with
regard to young children. Children clearly have no difficulty
dealing with all kinds of abstractions, and in classifying according

to abstract principles: simply listing "My best friends" or "My favorite pastimes" entails dealing with abstractions. The problem, again, is not with abstraction but with dissociation from the lifeworld of the child. Any use of language entails dealing with "abstraction."

Prominent among all classification systems is the forming of binary opposites, elaborating the poles, and mediating between the poles. Any classificatory system requires first the binary discrimination between what is to be included and what excluded. These binary discriminations will commonly not be opposites in any precise logical or empirical sense, but they will serve as conceptual poles for the purposes of organization and classification. Temperature is grasped intellectually by first discriminating "hot" and "cold"; these are not empirical or logical opposites, but they function as conceptual opposites between which one can begin organizing temperature concepts like "cool", and "warm", and so on. I will return to this in Chapter Four, and will here merely note it as another evident similarity between the *bonnes à penser* of oral cultures and of young children.

Young children's explanations also reflect a number of features noted in oral cultures. The logical rule of non-contradiction seems not to bind them so tightly, and their search for explanations seems more for a satisfying story into which to fit the *explanans* than for a logical account. Parents know only too well the experience of being in the midst of a carefully crafted scientific account of something a child wants explained and having it dismissed as clearly irrelevant to what was being asked. As is the case for the diviner or witch-doctor in an oral culture, or the scientist in ours, the child is looking for a wider causal context with unifying principles that help to account for the endless, and so intellectually uncontrollable, diversity of the world (Horton, 1970, pp. 131-71). But for the child and for the witch-doctor that wider context can be made up of a story that can meaningfully encompass the event or phenomenon to be explained. Empirical generalizations, theories, covering laws are the forms that lead to effective control over event and nature, stories can give us intellectual control and emotional satisfaction. Children also, of course, want common sense pragmatic explanations, but we need to be aware in our desire to provide scientific explanations that story-shaped intellectual control and emotional satisfaction have their values too. In an ideal educational scheme we will not have to sacrifice any of these.

Conclusion

I have tried to pull together and stitch together in this chapter a number of topics not usually dealt with in studying early childhood learning and curriculum. I hope you agree that the connections made between the *bonnes à penser* of oral cultures and those common in young children's thinking are genuine, not some straining of terms to support a fanciful hypothesis. I think some of the connections are fairly clear, though in some areas I have moved more hesitantly. One cause of the hesitancy is that the features of children's thinking I have been most concerned with are those which have in general been least enlightened by research so far. This kind of exploration, however, might provide some notches for research to get a grip on children's fantasy and imagination, and the various *bonnes à penser* of children's minds.

Making connections between the thinking of aboriginal Australians, Homer, and modern children invites skepticism, especially if one overdoes the comparisons, as is hard to avoid – or at least to seem to avoid – when drawing attention to the similarities of things usually seen in terms of their contrasts. The divide between orality and literacy, between mythopoeia and logic, between prerational and rational, between mythic and historical, and so on, have usually been seen as two forms of thought struggling for the human mind, and if one wins the other loses. The oral *bonnes à penser*, if this is the case, are thus rendered redundant by literacy. Even some of those scholars who have exposed the workings of certain crucial features of orality conclude that orality and literacy are "contradictory and mutually exclusive" (Lord, 1964, p. 129). This perpetuates Plato's view, as Havelock interprets it. Plato's distinction between the *philodoxoi*, who were caught up with appearance and personal meaning, and the *philosophoi* who were able to transcend those and see exactly what is the case in reality, set up an opposition we have tended to accept absolutely, where we might be a bit more discriminating. No doubt we have to lose some of the *bonnes à penser* of orality with the onset of literacy, but the educational task is to ensure that enabling people to see exactly what is the case, in as far as we can, does not dissociate whatever is the case from its personal meaning for us.

In oral *bonnes à penser* we have seen the roots, and the continued life, of the imagination. We will not sensibly pass this up for a dessicated literacy. We want literacy to flower with the imagination and have children discover that the shared forms and socializing conventions of language and literacy do not prevent us from retaining contact with our unique isolated consciousnesses, but provide a means of reaching out to others similar but never the same.

Children in their first few years recapitulate the acquisition of language and then of literacy. Language is the first disrupter of the infants' intimate participation in the natural world: "Language creates distance between the self and the object; language generalizes, transforming a unique perception into a common one; language transmutes realities into abstractions" (Coe, 1984, p. 253). That unique consciousness of reality, which is the birthright of each of us, can seem hopelessly lost if language becomes a purely conventionalizing instrument which persuades the child that its uniqueness was merely an illusion and that one is simply a socialized unit among others the same. Between the development of language and the development of literacy children live in an oral culture. Perfection, fulfilment, ripeness of this stage of development requires two educational achievements. The first is the discovery that language can be a fluid and flexible thing which does not need to obliterate the original unique consciousness, but can become the agency of it expression; this is one of poetry's functions. It can, with the success of this achievement, provide the child with the ecstatic sense of power that words have given humankind. Naming the natural world and experience right, where every word is at home, taking its place to support the others, is the beginning of our dissociation from nature and also of our power over it. Many mythologies, particularly African ones, describe Creation as taking place bit by bit as God names the parts of the world. Adam in Eden is given the power and ecstasy of naming the animals (a *New Yorker* cartoon showed a delighted Adam gazing up at a giraffe saying "I call you groundhog"). Again, Thomas Traherne, with his preternatural poetic memory of very early childhood conveys this sense of power:

> The city seemed to stand in Eden, or to be built in Heaven.
> The streets were mine, the temple was mine, the people were
> mine, their clothes and gold and silver were mine, as much
> as their sparkling eyes, fair skins and ruddy faces. The skies
> were mine, and so were the sun and moon and stars, and all
> the World was mine; and I the only spectator and enjoyer of
> it. (Traherne, in S. Egan, 1984, p. 73)

(If his parents, walking along by his side, were to wonder "What's
going through the little fellow's head?" the answer would not of
course be these polished phrases. But the feeling and the sparkle
and the brightness were surely there.)

The second educational achievement in mastering language is
to enable the child to discover that language can have a distinct,
dynamic life of its own. It is not merely something into which or
through which our experience can be expressed, but it is itself an
extension of our experience. It can initially be the means of a new
kind of aesthetic delight: its sounds can be shaped into patterns; it
can allow puns, jokes, stories, malapropisms; it can pour magical
meaning into voids, and spark meaning out of its combinations.

The same problems and possibilities recur with the achievement
of literacy. It can become a mass of conventional forms and clichés
that stamp the individual consciousness far back into the recesses
of the mind, or it too can become a liberator and amplifier for
each unique consciousness. The educational task is to ensure that
the socializing, conventionalizing skills of literacy are mastered,
but in a way that does not cut off or undermine its individuating
powers. And in addition it can become a further amplifier of our
experience. This book is an attempt to become clearer about these
things and to propose a curriculum and methods of teaching that
will encourage these educational achievements.

The implication of the previous two chapters, then, is that
the foundations of education are poetic. We begin as poets. The
logographoi in our cultural history, the wielders of rational prose,
came long after and built upon a heritage of poetic insight, organization of consciousness, and techniques for thinking. To become
subtle wielders of rational prose and of the mathematical language
which accompanied its development – in history, science, mathematics, social studies, and so on – we must first develop the poet
in each child. "Poet" is perhaps a dangerous word to use because
of its varied modern associations to different people; I mean what

Vico saw and what other scholars whose work I have drawn on in these chapters have tried to describe. Perhaps better might be to settle for a world like "imagination," though it too is vague and variously used. I mean the *bonnes à penser* explored so far, and to be explored further in the next two chapters. The sermonizing here has been to stress that in early childhood we are concerned with the foundations of education. To build them properly we need to be clear about the top floors, of course, but we also need to build proper foundations out of foundational material.

The *bonnes à penser* of orality that we will seek to develop will be influenced by the literacy and rational modes of inquiry and consciousness that are to succeed them. But our conception of that literacy and rationality will also be shaped by the orality from which they emerge. So we need to be sensitive both to the character of orality and to children's early *bonnes à penser* and to the direction in which they are to be taken. I will turn to the methodological implications in Chapter Five. For now let us explore children's thinking and sense-making further. We can leave behind the anthropologists and classicists and others, with thanks, and focus increasingly on children as we can observe them.

3

The Story Form and the Organization of Meaning

Introduction

When called to wash hands for lunch, and reluctantly accepting the inevitability of having to finish their game in the smurf village, children seek an ending. It may be a cataclysmic smashing of the village, or the destruction of Gargamel, or the assertion that all the problems of the morning are resolved. They seem to require a story-like sense of an ending. The fantasy-filled narratives concocted by the five-year-old in the kitchen, starting from the available props of a mixing bowl, a toy ring, and mummy's scarf, constantly seek out the rhythms and patterns of the story form. In common with, apparently, everyone else in the world, children enjoy a good story. The content of young children's stories is often different in important ways from that which typically engages adults. But the form of the story seems universal: it has a beginning which sets up an expectation, a middle that complicates it, and an ending that satisfies or resolves it. Or, to put it another way, in the beginning anything is possible, in the middle possibilities are gradually reduced and circumscribed, in the end the world of the story is complete and its possibilities reduced unambiguously to one.[1]

The invention of the story was a crucial stage in the discovery of the mind. What was invented was a narrative form that worked at increasing the memorability of its contents. In recognizing its power and refining it through millennia, people discovered something remarkable about how the human mind works. We are a storying animal; we make sense of things commonly in story forms; ours is a largely story-shaped world. Rational and empirical science inquiries, of course, are not generally story-shaped, seeking as they do to reflect the logic of their subject matter, but they provide in their results further material out of which we make stories. We seem to have to do this in order to make their results more generally meaningful. But even this is to concede too much; it is increasingly being realized, as in the quote from Niels Bohr in Chapter One, that physics does not expose purely the logic of reality, rather it exposes reality in terms already informed by our ways of making sense.

These are rather opaque observations. A crucial role of the story in oral cultures, we saw in the previous chapter, was to ensure that the main cultural messages were retained in living memories and that the rememberers were emotionally committed to those messages. But while we may be ready to acknowledge the persisting power of stories at even the most sophisticated levels of our literate culture, it seems obvious that they have not survived to play for us the same roles as in oral cultures. Indeed we might feel somewhat uncomfortable with a technique devised to enchant and commit the unreflective mind to the conventions and dogmas of a particular society. It is a technique designed to suppress precisely the reflective rationality that we prize so highly in education. Clearly we do not need stories to perform the pragmatic task of sustaining our social institutions, but equally clearly they remain of great psychological importance for us. Mind you, what made stories of social importance in the first place was the psychological functions they performed, so it is on these that we need to concentrate. In this chapter, then, I will explore just a little further what stories are and why they work, and what they work at. I will then consider their potential uses in education. In considering their educational uses I will consider implications both for the curriculum and for teaching, and then enlarge on those implications in Chapters Six and Seven respectively.

My hope is that the discussion in this chapter might make some points on which research can get some grip. Most educational writing about stories – with some notable exceptions – has been descriptive and classificatory, aiming to draw attention to particular kinds of children's literature or to argue for the educational value of particular kinds of stories at particular ages. Research on the whole has tended to focus on children's comprehension of elements within stories, or on the story as aiding recall (see, for example, Stein and Trabasso, 1981: Hilyard and Olson, 1982). Such research has tended to focus on the development of rational skills, largely ignoring metaphoric fluency, imagination, and the emotional crux which the story form is most particularly about. Research has, properly, focused on what it can get some kind of grasp on, but unfortunately this has tended to mean ignoring what is distinctive about stories. One result of this omission, through the effects research tends to have on educational practice, has been the use in research studies and then in basal reader series of rather vapid pseudo-stories or what might better be called event sequences. What is distinctive about stories is their power to evoke ecstasy, stimulate the imagination, fix affective responses to events and determine the meaning of their contents. It is these features that I will explore in this chapter, but these features are usually absent from research on stories, and are commonly lacking in the pseudo-stories of basal reading programs, and from instructional "stories" about, say, How Enrico spends his day in his Mexican village.

A touchstone of what counts as an adequate story for children might sensibly be whether the adult teacher or researcher will go back to that story for pleasure and be moved by it. As C. S. Lewis rather brusquely puts it:

> No book is worth reading at the age of ten which is not equally (and often far more) worth reading at the age of fifty – except, of course, books of information. The only imaginative works we ought to grow out of are those which it would have been better not to read at all. (C. S. Lewis, 1982, p. 15)

There is a danger of becoming altogether too high-minded about this, of course, perhaps in over-reaction to the terrible junk so commonly served up to children in basal readers. There is obviously a place for what high-minded adults consider junk-reading, but the problem at the moment is to fight for anything else. Anyway, this is an issue I will return to in Chapter Six. My point here is that educational research on stories needs to come to grips with what stories are, and my hope is that this chapter can contribute something of use to this enterprise. Fortunately Aristotle took an interest in this subject, so I can crib a fair amount from him and, fortunately too, this present inquiry can be satisfied with some relatively simple conclusions which seem to have been largely ignored in education.

My general argument so far has been that education should begin with what for convenience I am calling an oral foundation. This is a kind of truism until one spells out what "oral" entails – in this case those *bonnes à penser* indicated in the previous chapter. In other words, the kind of education Plato wanted to proscribe – the *mousike* of ancient Greece – and replace with initiation into rational modes of thought, I am suggesting should be seen rather as foundational to the achievement of rational modes of thought. As Eric Havelock puts it:

> If it is desirable that a large majority of a modern population be literate, can this be accomplished without a prior linkage to the poetic and musical inheritance – in short should children be rushed into reading before they have learned to speak fluently, to recite, to memorize, and to sing suitable verse available in their own tongue? (Havelock, 1980, p. 97)

While I will argue that a rich literacy does require a linkage to the poetical and musical inheritance, our complex modern society and complex modern consciousness are such that the seductively straightforward solution Havelock wonders about may be inappropriate. Delaying reading and recapitulating in a literal way the techniques of oral cultures returns us to the "culture-epoch" curricula of the turn of the century. It also recalls Rousseau's solution to the perceived problem of too early or too pressured initiation into rational disciplines: keep them away from reading. In our societies also any suggested solution is made more problematic by the different relationships between oral culture *bonnes à penser* and social classes (Heath, 1982). Normal initiation into different racial cultures stimulates and develops, and suppresses, different sets of oral *bonnes à penser* and some prepare better for particular forms of literacy and worse for other forms of literacy. This complication to any hope of a straightforward prescription will need attention too.

As mentioned above, when children's fantasy narratives wander on apparently interminably, they nevertheless seem constantly to be seeking out the rhythms and patterns of the story form. This is evident in children as young as two and three years. (See Ames, 1966; Applebee, 1978; Gesell *et al.*, 1940.) This may be in part due to children attempting to mimic stories they have heard, but such an explanation is inadequate to account for the apparent universality of the form in all cultures.[2] Alternatively, one may explain the impulse towards stories as a reflection of some fundamental structures of the mind. I will consider some reasons for accepting this latter kind of explanation, aware that it brings us into some rather sticky areas for inquiry. I will try to support some of the claims by drawing analogies between this inquiry into stories and their plots and linguistic inquiries into sentences and their syntax. We are now accustomed to the notion that the study of language and syntax can yield claims about mental structures, so analogies between those studies and this discussion of stories and children's understanding may make what follows seem a little less exotic.

The story form clearly provides a comfortable and hospitable environment for children's fantasy. I will consider why it provides so hospitable an environment and why children find stories so readily accessible, engaging, and meaningful. "Environment," we may note before beginning, is perhaps an appropriate word here. We know that things generally become meaningful within contexts, within boundaries and limits. Very generally we may say that young children's experiences of the world are such that they have very little sense of the limits, the boundaries, the contexts in which much of their experience is meaningful. And they have an urge to make sense of their experience, asking endless questions, eager to learn. The story is the linguistic unit that, as it were, brings its boundaries with it. Within the story, as within the game, the world is limited, the context is created and given and so the events of a story can be grasped and their meaning understood more readily than can the events in the less hospitable, imprecisely bounded world. Equally applicable to stories is Huizinga's observation about play and games; each "creates order, *is* order" (Huizinga, 1949, p. 29).

What is a Story?

I will begin with a partial definition, one that will need some unpacking: "a story is the linguistic unit that can ultimately fix the affective meaning of the events that compose it." A number of elements here have implications for children's learning and need elaboration. First, the story blends the disparate events that compose it into a unit of some kind; then stories fix meaning in some way; and the kind of meaning they fix, which is in turn to some degree definitional of stories, is "affective."

Let us take an event from a story: "She walked into the rose garden." By itself this event may set off more or less random associations, but its meaning is unclear. It has too many possible meanings, one might say. We know what the words mean but we don't know, most crucially for an event in a story, how to feel about it. Should we feel glad or sorry, ecstatic or horrified that she walked into the rose garden? If we add, "and she found the money," we begin to limit the possible meanings of the event, though not by much. As events are added to the story one by one the possible meanings are reduced until, in the end, only one meaning is possible. If we add events that tell us she had been desperately searching for money to give to her sad Irish grandfather, we might begin to feel, tentatively, glad that she entered the rose garden. Further events might reveal that the Irish grandfather is sad because his plan to hook all the local kids on heroin has not been going as well as he had hoped, and that he wanted the money to buy up a recent shipment of the drug. With this elaborated context we may now begin to feel sad or horrified that she entered the rose garden and found the money. When we know finally what to feel about the event, we know that we have reached the end of the story. In other words, we know we have reached the end of the story not when we are told that all lived happily ever after but when we know how to feel about all the incidents that make up the story.

A crucial aspect of stories, then, is that they are narratives that orient our affective responses to events. As we read a well-crafted story, the senses of expectation or puzzlement or fear that are set up in the beginning are played and shaped by the movement of the story. The story is like a musical score and our emotions are the instrument it plays. As long as we remain unsure how to feel about the events, we know we have not reached the completion of the larger unit. We know we have reached completion when we know finally how to feel about "She walked into the rose garden," and the rest of the events of the story. If we are to try to separate out the kind of meaning proper to the story, then, it is something that involves our emotions. Obviously such meaning required lexical meaning – knowing the proper referents of terms like "she" and "entered" and "rose-garden" – and also semantic meaning – making sense of the sentences as one reads or listens. Both are necessary to make sense of a story, but both are equally necessary to make sense of an essay. The kind of meaning that is unique to stories, and that stories are uniquely responsible for organizing, is what I am calling "affective meaning" (Egan, 1978a).

One reason why stories provide affective meaning is that, unlike the complexity of everyday events, they end. They do not just peter out or stop at some arbitrary point. What makes them stories is that their ending completes and satisfies whatever was raised in their beginnings and elaborated in their middles (Kermode, 1966). In doing this they fix the meaning of their contents; they show us how to feel about the events we have been following. In this, stories are radically unlike history. A problem with meaning in history is that we cannot fix our affective responses to events. They have too many sides, too many contexts, to allow the reduction of possible meanings to one precise meaning. As new things happen we constantly reassess the meaning of all past events. The only people who can fix for themselves *the* meaning of historical events, and who are therefore confident of how to feel about them, are ideologues who assert an ending which they claim is inevitable for the historical process. In an unsophisticated Marxist view, for example, the laws of history are known, and so the future progress towards the classless society is allowed to give meaning to the present stage of history. They then "know" the meaning of history by transforming it into a story. Knowing the end, they can know the meaning of all the event that are a part of the process. As Kafka pointedly observed, "The meaning of life is that it stops." The ancient Greeks made a similar observation: "Call no man happy until he is dead."

One attraction of stories is that they grant us the satisfaction, which history and our experience withhold from us, of being sure how to feel about events and characters. The world of the story, like the world of the game, reduces reality – of which humankind cannot bear very much – to a scale that mimics it on the one hand and allows us a certain comfort in dealing with it on the other. This attraction and its satisfaction seem to be felt keenly by children. The circumscribed worlds of story and game within which meanings are clear and determinate provide a haven from the conceptually less apprehensible world of everyday experience. While children's stories and games seem to be simpler than adults', articulated more starkly on binary poles of good and bad, love and hate, fear and security, and so on, they share with adults' the purpose, which is the focus of attention here, of fixing how to feel about the events that make them up. (Again, I am concerned here only with the basic story form. I realize that this analysis works less well or, rather, needs to be supplemented if we consider all the ambivalences built into sophisticated narratives, and if we consider the mixing of elements of history and present realities into fictional (factional) narratives. My point, however, needs only the simpler story form).

If we consider the kind of meaning children seem to find in their stories and fantasy worlds, and if we accept even some part of Piaget's image of the primitive nature of young children's logico-mathematical operations, we may see that the most prominent tools children have for making sense of things are strongly affective and moral. Children grasp the world, that is to say, by means of such concepts as good and bad and all the variants of these, with joy, sorrow and anger, with love and hate, with fear and security, and so on.[3] One is tempted to suggest that children's grasp on the world is affective and moral rather than logical and rational, but this would be to accept the restricted and misleading contrast inherited from the Greeks and criticized in the previous chapters. Rather, in young children what we call the rational and logical are intricately tied up with what we rather vaguely call the affective. In early childhood, thinking and feeling have not yet been schooled down divergent paths. Or rather, we might now say, the oral *bonnes à penser* most accessible to young children and most useful for making sense of their lifeworld do not find any advantage in systematically separating out thinking from feeling. One may say that we think with our feelings no less effectively and sensibly than with the particular cognitive tools usually focused on when rational thinking is referred to.

Common acceptance of the age-old distinction between the rational and the affective has not only tended to remove children's imagination and fantasy from educational discourse and research, but it has also inhibited educational inquiry from focusing on the possible Dionysiac contributions to thinking, on generating and elaborating the second, poetic, world apart from nature and encouraging greater precision of our emotions. Refinement and sophistication of our affective orientation to the world and knowledge is, I am arguing, a crucial and neglected part of education in rational thinking. The affective and the imaginative are not to be considered distinct elements from rational thinking; they are necessary *parts of* proper rational thinking. It is to the early development of these affective aspects of thinking that children's fantasy stories, and the story form in general, can contribute so richly.

I should qualify the use of "moral" here as well. Moral sense is also subject to development, and degeneration, and it would be simplistic to see young children's concerns with good and bad as no different from adults'. Good and bad, as love and hate, tend in young children to be used to discriminate between the people, things, and events that affect them in ways that cause in the relatively short term pleasure or pain. As Bettelheim notes concerning fairy stories: "A child's choices are based, not so much on right versus wrong, as on who arouses his sympathy and who his antipathy" (Bettelheim, 1976, p. 9). While I am qualifying things, I should perhaps qualify the starkness of Bettelheim's opinion here: assuming an adult's moral sense in a child is to not make a distinction where a distinction is proper, so Bettelheim's collapsing of children's morality to *nothing other than* sympathy and antipathy also fails to make a distinction where it is proper.

One implication of this discussion, then, is that the story form, which is responsible for organizing and fixing affective meaning, has more important contributions to make to children's learning than are made by its casual use in fictional narratives during Language Arts classes. Even people who accept the importance of stories, in other words, often fail to see that underlying them is a tool of immense power and importance for education. It is a tool that is under-used if it is wheeled out only during story-times that are separated from "real learning" and academic "work." If our concern is with the communication of meaning, and children seem able readily to grasp the world affectively, and the tool we have for affectively organizing meaning is the story form, then it would seem that use of the story form in the planning of lessons and units might yield some important benefits. Showing how this may be done is the subject of Chapter Seven.

Considering stories in the way the discussion in the previous chapter encourages – as *bonnes à penser* that can stimulate and develop particular mental capacities, as techniques to help thinking – enables us fairly easily to identify a first contribution they can make. They can stimulate and develop our ability to organize affectively a range of material into coherent and meaningful units. Learning to follow a story *is* acquiring this capacity. And learning to follow a story is in part a matter of finding appropriate objects onto which a mental predisposition can latch; our "story sense" is shaped and developed by the particular stories available to it in our cultural environments – a topic to be pursued in Chapter Five. Acquiring the capacity to identify and abstract from the flux of experience particular facts and events and to imagine others, and giving them coherence and meaning by organizing them in terms of an affective pattern or emotional rhythm is a basic form of human sense-making. This echoes Rosen's conclusions that stories are "a primary and irreducible form of human comprehension" (Rosen, 1986, p. 231).

Considering stories in this way also leads us towards criteria for identifying what are good stories for young children. Such criteria are based on something rather more tangible than typical, and typically rather vague, aesthetic criteria. The aesthetic after all becomes utilitarian when we can more precisely identify the psychological capacities it helps to develop. Initially we can conclude that the best stories for young children will be those that stimulate vivid and diverse images and organize them into an affectively gripping pattern. But this is to touch on only the most general features of stories. Even a relatively superficial inquiry such as this can push on a little further. I think we can uncover further principles about what stories are and how they work that carry implications for curricula and teaching. Let us consider a few analogies between stories and sentences to provide us with more *bonnes à penser*.

Stories and Sentences

It might help to clarify further what I mean by the story form if we consider some analogies with the more developed analyses available in linguistics. A better sense of the role of the story form in organizing the affective meaning of events might come from a comparison with the role of syntax in the sentence. That the story is a macro-level linguistic unit with analogies to the micro-level of the sentence has been a commonplace of poetics for some time. G. L. Permyakov has argued that "the differences between units within the sentence and beyond the sentence are quantitative" (Permyakov, 1970, p. 56). Tzvetan Todorov has argued that "the relation between [language and discursive narratives] is not only functional but also genetic. Discursive forms are transformations of linguistic forms" (Todorov, 1973, p. 164). Even more starkly, Roland Barthes tells us that the story is simply the sentence writ large (Barthes, 1966). A. J. Greimas and Todorov have followed up these arguments in analyses, not always nor equally successful, in which they equate grammatical "functions" with story "actants," and grammatical cases with roles in a story narrative (Greimas, 1966; Todorov, 1969). It is clear also that some of these literary theorists see the structures they derive from analyses of language and narratives as indicators of fundamental mental structures. We do not of course have to find such general claims persuasive to acknowledge that there may be *some* useful analogies drawn between the sentence and the story.

Consider this analogy:

Sentence : Syntax :: Story : Plot[4]

This suggests a distinction between the concrete or surface level of content, whether the particular words of the sentence or the particular events of a story, and the set of underlying abstract rules which orders the surface level and determines its meaning. Where I have used the term story form, then, I might instead use, as in the analogy, the term plot. The form underlying the story is its plot.

Consider this further analogy:

Morpheme : Syntax :: Event : Plot

As syntax determines how morphemes – the smallest meaningful units of language such as affixes, base words, inflections – are organized to make meaningful sentences, so plots determine the organization of events into meaningful stories. Earlier we saw that the kind of meaning created by events when organized within the macro-linquistic unit of the story was what I called "affective." The kind of meaning syntax is responsible for creating is what may be called semantic. As when listening to music we hear melody, harmony, and rhythm together, so when reading a story we attend to various kinds of meaning. We attend to, at least, lexical, semantic, and what I am calling affective meaning together. Lexical meaning derives from knowing what "she" and "walked" and "rose garden" refer to; semantic meaning derives from understanding "She walked into the rose garden" in its narrative context; affective meaning derives from following with out gut, as it were, the rhythms of emotion that resonate from the event.

Consider, then, these further analogies:

Syntax : Semantic meaning :: Plot : Affective meaning
Sentence : Semantic meaning :: Story : Affective meaning

So the linguistic unit within which the meaning of events is determined is the story, the kind of meaning determined is affective, and the element that determines affective meaning is the plot. As sentences are made up of words that could have many meanings in different contexts, so events apart from any context could have many meanings. The possible reactions to "She walked into the rose garden" are many. The function of syntax in organizing the words to express a specific semantic meaning is to restrict by context the possible meanings till each word is used with a single precise meaning. Similarly, plots organize events into a story in such a manner that all but one affective response is inappropriate. This helps explain why young children, who find ambiguity difficult to deal with and who seek clarity in how they should feel about events, find stories so engaging and their meaning so accessible. It provides also another way of making the perhaps obvious point that understanding the force of a story requires that the lexical and semantic levels of meaning are also clear.

Another analogy of interest concerns the way sentences and stories are stuck together. I am not sure we have a specific term for how words are ordered in sequence in a sentence but events are ordered in sequence in a story by causality. One scene or event follows another by building coherently towards the overall unit. Causality in stories is not determined by any obvious logical principle but rather by affective connections; one scene follows another, taking their places in the affective pattern. The graveyard scene in *Hamlet*, for example, is not causally required by any logical ties with what precedes it, but takes its place precisely in the affective causal sequence of the play. Affective causality is, of course, parasitic on our conceptions of "real-world" causality, but we do not have direct access to reality, only to our ways of representing it. So affective causality will complicatedly entail conceptions of logical causal sequences, though the simpler the story they operate in the more dominant will be the affective component. This will be evident in the degree that events are represented as directly caused by individuals' emotions.

To take the general point of this section further we might consider this analogy:

Story : Plot :: Essay : Argument

In each case of Sentence : Syntax :: Story : Plot :: Essay : Argument, we have a concrete, surface content organized by an abstract set of rules. The fact that sentences, stories, and essays, despite their infinite diversity and originality, are comprehensible to other people suggests that at the level of syntax, plot, argument, there are limited structures to which everyone has access. This encourages some people to consider syntax, plot, argument, less as properties of narratives and more as properties of minds. Analyses of syntactic structures are assumed to reflect, after whatever degree of transformations, structures of the mind. We do not need to get into the complex and fundamental arguments between empiricists and neo-rationalists which these kinds of claims raise. (Though it is perhaps worth noting in passing that the rather rigid empiricism of much educational research on topics related to story comprehension has prevented that research from drawing on the much greater theoretical sophistication of neo-rationalist studies of stories.)

My point here is simply to stress that underlying stories there are abstract forms, plots, sets of rules that determine the structuring and organization of events to create a particular kind of meaning. And I will go on to argue later that such forms, plots, rules, can be abstracted from fictional stories and used to organize any kind of content, academic or experiential, in order to make it more accessible and meaningful to young children.

Stories and Other Contexts

The story, then, is the linguistic unit that carries its context around with it. Within the story each part is placed within the context of the other parts, and so its meaning is clarified and supported. In education, our concern to communicate meanings clearly has led to the importance of context being stressed a number of ways. Given the importance I am claiming for the use of the story form in teaching, it would indeed be surprising if no one had noticed it before. Of course, all educational thinkers have noted the importance of coherently organizing knowledge in teaching. While I am not aware of anyone making quite the points I am making here and will develop in subsequent chapters, there have been a number of people making related observations and supporting them empirically – many more people than I will mention here.

One product of recent research has been the development of what is often called "schema theory." This derives from the discovery that learning is significantly improved if what is to be learned is embedded within a context or schema that is meaningful to the learner. Its origins are to be found in F. C. Bartlett's study of memory functions (Bartlett, 1932). He discovered that adults' recall of stories was often far from verbatim. According to the previously popular "trace" theory, memories should be stored replicas of earlier experience. But adults' recall of stories often involved inventions, confusions, and blendings of information. It seemed to Bartlett that his subjects constructed expectations about what would happen from past experience of other stories and somehow used these structures or frameworks in making sense of the story they were hearing. These frameworks or structures he called "schemata."

A more recent formulation of the basic principle of schema theory runs as follows:

Whatever our age, whatever our language, whatever our
cultural background, we function psychologically by building

systematic *representations* of experience, which provide both
an interpretation (or structuring) of the past and a system
for anticipating the future. . . . How to describe these
"representations of experience" is the primary issue which
divides competing schools of psychology. For our purposes,
it is enough to recognize that a system of representation
is a mental record of our past experience. (Applebee,
1978, p. 3)[5]

Whatever the source of schemata, my concern here is simply to
note the accumulating data generated by research using schema
theory which testify to the importance of contexts for the learning
of meaningful material (Anderson, 1977).[6] Schemata as they are
generally understood in research on language learning and recall
are obviously not the same entities as plots as that term is used
in the section above. In the terms and distinctions used above,
schemata seem most commonly to be some kind of mix of plots,
syntax, and surface content. But important similarities exist,
expressed well in Applebee's argument about one of the values of
stories: They extend

the relatively limited experience of young children. The
stories they hear help them to acquire expectations about
what the world is like – its vocabulary and syntax as well
as its people and places – without the distracting pressure
of separating the real from the make-believe. And although
they will eventually learn that some of this world is only
fiction, it is specific characters and specific events which
will be rejected; the recurrent patterns of values, the stable
expectations about the roles and relationships which are part
of their culture will remain. It is these underlying patterns,
not the witches and giants which give them their concrete
form, which make stories an important agent of socialization.
(Applebee, 1978, pp. 52–3)

Even here, however, when Applebee uses phrases like "recurrent
patterns" or "underlying patterns" or "the vocabulary and syntax
of the world," he seems to be making only a partial form/content
distinction. The underlying patterns and so on are not, in his view,
abstract plot structures but rather are still a kind of content – the

content of particular values, roles, and relationships of a particular culture. I am recommending that we take one step further in distinguishing between the content of stories, and schemata, and consider, as it were, their grammar (see Prince, 1973). This is the crucial step that will allow us to consider the power of the form underlying stories and other schemata, and will allow us to pry it loose from the content of fairy stories or fantasy, and apply it in addition to making meaningful those thing we wish to teach. It is this more radical step that I am suggesting here is sensible and that I will later take into practice.

Another source of suggestive empirical findings comes from the work of Renée Fuller. Initially she set out to develop a method to teach children with superior abilities to read. By chance the method was used also with severely retarded students and achieved remarkable success. The key features of her Ball-Stick-Bird method (Fuller, 1974, 1975, 1982), at least in the context of the present argument, are the uses of "code approximation" and stories. Code approximation means simply that children are taught not to try to work out each element – letters, syllables – precisely in sequence before moving on. Rather they are taught that English spelling is a sloppy code, and that the right sound of a letter in a particular word should be felt for in the context of the whole word or sentence. Similarly the correctness of particular words can be assessed for appropriateness within the context of a story. Relatedly, she reports that "tests in which words are embedded in a sentence had significantly higher scores than tests where the same words were presented in a word list" (Fuller, 1979, 1982).

Fuller explores various explanations of the evident successes her Ball-Stick-Bird method achieved even with subjects whose IQ on the Stanford-Binet test measured as low as 20. She concludes that a crucial cause of the successes was that her reading tasks were all within the context of stories, and the stories

> functioned to anchor the "bits" of information, and seemed to help their intellectual cohesion. The stories had not only motivational value . . . but they made it easier for the subjects to understand what they had to learn and why. Reading came to resemble a game for which they were being given the rules in the process of playing. (Fuller, 1979, p. 2)

From the results of her work she goes on to argue that story cohesion is the fundamental unit of cognition, speculating that the reason for the failure of Lashley's (Lashley, 1963) search for the basic unit of memory and learning was that he was looking for what we might call, anticipating a later section, disembedded units. Fuller argues that the story, rather than contextless bits of information, form the "engram" of our species.

> Story cohesion, as the basic form of intellectual cohesion, is earlier in development and cognition than we had thought possible on the basis of IQ tests. Because these tests have determined what we think is intelligence, their importance has frozen educational techniques into the pattern of turn-of-the-century education. (Fuller, 1979, p. 3)

Notions of what intelligence is have in this century been derived from psychological theories, though the older intuitive sense of intelligence resists being entirely collapsed to what is measured by some instruments derived from some theory. If we did not retain this more intuitive sense of intelligence, we would of course have nothing against which to measure the adequacy of the psychological theorists' notions. Nor would we have an incentive to improve the sophistication of the psychological theories or their measuring instruments. Once some measuring instrument derived from some theory becomes useful for discriminating among, say, students in schools, then the practical value of this leads to increasing the influence and power of the theory's notion of intelligence. Piaget's theory yields a rather different notion of intelligence from that inherent in, say, the Stanford-Binet tests. As instruments are refined for discriminating among children on the basis of Piagetian notions of intelligence, so we will see the theory's influence become more pervasive in education. It is not simply that teachers teach towards what the instrument derived from these theories measure, though of course this does happen extensively, but more pervasively we begin to think of the processes that can enhance those particular notions of "intelligence" through the schooling system as identical with education.

If Fuller is right in her claim that the ability to comprehend stories is more basic to human intelligence than anything that is measured in the contextless tests common in measuring IQ or, it should be added, in the contextless Piagetian tests of logico-mathematical development, then we are ignoring a basic aspect of human intelligence in our testing procedures and we are being influenced to teach towards a restricted set of intellectual skills and away from others of possibly greater importance. The story is the archetypical form in which bits are organized together into a greater coherent whole. The ability to organize parts within a whole and into larger wholes is, of course, of great importance in nearly all significant "real-world" intellectual tasks.

(In passing, as a related aside, it seems worth recalling the numerous theories about dreaming and the importance most of them accord this experience in our lives. What is often insufficiently noticed in such theories is one of the most obvious features of dreams – we are telling ourselves stories. As with stories in our waking lives, it is the uncompleted ones that we tend to remember. They are the broken narratives whose content has not been affectively organized – we are left not knowing how to feel about them; expectations have been created but not satisfied. The story's role in affectively organizing experience and imagined events goes on even in sleep. But also a very large amount of what we consider our thinking is a matter of shaping memories, hopes, fears, imagined events, etc., into stories.)

A third related set of studies is reported in Margaret Donaldson's *Children's Minds* (1978). She observes that "there exists a fundamental human urge to make sense of the world and bring it under deliberate control" (Donaldson, 1978, p. 111). She observes also that in everyday situations nearly all children show an impressive practical intelligence, but then often quite suddenly they seem remarkably stupid in their inability to deal with what seem like quite simple intellectual tasks. We might also characterize this by saying that many children have highly developed oral cultural capacities but have not developed the capacity to dissociate thought from their lifeworld.

Let us consider, for example, the classic Piagetian experiment which is supposed to show that young children cannot "decenter," cannot, that is, take a viewpoint other than their own. The classic Piagetian task uses a model of three mountains that differ from each other by colour and by some other prominent features. The child sits on one side of the model and a doll is put on another side. The child is then asked what the doll can see. Various means are given for the child to respond, such as selecting the doll's view from a set of photographs taken from different angles. Typically, until about ages eight or nine, children will fail at this task and younger children very commonly select the picture taken from their own viewpoint. Based on such findings Piaget has built crucial parts of his theory of young children's egocentrism, inability to "decenter," and so on.

Martin Hughes devised a different form of the Piagetian experiment. It involved a model with walls which hid parts of the model from particular sides. He then used two dolls, one of a policeman and one of a little boy. The policeman was placed at different positions at the edge of the model and the subjects were asked where the boy would be invisible to him. Almost invariably the children found this task easy. Even when there were two policeman dolls and the subjects were asked to place the boy doll so that it could not be seen by the policeman, 90 per cent of the children between three and a half and five years were correct in their responses.

The logical form of Hughes's experiment was identical to that of Piaget. The results, however, were dramatically different. Why? Donaldson's answer is that Piaget's task was set in contexts totally "disembedded" from the world that was meaningful to children. Hughes's similar task differed only in being "embedded" in a context of meaning shared by the child.

This, and the series of similar experiments Donaldson reports, raise two challenges. The first is aimed at Piaget's theory – at its claim that children lack certain skills because they have not developed certain logico-mathematical structures and consequently at the whole stage-developmental sequence because it is articulated in terms of these structures. The second challenge is to those educational practices, and curricula, which are insensitive to children's need for "embedding" new information or skills in meaningful contexts. (As argued earlier, "meaningful context" need not be interpreted in terms of the *content* of children's everyday experience.)

It is clear that the kinds of skills measured in IQ tests, with which schooling success is so complicatedly intertwined, lead to favoring children who are more successful at performing tasks that require what Donaldson calls "disembedded" thinking. That is, those children who can more readily "abstract" their thinking from the everyday world of human purposes and intentions do better.

The kind of intelligence inherent in this skill is most highly valued in our schooling systems.

This does not mean, of course, that such thinking is not indeed of the highest value. Nor does it mean that we should in any way discourage "abstraction," or reflective theoretic reasoning (Tulviste, 1979). It means rather that we should recognize that it is a kind of thinking which young children do not use readily during their "oral cultural" years. Learning to think in a "disembedded" way is a difficult achievement and is perhaps the most important general intellectual capacity to be mastered in the early years at school. We will be able to further this capacity only accidentally if we are unaware of it, and unaware of how it becomes differentiated from the more common – "oral" – forms of young children's thinking. Furthering this capacity requires two distinct educational achievements, I think. First, the adequate development of the oral foundation on which it can be built – and this is the topic of this volume – and second, the stimulation of reflective capacities and theoretic reasoning – which is the topic of the next.

Here we need to understand how to embed new information in contexts that are meaningful to children. What is the crucial feature that made Hughes's task so easy for children while Piaget's was so daunting? Boys hiding from policemen is, of course, a common element of stories. The story, then, to put it only half-facetiously, carries its own bedding around with it. The task to be faced here is how to embed curriculum content into story-like contexts which will ensure greater understanding of whatever is to be taught.

This section is not intended to provide an exhaustive description of empirical support for my claims. Rather I have touched on just a few areas where empirical results most *suggestively* argue for the importance of meaningful contexts for enhancing children's learning. Orienting, meaningfulness, pattern, form, fitting things together, embedding, organizing: these are, to return with more *bonnes à penser* to the observation made in Chapter One, all functions of what Aristotle called the *mythos* of a narrative or argument or play or any general set of words. If the *logos* is the text, the surface level of content, there is underlying this and giving it order and coherence, life and meaning, a *mythos*. The *logoi* are the bits, the *mythoi* weld them into a greater unit and thereby create a more general meaning. We tend to be insufficiently sensitive to the *mythoi* that children use to organize the *logoi* of their experience.

Again, it is Apollo's logical realm that our schools attend to most fully, and we pay too little attention to Dionysus' subterranean factories of meaning.

Stories in Education

Well, I've dragged you through a somewhat heavy-handed and repetitious introduction to this section. But even recollecting in the tranquillity of revision it seems worth keeping the previous sections in place because, while not making particularly original points, they do emphasize the importance of something rather neglected in education. My purpose in this section, then, is to elaborate a little on some educational implications of the above discussion of stories and prepare for the fuller elaboration in Chapter Six and Seven. Some of the implications are fairly obvious, others might do with teasing out a little.

The story is a technique for organizing events, facts, ideas, characters, and so on, whether "real" or imagined, into meaningful units that shape our affective responses. It is a basic conceptual tool for providing coherence, continuity, connectedness, and meaning to its content, and building from their coalescence a further level or kind of meaning. Stories, after whatever transformations, reflect a mental predisposition. One implication of these conclusions for education is that we would be sensible and courteous to organize what we want to teach children in this form that can make its contents engaging and meaningful. This is one of the implications that might do with teasing out a little.

The trick here is to abstract elements of the story form from the typical content of, say, the classic fairy-tales and see how those elements might be used to shape the content of lessons or units of study across the curriculum. Important elements of such stories that we have already considered include a beginning that sets up an expectation; this expectation has an affectively engaging quality, and such a quality is most commonly achieved by setting binary opposites into conflict with one another. The central part of the story involves the elaboration of this binary conflict, and the end comes with its satisfaction or resolution or mediation. If we concentrate on just these principles and consider how we might convert them into a technique for use in planning teaching, an initial general implication concerns our very approach to our subject matter. We must start seeing knowledge of the world and of human experience as good stories to be told rather than, or as well as, sets of objectives to be attained.

The beginning, then, involves searching the content for what is most affectively engaging about it. We may phrase this as asking what is most important about it or why does it matter. We must locate, that is, what is of deep human significance about our subject. Saying simply that children ought to know it in order to become educated is insufficient. That responds excessively to the Platonic insight and ignores Rousseau's. (Identifying fabulously engaging material peripherally related to our topic responds excessively to Rousseau's and ignores Plato's.) We must, these principles imply, find what is most important about the topic and frame that importance in the form which children are predisposed to find engaging and meaningful.

Such an approach may seem possible in history or social studies, but more remote from science and mathematics. I think, rather, that the main reason mathematics and science seem to present such difficulties to so many children is because their place in human understanding is still taken in largely unreflective educational practice in a nineteenth-century positivist sense. Mathematics and science need to be embedded in contexts of human meaning, with their hopes, fears, intentions – the human emotions among which they came to birth, continue to progress, and that gives them life and meaning. Of course we can impress mathematical and scientific facts and operations into children's superficial memories without any of this. But, as has been pointed out by educationalists for centuries, this achievement is educationally useless. The problem is to engage children's understanding in such a way that the material sinks into that ever-active level of memory˙ discussed in the previous chapter. That engagement of understanding, I am arguing, is accessible to young children by presenting material in a manner that draws on the elements of the story form.

If in Science we are required to teach a unit on Heat, for example, it is not enough – either in terms of courtesy or of pedagogical sensitivity – to organize the knowledge we want acquired into a neat logical sequence – setting up perhaps a set of interesting experiments whose results build gradually the basic knowledge about Heat that constitutes the objectives of the unit. The implication of the discussion of stories is that we must first embed the topic in a context of human meaning accessible to, and vividly engaging for, the child. We must begin by finding something that is affectively important about Heat, and finding a way, perhaps by means of binary opposites, of embodying that affective importance in clear and engaging terms.

The question about identifying the affective importance of the topic is not to be interpreted in some "childish" sense. Rather, the teacher can ask simply what he or she finds most affectively important; at what point does the topic engage an emotional response in him or her. The educational scheme I am outlining in these volumes is one in which we accumulate capacities. We do not properly discard capacities as we grow older. There are inevitable losses but the understanding of the young child is not a kind that we properly leave behind, so within ourselves we can identify affective responses to topics that are equally accessible to children. And, another feature of this layered scheme, the initial layer is one in which we lay down many of the most important bases of human understanding, particularly those in which affective orientations to the world and to experience are established. So, when we seek within, as it were, for what is affectively engaging and important about Heat, we can safely do so in the most serious sense we know. It is there that we can locate what will also make it affectively engaging to children.

Let me quickly sketch an outline for a unit on Heat that uses the principles identified above. One way of answering the beginning question is to see Heat as destroyer or Heat as helper. How can we body forth these destroyer/helper opposites in conflict in a way that will enable us to show vividly the content of our unit in an engaging and meaningful way? We might begin by setting up our context, preparing the bedding, for the facts, experiments, and so on. And we might borrow the way the Greeks did this for themselves in their mythological representations. (These, remember, are the bases on which their rational and scientific inquiries grew.) So we might begin with the myth stories that explain affectively the vital importance of heat to human life, and its dangers. We can thus tell the stories of Prometheus and Zeus, and of Sol and Phaeton, and see Haephestus limping around his constructive workshop. The daring of Prometheus, giving fire to humans, and the terrible punishment of Zeus, show the importance control of heat has played in human civilization. It is a power that has made us like the gods. Phaeton's escapades show what destruction can follow when this terrible servant gets out of control.

The middle of our unit needs to elaborate the theme of Heat as destroyer/Heat as helper. The middle of the unit needs to be seen as like the middle of a story. It is not to be developed by simply putting in various relevant content in some logical sequence. Rather the teacher must think more as a story-teller developing a theme. So the content selected will be influenced by the theme. We will choose as experiments, for example, not so much those that get at key facts, but those that expose key facts in light of our theme. It is what they expose about the constructive/destructive forces of Heat that matters now. (Obviously we could have chosen different binary pairs and consequently developed different themes.) Experiments with heating water and generating steam can tie in with the stories of Hero of Alexander's steam engine and then that of James Watt. These stories need to catch the human purposes, hopes, fears, struggles, of the individuals, and embed their discoveries and inventions in them as they relate to our theme. Experiments using silver or matt black reflectors over glasses of water and measuring the temperature of the water after they have stood in the sun for some time can be engaged with the theme through wondering how space ships and astronauts can best be protected from Sol's burning rays in space. And so on. The difference in this approach is more a matter of context, and its affective quality, than in the typical content of such a unit.

A conclusion to such a unit might come in considering the constructive and destructive potentials of Heat in nuclear power. This urgent present issue is still grasped in the terms given vivid form in the ancient Greek myth of Prometheus and Zeus. Nuclear energy promises a promethean gift to human beings, but Zeus may wreak vengence for our attempts to harness his godly power. The myth catches, that is, a way in which we still affectively orient ourselves to the constructive and destructive potentials of Heat.

This sketch of a unit is not intended to be any more than an indication of how it is possible to take some of the principles of the story form and turn them to pedagogical use. In Chapter Seven I will elaborate this further, constructing from these principles a framework or model to guide lesson and unit planning, along with some examples worked out in more detail.

Less opaque implications for education that follow from this discussion of the story form involve children's developing such capacities as establishing a sense of coherence and of causality among events and a flexibility in the understanding and use of metaphor and other tropes. The story, I argued, is the archetypal form in which narrative bits are pulled together into coherent wholes to create a larger meaning. This is a fundamental feature of our sense-making. We see it in embryonic form in very young children's chattering narratives and in another form in sophisticated theories in the physical sciences. Our minds, that is, do not simply mirror the world, they construct an image of it out of mind-stuff – concepts, or whatever we want to call it. That constructing is our ever-active sense-making, which involves crucially the constant and shifting coordination of contexts and contents, the making of our images of the world in the context of our patterns of understanding and our emotions, and so on, and the matching of these with the further knowledge we derive from the world (Gombrich, 1960). The ability to follow a story entails the most fundamental form of this process. We assume its existence in young children when we tell them the story of Cinderella or Robin Hood, confident that the story will generate a kind of pleasurable, satisfying meaning. This basic capacity is not something we learn, it is something we *are*. We do not, then, need to teach it. What we can usefully do is stimulate it, elaborate it, and develop it, and the instruments we have for achieving this desirable enlargement of capacities are the classic folk-tales and myth stories from around the world. This is the basis for including in the early childhood curriculum a large component given over to telling fictional stories. Some children will hear these at home, of course, but we can be a little more systematic in constructing a curriculum of stories.

This is a point different from the expansion of knowledge that the content of stories can provide, and it is somewhat different from Applebee's point about the socializing role of stories. My point here is that becoming fluent in the underlying grammar of stories *is* the development of a fundamental intellectual capacity out of which other coherence-establishing skills can grow. That underlying grammar requires exposure to many and diverse stories, especially those that have the ecstasy-inducing qualities mentioned earlier.

Perhaps I can show how stories can stimulate and develop capacities for organizing meaning and establishing coherence more clearly by focusing on just a single feature, such as, for example, causality. By putting events together in stories we generate particular causal schemes – we assert that the sequence of things in the world of the story works in a particular way, by particular rules; these events cause these emotions in people which cause them to do these thing which cause these results, and so on. In very simple stories, for example, emotions such as anger or pleasure or envy, or whatever, are represented as directly causing events. As our story-sense, our sense of the grammar of stories, becomes more sophisticated, fed by many stories, so the conceptions of causality inherent in such stories become more sophisticated. That is to say, following increasingly sophisticated stories is among other things, the development of one's conception of causality. Increasingly, simple emotions give way to more complex emotions as causal elements responsible for moving events along, and the logic of events themselves carries an increasing responsibility for the causal movement of the story. Initially stories involve largely what I have called affective causality, but this is somewhat parasitic on notions of plausible real-world causality. It is, again, in the enrichment and sophistication of this affective causality that logical and scientific conceptions of causality are hatched. They are not independent entities, as though the latter set could be available for development however primitive affective causal conceptions remain. Historical causality, for example, involves even at its most sophisticated a residue of the kind of affective causality to be found in fairy stories (Gallie, 1968; White, 1973). We can see a continuum of increasingly refined conceptions of causality from fairy story to simple historical narrative to scientific theory. The further along one moves on this continuum the more precisely less is explained, the further back one moves the more generally and imprecisely more is explained (or is attempted to be explained). The educational point, however, is that one cannot expect the child with an impoverished sense of affective causality adequately to develop more refined conceptions of causality.

Much the same might be said about metaphor and the development of a whole range of thinking skills. If we conceive the logic of metaphor as quite distinct from the logics of rational inquiries then one might assume it is possible to stimulate and develop the latter without bothering to attend systematically to the former. If one conceives the logics of rational inquiries as growing out of, as refinements of, the logic of metaphor – which is the argument of this book – then one's educational conclusion must be to attend systematically to the stimulation and development of the prerequisite logic of metaphor. Here, again, becoming increasingly familiar with stories which rely for their meaning on rich and fluent metaphorical moves and connections entails development of one's metaphoric capacities. As for children's conceptions of causality, of course, stories are not the only way to stimulate and develop metaphoric capacities, but they can be potent instruments when chosen carefully.

These are a few implications that follow from some formal characteristics of stories. Such formal characteristics are discussed much less in education than the fictional contents of stories. About this latter there is a rich literature, some parts of which I will simply echo in noting other uses of stories in education.

On the borderline, as it were, between formal or structural features and matters of content, C. S. Lewis describes the sequence of events in stories as "only really a net whereby to catch something else. The real theme may be, and perhaps usually is, something that has no sequence in it, something other than a process and much more like a state or quality" (Lewis, 1982, p. 18). Lewis argues that a main delight of the best stories is their creation of unique and new feelings, sensitivities, perceptions, ideas, by an intoxicated immersion in other worlds. They evoke in the sequence of events a "hushing spell on the imagination," a sense of wonder, an empathy with characters in the poetic world alongside that of nature. The particular feelings of wonder are what remain after the details of the stories may be forgotten. We can perhaps locate, if we try, the sense that "pirate" had for us as children, or "giant" as even younger children, or the "Hobbitry" of Tolkein's Shire. The "intolerable pressure, the sense of something older, wilder, and more earthy than humanity" (Lewis, 1982, p. 9) still cleaves to our early childhood sense of "giant," at least it will do so if we first encountered such creatures in the great fairy stories, rather than in some "cute," bowdlerized version. (This seems to conflict with Applebee's point above: for Lewis it is precisely the witches and giants that are important in expanding our grasp on experience.)

This is just one way of touching on the role of stories in stimulating and developing the imagination. Here I will only repeat the point made above: if our educational aim is to produce creative engineers, homemakers, politicians, writers, scientists, and so on, then we must attend to cultivating the ground from which that creativity grows. The enlarging of our sense of the possible, the capacity flexibly and fluently to imagine what is not, the stimulation of a sense of engagement by and wonder at the world and its possibilities, are parts of what the great stories can contribute to in individual development. (On imagination and education see Egan and Nadaner, 1988.)

A further educational use of stories is the more prosaic one of drawing in to the bright circle of their recognition a huge range of knowledge about the world – the distinctive character of particular places; flora, fauna, and geographical details, people past and present, and (the point Applebee makes above) a set of norms, values, and expectations attached to roles and relationships within one's culture. One might enrich this by adding Ted Hughes's observation that stories are

in continual private meditation, as it were, on their own implications. They are little factories of understanding. New revelations of meaning open out of their images and patterns continually, stirred into reach by our growth and changing circumstances (Hughes, 1988, pp. 34, 35).

Stories can expand both knowledge and experience, but can do so in an exploring, enriching way (Rosenblatt, 1976). They can both enhance the meaning of the particular places in which they are set, and can enrich one's perception of the human possibilities of similar kinds of places. A common difficulty for early settlers in North America was their sense of the natural environment as alien. After all, the landscape of Europe had been infused with human meaning by being the setting of so many stories. So they incorporated Indian legends and wrote their own stories and songs and poems about their new environment and experiences; they shaped their environment, humanized it, and made it comprehensible.

But the primary stuff of stories is human emotion. As the landscape becomes humanized in the context of human hopes, fears, loves, hates, and so on, so even more vividly do we understand other characters through the behaviors caused by these common emotions. Stories have the power to enable us to feel with others. We can see the world through others' eyes, through their emotional responses to events. As stories become more sophisticated the range and complexity of emotions that move the story along, and move the emotions of the listener or reader, are expanded. This entails the expansion of sensibility and sensitivity. Out of these, in part at least, grows our moral sense.

As I noted above, these points merely echo an extensive literature on the educational uses of stories and children's literature in general.

The way I have made these points perhaps suggests that I imagine children as simply passive absorbers of stories which then work these magical effects regardless of children's intelligence, activity, social and cultural background, and so on. I don't. I am here discussing the potential contributions of stories and will at various points later pick up on the various practical circumstances which affect the realizing of these potentials. Here I might mention in passing the value of young children not being merely recipients, but also makers, of stories. There are educational values in encouraging children to tell and write stories. (The seeming anomaly of expecting children to write as a part of developing capacities of "orality" will be discussed in the Conclusion to this chapter.) Whether telling stories or reciting them to tape recorders for joint listening with friends or teacher or writing them down, each child can begin to learn how to use the conventional forms and contents of simple stories in ways that locate and follow the rhythms of his or her own "voice." The main educational value in making stories lies in learning to create and shape events in a commonly comprehensible form that bears the stamp of one's "hidden self," in Matthew Arnold's sense, that enables one to express and enlarge one's unique, isolated consciousness. The great stories can evoke ecstasy when heard; one's own stories can generate ecstasy in capturing and expressing one's true voice, one's true self. The externalized story can help us to achieve this. Ecstasy from stories heard is relatively easy; learning to make stories that generate for oneself such ecstasy is very hard work. Practice, revision, practice, guidance, practice, practice, appreciation, and more practice. But we have years and a curriculum. "Ecstasy" and "hidden selves" may no doubt seem rather far removed from the real world of basic skills teaching. My argument, of course, is that these things are much, much more practical approaches to developing literacy, and numeracy, than the skills development procedures that are so common at present.

Conclusion

I will take a circuitous route back to stories in order to address some questions that should not be ignored any longer. I need to sort out the apparent contradiction between my claims that this foundational layer of education, this mythic understanding, is primarily to be concerned with developing the *bonnes à penser* or orality and the claim above that this can be aided by having young children write stories of their own. At the beginning of this chapter I suggested caution about accepting Havelock's implied recommendation that linking literate rationality to its oral and poetic source required delaying the teaching of reading and writing until children had learned "to speak fluently, to recite, to memorize, and to sing suitable verse available in their own tongue." As literature is not, to use Peabody's phrase again, the invention of literate people, so too, I want to argue, orality can be stimulated and developed by products of literacy in literate people.

This argument turns on the rather obvious fact that "literacy" and "orality" are very general and rather imprecise terms. (If we define "literacy" in precise performance terms all we will miss is the point. We can, of course, give a behavioral definition to the term but that will only make it necessary to find a new term for what "literacy" at present properly means. This attempt prematurely to give precise behavioral or performative definitions to concepts common in educational discourse has done serious mischief to the ability to talk sensibly about such things as intelligence, learning, creativity, skill, knowledge, etc. A kind of linguistic Gresham's law operates, in which the crude and bad sense drives out the complex and good.) It it not literacy *per se* that directly causes reflective thinking; rather, internalized literacy permits, and I think it fair to say, inclines one towards cumulative forms of reflective thinking. Literacy, that is to say, seems to be a necessary but not sufficient condition for reflective thinking. What else is required for sufficiency is a matter much in dispute at present (see, for example, Baumann, 1986; Goody, 1982, 1986; Heath, 1983; Scribner and Cole, 1981; Street, 1984). "Orality," even more than "literacy," is an imprecise term. We do not know, that is to say, precisely what each refers to; what range of intellectual capacities constitute either. Consequently we cannot say precisely to what degree they are mutually exclusive, overlap, and so on.

Nothing of what we know about literacy and orality at present, however, entails the conclusion that we must keep children from reading and writing in order to encourage further developments of orality. For example, a young child learning nursery rhymes and singing games by reading, who then recites them and introduces them into games with friends and siblings, is not necessarily being inhibited by literacy from the further development of some capacities of orality. I don't want to get too dogmatic about this because it is in part at least an empirical question. Until it is resolved, however, it seems reasonable to resist the attractive literal recapitulatory idea proposed by Havelock.

Possibly my argument can be accommodated to Havelock's by means of an observation that both he and Walter Ong make about the introduction of literacy on the one hand and printing on the other. In both cases there was a considerable delay between the introduction of these technologies and the realization of their revolutionary potentials for restructuring thought. In each case their initial use was to mirror the forms of thought they were destined to supersede. In the case of writing, Havelock has argued that, despite its appearance centuries earlier, it was not until Plato that its full transforming potential was realized (Havelock, 1963), and Ong has argued that the restructuring potential of print was not fully worked out until the Romantic movement (Ong, 1971, 1977, 1982). It is again an empirical question whether similar lags – reminiscent of Piaget's *décalages* – occur in the case of individuals' acquisition of literacy. The question is complicated by the remaining imprecision of "literacy", of course, but also by literacy being acquired today largely mediated by print and by handwriting whose form, structure, alignments, etc., have been influenced by print, as well as in social contexts permeated by assumptions of literate competences. But even so, to put it extremely, it seems most unlikely that the potential restructuring of thought which literacy can allow takes place as soon as children begin to master reading and writing – like water suddenly boiling, restructured into is constituent gases. Rather, internalizing literacy might better be likened to the gradual heating of water until after some time it reaches boiling point, until the social and pedagogical conditions allow the restructuring of thought. For reasons I will go into in the next volume, I suspect that we will discover empirically – once we get sufficient conceptual clarity for relevant and effective empirical research to proceed – that a child who is taught to read and write during the fifth or sixth year will not begin to exploit the capacities of literacy fully – what I will call Romantic understanding – till the seventh, eighth or ninth year.

Literacy by itself, to say it yet again, does not *cause* this profound restructuring of thought, but it was the historical agent which crucially stimulated the development of a whole range of techniques of thinking which are assumed in typical schooling, and it is exposure to this range of techniques that encourages the development in individuals of reflective rationality and disembedded thinking. There remains, however, considerable vagueness in identifying what these techniques are, what sequence they might best be acquired in, why schooling and reflective reasoning are relatively easy for some children from certain backgrounds and so difficult for others, and so on.

"Literacy," then, is a kind of shorthand term for this range of thinking techniques. It is also perhaps a bit of a red-herring, or potentially so. The danger is that the term is very closely allied in education with reading and writing "skills," and however much one tries to imbue it with the kind of sophistication and complexity that is a part of, say, Ong's or Havelock's usage, there will always be the temptation to see literacy, in the simple-minded skill sense, as directly causing reflective thinking and the general restructuring of thought. The focus on literacy, in Ong's and Havelock's sense, has, however, been immensely important for education because it has at last provided some conceptual grasp on a range of problems that have been, and have long been recognized as, crucial but very difficult to come to grips with. At about age seven children who are going to be successful in the education system begin to go through a significant restructuring of thought. This has been described in many different ways, depending on what aspects of children's thought has been the focus of study – abstract reasoning, concrete operations, theoretic syllogistic reasoning, disembedded thought, and so on. Children from some cultural backgrounds find this restructuring relatively easy, others find it very difficult and make it only partially or hardly at all. People in oral cultures also seem to make it hardly at all. What the detailed study of historical literacy has made clearer are some of the conditions that help or hinder this transition in thought, and it has done this in a way that allows us to remove the problem some way from the ideologically loaded nexus in which the debate has often been conducted. So while "orality" and "literacy" are in the end probably inappropriate terms to dominate the characterization of the educational problem, they are immensely valuable for helping to get a better grasp on just what the problem is and how we might go about solving it for all children, regardless of culture or racial and sub-culture. This is all part of the aim to make the school more an agent of the traditional pursuit of truth rather than a combat zone for class warfare.

This may seem in danger of escaping from the theme of stories altogether, but I want to connect it very precisely with my theme by reflecting on "What no bedtime story means." This is the title of an article by Shirley Brice Heath (1982). What she described in that article, and more extensively elsewhere (Heath, 1983), are the differences in different communities in their general linguistic interactions with children. For present purposes it is possible to disregard her detailed empirical characterizations and resort to a reduced and simplistic typology: in one community we can see the deliberate preparation for the forms of thought that lead to a relatively easy restructuring of thought about age seven and so to success in school; in another community we can see a development of the techniques of thinking common in oral cultures without preparation for "literate" restructuring. In the former case we tend to find a suppression of "orality" in order to restructure thought as fully and as early as possible.

Let me now bring this together with Havelock's argument. I obviously think Havelock is correct in his suggestion that children need to develop the capacities of "orality," but I also think that it is quite possible to begin developing "literacy" in such a way that it can contribute to young children's ability "to speak fluently, to recite, to memorize, and to sing suitable verse." The important point Havelock makes is that our objective for the initial years of schooling must be to develop the "poetic" foundations of education, to bring childhood to ripeness within the child. My complementary point is that this must be achieved in a manner that accommodates to our sense of the aim of education. "Orality," "poetry" – mythic understanding – is a constituent of education, not a step on the path to somewhere else. It is the foundational layer on which other forms of understanding will grow and with which they will coalesce once formed – a difficult metaphor because education is neither a mechanical nor an organic process.

In the simplistic typology derived from Heath's studies we may see that our educational prescription for each case will be different. In the former case we will need to ensure a greater emphasis on stimulating and developing the *bonnes à penser* of orality, because without these the *bonnes à penser* of literacy that are being forced will lack life and meaning. In the latter case we will need to ensure a greater emphasis on shaping the highly developed "orality" in the direction of "literacy." My point here is not to offer realistic prescriptions, but simply to make clear that my generalized treatment here, and my ideal curriculum later, are not to be seen a impervious to the complex realities of everyday schooling. Rather, getting clearer about the forms of thought involved in "orality" and "literacy" gives us further help in making practically useful prescriptions to enable the fuller educational development of all children.

My argument in this chapter is that the story is of crucial importance as a foundation of all sense-making. All children, then, need to be exposed to powerful stories with the characteristics identified above and to be discussed further in later chapters. Those children whose home-life is full of such stories may need less exposure in schools than those children whose homes are impoverished in this regard.[7] (The general curriculum prescription will need to be accommodated to the particular capacities or *bonnes à penser* stimulated in different sub-cultures.) The form of stories gives us clues about how to make material we want to teach more engaging and meaningful to children. The content of the great stories of the world helps to simulate a range of basic capacities – intellectual, affective, moral – that can form a significant part of the foundation of education.

4

Some Further Characteristics of Mythic Understanding

Introduction

One difficulty in writing this book is an ever-present uneasiness caused by the inability to do more than touch on a small range of what constitutes Mythic understanding. And even the topics I touch on, such as stories in the previous chapter, have ramifications that go far beyond what can be encompassed within a single chapter. The choice of topics for discussion is determined by the attempt to bring into prominence certain features of children's thinking which are not at all contentious but which, perhaps in part, even for that very reason, have not figured prominently in educational discourse and research. What I am doing, then, is more in the way of pointing at some things and then trying to show that they have important educational implications. This is not at all to depreciate the importance of those features of children's thinking that are enlightened by mainstream educational research, but rather to argue that a balanced picture of the child as thinker and learner needs more appreciation of what I am pointing to as key features of Mythic understanding. Research has, for example, focused in great and ingenious detail on the embryonic forms of rational skills but has not equally enlightened, say, metaphoric capacities. There is no problem at all in enlightening first what our available research methods are good at, but there is a problem when we assume that what is enlightened forms a disproportionate part of the phenomena we are trying to understand.

My overall aim is to outline a scheme of education that is sufficiently clear, detailed, and distinct that it can be implemented in classrooms through teaching practice and a revised curriculum, and that it can be evaluated. What determines the extent of the discussion of features of Mythic understanding, then, is the need only to establish what will suffice for these purposes – however much more could be said about stories, metaphor, affective organizers, and so on. To achieve this aim it is, incidentally, necessary to go at least into enough detail to make the distinctive features of the scheme plausible and to encourage a somewhat uncommon way of thinking about children's early education. These, then, are the considerations that have determined the topics to be dealt with in this chapter. I will sketch, even more economically than with the story form, some other features of Mythic thinking, all of which have been at least mentioned in the first two chapters but all of which need, I think, just a little more development to sustain the implications to be drawn in the final chapters.

Binary Opposites

I have mentioned binary opposites in each chapter so far, and give a section to the topic here because it is one of those features of young children's thinking that has been noted by a number of educational writers and has figured in significant educational research but whose importance and implications for educational practice seem to me never to have been adequately drawn out. It is, not coincidentally, one of those topics that have figured in the three main sources I have been using; empirical observations of the everyday language, stories, and games of young children, studies of oral cultures, and the Greek foundations of our forms of rational inquiry. I will, then, draw as briefly as seems prudent on each of these areas to establish what I mean by binary opposites and to indicate why they are important for the foundational layer of education.

The term itself, taken from Lévi-Strauss's use (1966a, 1969), is a bit problematic because most of the binary discriminations referred to are strictly neither empirical nor logical opposites. "Hot" and "cold," to use an example to be developed later, are not true opposites; the two sensations are not the reverse of each other and the intensification of both produces a sensation of burning. But in the end I think the term is justified, and useful, because it draws attention to the way we generate oppositions in the construction of thought. So I will stick with "binary opposites" rather than a more non-committal term such as "binary discriminations" or "polarizations," on the understanding that "opposites" is not to be interpreted in a strict logical or empirical sense but is to be recognized as a rather complex but very common feature of thinking, one commonly tied in with our metaphoric capacities. That is, the oppositions are commonly metaphorically so, rather than logically so. As Ogden puts it:

> Opposition is not to be defined as the maximum degree of difference, but as a very special kind of repetition, namely of two similar things that are mutually destructive in virtue of their very similarity. They are always a couple or duality, opposed as tendencies or forces, not as beings or groups of being nor yet as states. If we regard Concave and Convex, Pleasure and Pain, Heat and Cold, as opposites, it is by reason of the real or assumed contrariety of the forces which produce those states. (Ogden, 1967, p. 41)

The prominence of such binary opposites in young children's thinking is evident to the most casual observation. Bettelheim points out that the "manner in which the child can bring some order into his world is by dividing everything into opposites" (Bettelheim, 1976, p. 74). And indeed we see this in the structure of stories, games, and the fundamental classifications of experience – big/little, love/hate, brave/cowardly, good/bad, fear/security, dominance/submission, and so on and on. This prominence some see as simply a logical matter that impinges on our psycho-logy: "Logically, we express . . . elementary differentiation in the form of contradictories, A and not-A, and it is certainly true that the ability to distinguish, together with the ability to perceive resemblances, is basic to all cognitive processes" (Hallpike, 1979, pp. 224, 225). Lévi-Strauss, notoriously, has made the search for binary opposites in myths the starting point of analysis because it exposes the most fundamental structural features of thought: "duality, alternation, opposition and symmetry, whether presented in definite forms or in imprecise forms, are not so much matters to be explained, as basic and immediate data of mental and social reality which should be the starting-point of any attempt at explanation" (Lévi-Strauss, 1969, p. 135).

At the most basic levels, then, we constantly find binary oppositions used to discriminate features of the environment and of social life:

> Binary oppositions are intrinsic to the process of human thought. Any description of the world must discriminate categories in the form "p is what not-p is not." An object is alive or is not alive and one could not formulate the concept "alive" except as the converse of its partner "dead." So also human beings are male or not male [or female or not female], any persons of the opposite sex are either available as sexual partners or not available. Universally these are the most fundamentally important oppositions in all human experience. (Leach, 1967, p. 3)

It is easy to see why the process of forming binary opposites is so useful in beginning to make sense of the world or of experience: "When once an opposition is established and its principle understood, then either opposite, or any intermediate term, can be at once defined by opposition or by degree" (Ogden, 1967, p. 20). Some basic discriminations, perceptual and cognitive, between figure/ground and self/world seem to be evident near the beginnings of life (see, for example, Banks and Salaparek, 1983; Gibson, 1969).

When we look to the historical beginnings of our rational inquiries we similarly find binary oppositions prominent. Heraclitus thought (as far as we can make out what he meant) that the essential qualities of the world and experience were Flux and Becoming, and that these were a product of the union of the binary opposites, Being and Non-being. To the Pythagoreans ten fundamental opposites were evident in the structure of the world (limited/unlimited, odd/even, unity/multiplicity, right/left, masculine/feminine, quiescence/motion, straight/curved, light/dark, good/bad, square/rectangle). Wherever we look in the ancient and medieval worlds we find such opposites used in ordering the way people think about the world and experience. In St Augustine's City of God "Contra malum bonum est, et contra mortem vita:

133

sic contra pium peccator" (As bad is opposed to good, and death to life, so the sinner is opposed to the pious). Initial unities cleave into opposites and the opposites yield mediations. (Le Goff has shown the birth of purgatory from heaven and hell (Le Goff, 1984). Binary opposites are prominent and fundamental tools in the "folk-taxonomies by which we bring order and understanding into a complex universe" (Goody, 1977, p. 36; see also Lloyd, 1966).

Let me add some further support to the claim for the fundamental importance of binary opposites in human learning. Derek Bickerton has made a comparative study of the genesis and development of children's language and that of "new" creole languages from various pidgin languages (Bickerton, 1982). Pidgin languages are those crude makeshift means developed by groups of different language speakers in order to communicate.[1] Thus African slaves from different language groups put together on plantations had initially to devise a pidgin language. Japanese, Tagalog, Chinese, Portuguese, and Hawaiian speakers developed a pidgin working on sugar-cane farms in Hawaii. After some generations the pidgin is developed into a creole language; this is a language with a stable structure and syntactical rules that differ from those of the initial languages and from the pidgin forms.

Among the conclusions of Bickerton's study is the Chomskian observation that we must have a "bioprogram" for developing language. It cannot be generated simply from "inputs"; too much is learned too quickly from too small input. Bickerton is particularly interested in the kinds of mistakes young children make, and do not make, in learning their native language, and in the kinds of changes one finds in moving from a pidgin to a creole language. While much of this is fascinating, the principal point of interest to my present argument is Bickerton's finding that basic to all human communication and at the root of all language and language learning are four binary distinctions.

The first is specific/non-specific. ("A dog just bit me"/"Mary can't stand a dog in the room.") Children learn such distinctions without making errors. The second is state/process. Children learn easily and without error that the ending "ing" can apply to verbs which denote a process and not a state. Thus a child may say "I eating" but not "I being there." The third is punctual/non-punctual. This distinguishes between single events ("I hit") and repeated or habitual events ("I live"). The fourth is causative/non-causative.

Children learn without error when the causal role of an agent is indicated by an inflection on the subject of the sentence.

Whether or not a bioprogram or Chomskian Language Acquisition Device exists, however, is of less concern to my present argument. For Bickerton and Chomsky such a bioprogram is offered as an *explanation* of the phenomena they describe. Of more interest for my argument are the *phenomena* Bickerton describes, whether or not the innate bioprogram is the best explanation of them. What remains is the fundamental importance of binary operations at the most basic levels of learning. Whether the same processes are later used in learning more superficial cultural content – necessarily or contingently – is open to question and to empirical testing. The fact that we see the basic binary discriminations operating at the most basic level of all language learning adds some plausibility to my claim of its being a process that young children use commonly and easily.

A somewhat different, but clearly related, set of claims may be found in Roman Jakobson's work on language learning. While some aspects of Jakobson's work on phonology has come in for criticism, Chomsky argues that its continuing importance to linguistics "lies not in the formal properties of phonemic systems but in the fact that a fairly small number of features that can be specified in absolute, language independent terms appear to provide the basis for the organization of all phonological systems" (Chomsky, 1968, p. 65).

Jakobson pointed out that in all languages there is a fundamental opposition between consonant and vowel sounds, and that in learning to talk children begin by gaining control over the basic set of vowel and consonant categories in a standard sequence, elaborated on the basic binary discrimination (Jakobson and Halle, 1956). The discrimination is made on two binary oppositions between the high-energy noise of the vowel and the low-energy noise of the consonant, and the loud-compact noise of the vowel and the soft-diffuse noise of the consonant. So first there is the discrimination between the undifferentiated consonant and vowel sounds. The next further discrimination within these categories is based upon pitch: the low-frequency consonantal pitch producing the "p" sound and the high-frequency producing a "t". These are then mediated by a high-energy velar stop consonant "k". Thus we may represent the basic consonant triangle as follows:

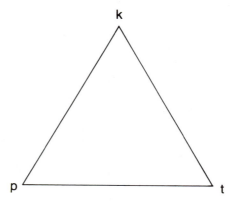

Similar discriminations on the same high/low and compact/diffuse bases within the verbal category may be represented as follows:

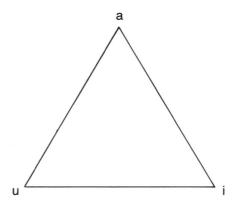

This all may be represented in the following diagram:

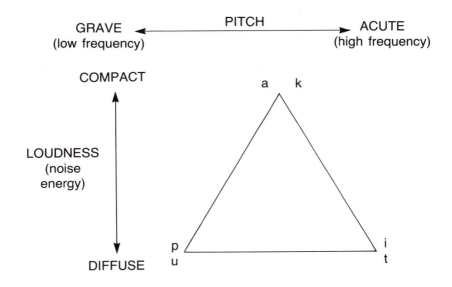

Children universally progress in controlling the available repertoire of phonemic discrimination in pretty much the same way. This path is followed rather than any other, it is claimed, because the brain, in association with the architecture and musculature of the various organs used in talking, is so structured as to be predisposed, or "programmed," to do it this way. This structure then, as represented in the vowel–consonant models, outlines a necessary process followed by all human minds. Here, as we saw with plots and stories in the last chapter, we see a method that focuses on a relatively restricted underlying structure that organizes the infinite variety of possible sounds. If we focus only on the surface sounds, noting the endless shades and differences across cultures, then we will be unable to see the patterns or structures that underly, and apparently determine, them.

The arguments supporting the universality of the polarizing/mediating model are made much more elaborately in the work of Claude Lévi-Strauss. Lévi-Strauss drew on Jakobson's work in his investigation of kinship systems and, more elaborately still, of myths.

Basic discriminations, such as between one's own species/another species, dominance/submission, sexual availability/unavailability, food/not food, are common to nearly the whole animal world. So while a dog may *learn* whether x is a food or not a food, it knows by instinct the difference between food and not-food; having determined which x is, the dog instinctively treats it in appropriate fashion. Such discriminations are necessary for survival in the world of nature. However, in the cultural world survival as a cultural animal requires more elaborate discriminations, and for a complex society to function harmoniously each member of the society must recognize these. Now, despite much argument to the contrary, there is nothing instinctive about being English as distinct from, say, French, but the basic predispositions that condition people everywhere to develop into members of a society, it is claimed, may be considered to be instinctive, "programmed." Furthermore, the kinds of discriminations that are learned in various cultural codes, like language, clothing, food, kinship, while eventually existing in myriad different forms are all nevertheless elaborated according to the same principles – principles encoded in the structure of the mind and exposed in an isomorphic structure that can be uncovered in the ways we categorize and organize and learn the content of our culture. Lévi-Strauss argues that underlying the diversity of forms of cultural behavior, such as we see for example in systems of kinship, modes of cooking, languages and mythologies, there are common and relatively simple structures that determine the basic empirical discriminations on which the overt behavior is then elaborated.

As a simple example, Lévi-Strauss takes the variety of forms of cooking evident around the world. He sketches a "culinary triangle" patterned on Jacobson's vowel–consonant triangle (Lévi-Strauss, 1966b, pp. 937–40). He uses cooking as an example because cooking is, with language, a truly universal form of human activity. The basic empirical discrimination made, he suggests, is between *the raw* and *the cooked*, and these are mediated by *the rotted*. Thus the two poles along which our mental organization of food will be formed are normal/transformed and culture/nature. This has been developed on the basis of empirical observation, and may be represented thus:

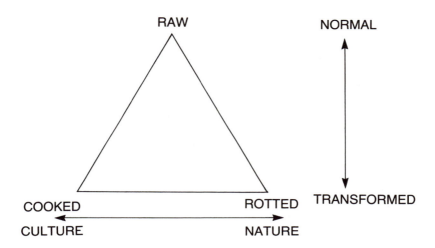

Put briefly: *the raw* category represents, ideally, food that is eaten in its natural state – though humans tend always to do something to it: peel it, scrape it, season it. *The cooked* is food transformed by cultural means – i.e. the use of some kind of implement or pot. *The rotted* is food transformed by natural means. (Many cultures show a marked preference for rotted foods. Lévi-Strauss mentions the French predilection for "rare" cheeses as an example.)

The principal categories are "empty," and their function is to delimit the semantic field "from the outside," i.e. the object of analysis is not the kinds of foodstuffs but the categories and their structural relationships. For example, even in the consonant triangle the phonemes "k," "p," "t" are ideal types, representing empty positions that each language fills with its closest distinctive sounds. What the analysis is concerned with are not the actual sounds of any language but the ideal categories that may be abstracted from empirical observation. So each culture may tend to have slightly different concepts of what constitutes the raw, the cooked or the rotted.

It might be useful to draw an analogy between the orienting and perspective-establishing function of binary opposites in our thinking and the binary structure of our other sense-making organs. If our concern is the content of our visual field we will not be drawn to realize that what we see is a mediation between the views from two eyes. While the binary structure of our vision is crucial in providing perspective for what we see, the complexity of our visual field, and the fact that we attend to what we see not to how we do the seeing, means that we tend to forget that we are putting together two views. The complexity of our thinking, and in the present case children's thinking, and the fact that we attend to the content of thought rather than to any of its structural features, means that we tend to overlook the powerful binary opposites we often use to orient and to provide perspective for our thinking.

Well, this analogy – not I think a particularly strained one – and the previous examples are here to suggest that my insistence on the importance of binary opposites is not some exotic oddity. In making sense of the world at the most basic levels we find the binary/mediation principle at work. It seems to be a crucial tool, and one that has been somewhat neglected in education. Something like it, and something whose elaborate theoretical development can connect what I am pointing at with sophisticated intellectual processes, is Piaget's conception of equilibration (Piaget, 1978). It would be a mistake, I think, to try to collapse the polarizing/mediation to simply a form of equilibration, in Piaget's sense. What I am pointing at is in many ways much grosser than the process Piaget has elucidated, but it is at a level from which some fairly straightforward educational implications can be drawn.

There may seem some redundancy in quoting so many and such varied authorities to establish what some take as an obvious logical point and others as an obvious feature of our psychological make-up. I do so simply to reiterate something that is perhaps so obvious that we tend to forget it. My argument is that attending to the use of binary opposites in children's thinking, and in human thought in general, might help us towards an ordering of subject matter that is in accord, rather than at odds, with the way children most readily make sense of things.

Now for the qualifications: I am not crudely suggesting that we present everything to children in binary terms. The point about binary opposites concerns initial access to knowledge. The point about education is to develop knowledge to better reflect the world and experience – not the simplest structures whereby we begin to grasp them. One may say that the educational point is not so much the use of binary opposites as, rather, their mediation.

As Goody notes about the binary structures of folk taxonomies, "the order is illusory, the meaning superficial. As in the case of other binary systems, the categorization is often value-laden and eccentric" (Goody, 1977, p. 36). Binary opposites are wonderfully effective for getting an initial grasp on the world and on experience but if they dominate too long, they ensure inappropriate reductions and simplification – as, for example, in those whose thinking about their nation's foreign policy is dominated by the seductive binary opposites good and bad. "Such [binary] relationships are good for thinking, but reality does not always follow suit; a certain stubbornness of the facts remains" (Burkert, 1985). In education that stubbornness of the facts is one of our guides, but so too is the structure of children's thinking. The task, then, is to see in what way we can acknowledge the importance of binary opposites in making knowledge more readily accessible to children while remaining faithful to the stubbornness of facts.

If we look at everyday children's thinking, as evident in fantasy, stories, and mundane empirical discriminations, we can see further some of the roles played by forming binary opposites and mediating between them. One of the most striking features of young children's preferred stories, and that which invites us to use the term fantasy about them, is their fantastic content. Their underlying form is common to all stories; it is those talking bears and rabbits and worms that make them distinctive. A theory of learning that proposes that children make sense of the world and of experience by starting with, and only with, the content of their everyday experience and then working gradually outwards has considerable difficulties dealing with the fantastic content that brims over in children's narratives and in the stories they prefer from ages roughly four to six.

How can we account for the fantastic content of children's fantasy? There is nothing in their experience that would suggest the plausibility of talking middle-class bears. Of course they hear stories that include such creatures, chatting with worms and trees as they push baby bear in a stroller through the woodland-town. And of course their fantasy narratives are full of ideas and creatures either derived from or composed of things they have seen and heard. That is, even though the content of their fantasy is obviously constructed in some way from the content of their experience, this still leaves unexplained the fact of fantasy. Why are middle-class talking bears and the rest so readily engaging at this age?

It is surely quite inadequate to explain fantasy as something foisted on young children by adult story-tellers. That fails to explain why, of all the products of adult story-tellers, fairy stories with impossible creatures are so consistently and powerfully engaging. The similarity between children's fantasy creatures and those in the world's myths and folk-tales also argues that these impossible creatures are not trivial or accidental parts of children's thinking. The answer offered below deals with only a part of the question, but it is the part that I think has interesting implications for education.

The part not dealt with involves the kind of explanation of children's fantasy given by Freudians or Jungians. Whatever one makes of claims about fantasy being a primary process activity operating according to the rules of substitution, displacement, and so on, or being a spontaneous irruption from the unconscious that may become the subject for active imagination, they address an aspect of the problem that has, of course, major psychological, psychoanalytic, and therapeutic implications. These are issues addressed at length by Bettleheim with regard to folk-tales. He argues that the fantasy of folk-tales talks *directly* to the child's mind about the great issues of life which the child lacks the conceptual apparatus to grasp in realistic terms: "Like all good art, fairy tales both delight and instruct; their special genius is that the do so in term which speak directly to children" (Bettelheim, 1976, p. 53).

But my interest is a very narrow one – I am not at all trying to explain generally why the content of such fantasy is as it is. Rather I will be looking at just a part of the problem and offering an explanation of just one feature of fantasy content.

Not only is the content of children's fantasy interesting, and important to explain, but also changes in its underlying form help to explain something of how children move from fantasy towards reality. We may readily see simple binary opposites everywhere in young children's narratives and stories. Characters are good *or* bad, clever *or* stupid, industrious *or* lazy. Bettelheim notes that "since polarization dominates the child's mind, it also dominates fairy tales" (Bettelheim, 1976, p. 9). The use of this polarization according to Bettelheim is that it enables the child "to comprehend easily the difference between the two, which he would not do as readily were the figures drawn more true to life, with all the complexities that characterize real people" (Bettelheim, 1976, p. 9). Of particular interest to educators is the process whereby those complexities become comprehensible to those children who earlier showed a marked preference for grasping the world and experience in terms of binary opposites.

If we consider how children learn and conceptually elaborate something fairly straightforward like, say, the temperature continuum, we see that they often begin by learning "hot" and "cold." This does not mean that they cannot feel an infinite continuum of temperatures, it is simply that the polar opposite concepts are learned first. Thereafter children learn "warm" or some such term. That is, they learn a mediating concept between the poles. They then learn concepts that mediate between "hot" and "warm" – "pretty hot" – and "warm" and "cold" – "cool." The meaning of these terms is relative to the child's body temperature: i.e. this feels hotter, or much hotter, than my body; this feels colder than my body. Later still, children learn the temperature continuum as a set of arbitrary numbers. This does not displace the concepts of "hot" and "cold" and the rest; rather it embeds them in a context removed from the personal referent of body temperature, and indicates that when "hot" and "cold" are used their meaning has to be seen as relative to something. Similarly, the initial "good" and "bad" polar opposites are good or bad relative to the child's feeling – the daddy who insists they stop playing smurfs and wash their hands for lunch is "bad daddy," meriting a smack on the way past if they think they might get away with it. The poles become conceptually mediated by the acceptance of characters and events that are neither bad nor good but in between. Again, the concepts "good" and "bad" do not disappear as this moral continuum becomes increasingly elaborate, but they are perceived as more relative and become embedded in moral schemes more or less removed from personal pleasure and pain.

So why middle-class bears? Children do commonly seem to use the process described above to make sense of their world. If one looks at the world through children's eyes, one sees some very prominent and puzzling matters that need to be accounted for. There is, for example, a distinction between things that are natural and things that are cultural. The cat and the guinea-pig do not have clothes and won't talk back intelligibly, nor do they make chairs and tables for themselves. Also there are things that are alive and things that are dead. If we mediate between nature and culture we get talking, middle-class bears, among other things. If we mediate between life and death, we get gods, spirits, ghosts, and so on. Middle-class bears are both natural and cultural, as ghosts are both alive and dead, as warm is both hot and cold. So the common process by which children come gradually to make realistic sense of the world, grasping first extreme opposites and mediating between them until they generate conceptual continua that mirror perceived continua in the world and in experience, works less well when it is used to make sense of discrete empirical categories. Attempts to mediate between life and death, or nature and culture, may generate enormously elaborate worlds of fantasy creatures and events and beliefs, but the grasp on reality comes with the realization that there is no empirical category between nature and culture, nor between life and death. In this realization we learn that nature and culture, and life and death, are discrete categories. These are not simple lessons, of course. They are, however, important in the transition from Mythic to Romantic understanding, as I will discuss later in this chapter.

When Bettelheim discusses the prominence of binary opposites in fairy-tales he makes what seems an obvious point: "Before a child can come to grips with reality, he must have some frame of reference to evaluate it" (Bettelheim, 1976, p. 117). The temperature continuum is an empirical reality and "learning it" means mastering a set of concepts that allows one to name the set of discriminations found useful in one's culture. It is likely, for example, that an Inuit child might learn a larger number of discriminating concepts towards the lower end of the continuum than might a child in a tropical desert region. Similarly a child in a scientific culture such as ours is required not just to learn the basic set of temperature concepts that are commonly used in our daily lives but also to move beyond these to understand temperature in the abstract form represented by a thermometer. This abstract and arbitrary way of referring to temperature allows us in theory to make an infinite number of discriminations corresponding with the infinite degrees of the empirical temperature continuum. We may thus denote a temperature of 17.38652 degrees Celsius, which is discriminated from 17.38653 degrees Celsius.

The world is made up of many such continua, and a major difference between education in our culture and initiation into other cultures is that we require children to learn "abstract" or disembedded ways of representing empirical continua and arbitrary schemes for measuring them. In a "primitive" culture it might be enough to learn fewer than a dozen concepts that discriminate weights or speeds or colors or whatever. (Though in some cultures dozens of discriminations might be available in the language for kinds of snow, to choose a popular example. See Goody, 1977; Lévi-Strauss, 1966a.) We require, however, that children not only learn utilitarian concepts but also "abstract" means of representing empirical continua. This is not easy for most children and is a part of what has been a focus of concern so far. Common tools for teaching such thinking involve those disembedded problems that begin: "If it takes three and a half men sixteen days to dig five and a quarter holes. . . " Solving such problems requires an abstraction of our thinking from the reality of digging holes, and we can feel the strain of moving from the everyday language of intentions and events to dealing with such problems. We have to learn first that it is meaningless, from the questioner's point of view, to ask why they are digging the holes. One difficulty with such problems is that they often seem to assume the skills they are designed to teach. What we lack is any clear understanding of the move from embedded to disembedded or from contextualized to decontextualized thinking.

We tend to reward most highly those who can deal best with disembedded thinking because it is a crucial skill for a technologically based civilization. Nor should we, of course, in stressing its difference from everyday thinking, depreciate it. There is a sense in which this abstracting ability, and ease in dealing with the abstractions in their own terms, and ease in referring the abstractions back to the events and materials of the world, is the most "realistic" kind of thinking. That is, if our concern is to gain real control over things in the world, then conceptual schemes that best represent that reality are the most realistic. At least, this belief is implicit in our ideal of educating children to deal easily with "abstraction."

Early steps in learning many important things about the world, then, may be seen in the binary opposite discriminations evident in young children's fantasy. Whether or not we can show empirically that children invariably develop their conceptual constructs by the process of first framing binary opposites and then mediating between them, we can see that there is a powerful logical plausibility that such a process is followed in learning certain kinds of things. The initial "frame of reference" the child constructs to deal with perceptions of temperature would seem necessarily to involve the points at which temperature becomes significant, i.e. when it causes discomfort. We do not notice temperature when it is what we call temperate. This first noticing and discriminating hot and cold seems a matter of logical necessity (although it is an empirical question whether children learn the terms "hot" and "cold" first). It is by means of binary opposites that we begin to get control over the conceptual field.

The further argument supporting the claim that this polarizing and mediating process is general and common in young children's learning is the very fact of fantasy. Fantasy is made up of the mediation between empirical categories: middle-class talking bears are mediations between nature and culture, as ghosts and spirits are mediations between life and death, as warm is a mediation between hot and cold. These mediating categories that children engage so readily are not so readily discarded in cases where the mediating category does not reflect something real in the world. "Warm" becomes a straightforward part of a child's conceptual apparatus as its referent becomes clear by social interactions. Middle-class talking bears become accepted as fictional conventions when it becomes clear that there are no talking bears in the real world. But the fictional convention is not casually discarded; even though children may not believe in the empirical reality of their fantasy creatures, yet such creatures maintain for some time a conceptual hold. We recognize children's acceptance that fantasy creatures do not exist as a step towards a better grip on reality. In cases where empirical evidence is hard to find, however, the persistent belief in such creatures is often hard to shake. Those half-human, half-animal Yetis or Sasquatches persist in every niche where empirical evidence is absent. Similarly gods and ghosts and spirits persist in the claim that there does exist a world where the dead are alive, or that there are mediating creatures between death and life. Either spirits, ghosts, and gods exist or they do not exist. Whichever is the case is not my concern here; what I am concerned to indicate is that the category of creatures who are both alive and dead is not one established routinely by empirical methods, but is rather one that is generated by mediating between the empirically discrete categories of life and death. Giving up belief in ghosts, say, is also usually considered a step towards a more realistic grasp on the world.

The dissolution of the mediation-generated category of ghosts tends to occur at about age five, six, or seven in our culture – though a lingering suspicion often persists in that no one can prove that ghosts do not exist. This is partly an age-related matter, becoming familiar with the conditions of reality that exclude ghosts and include politicians. The age of such enlightenment, however, can vary enormously depending on how much the cultural environment encourages or discourages belief in such mediated categories. In some cultures there is enormous pressure to believe in ghosts, even though there is no empirical evidence of their existence. Many empirical phenomena, not otherwise explicable, are attributed to ghosts, there are numerous claims of people seeing them, and so on. In our culture there is often a fair amount of pressure to persuade young children to continue to believe Santa Claus really exists. We exert a small cultural pressure to preserve a number of such "cute" mediated category confusions until about age six or seven. If children persist in such confusions thereafter we tend to become a little concerned and insistently assure them about what is real and what is not.

So from a focus on children's fantasy, and on the pervasiveness of the process of forming binary opposites and mediating between them, we can see clear cases where the conceptual process is so powerful that it overrides empirical perceptions. It energetically generates impossible creatures and conditions in the cognitive space between discrete empirical categories. The monsters of children's play and the fairy creatures who inhabit the garden or come to "life" around the dress-up box are not the product of perception-dominated thinking. These are cases where we could argue that, contrary to the common claim, children's thinking is conception-dominated. The "developmental" process here is in the direction of enabling empirical perceptions to break the hold of conceptions – not the other way around. We do obviously see cases of perception-dominated thinking in young children. The mistake is in seeing this as indicative of the whole of children's thinking.

So I have suggested that, in moving towards more realistic forms of thought, we may see a basic learning process or model being repeated on quite different kinds of content. In the case of continua, such as temperature, we see binary opposites and mediation until the child "breaks into" understanding abstract and arbitrary ways of representing the continua – one of the chief methods of doing this involves numbering. In the case of discrete empirical categories, the binary opposites represent first the discrete categories – such as life and death, nature and culture – and mediation creates categories for which there is no clear empirical referent. The mediation process may spin enormous complexity and variety of entities and the step into a more realistic view of the world is made by not abstraction, but by recognizing that the mediated entities do not exist (though this might well be seen as a form of abstracting thought from the categories given by cognitive processes). In both cases, however, the underlying process seems to be much the same.[2]

While a considerable part of the hold of fantasy over young children's mind may be due to the kind of explanations given by Freudian or Jungian or other psychologists, I am arguing that a considerable part is also due to these impossible creatures and events being the product of the learning process that works so well in making sense of so much of children's experience of the world.[3] Whether that polarizing and mediating process is a necessary or natural one – generated by the geometry of our minds' way of learning – or whether it is simply a common one used often because it works well, is not my concern here. All that matters for my present argument is acceptance that this process is a common and quite general one evident in how young children organize the world in order to learn about it. Indeed for my argument here, even less needs to be granted: it will be sufficient if it is accepted that the process of moving from binary opposites towards more elaborate representations of reality by means of mediation and further mediation is a *possible* and efficient way of learning certain kinds of things.

In a number of the cases considered above the use of binary opposites in first gaining a grasp on knowledge is not done in a way that overrides "the stubbornness of the facts." Indeed, it provides access to the facts – not in any degree of complexity, but in a way that need not falsify them. I have discussed this topic at some length because it will form an important part of the framework for planning teaching. I gave some hint of its role in the example on Heat in the previous chapters, and I will leave it now to be picked up in Chapter Seven where its implications for teaching will be drawn in more detail. My general point here is simply that we might wisely pay more systematic attention to a procedure of learning that is so pervasive and so powerful.

Imagination

It may seem disproportionate to give a lengthy section to discussing binary opposites and then here to pile together in considerably less space centrally important constituents of Mythic understanding. The more extensive treatment of binary opposites is due to the part they will play in the framework for planning teaching, and the need to justify something relatively unfamiliar in educational discourse. The set of items to be mentioned in this section are more familiar and are discussed in various places (not least in Egan and Nadaner, 1988). In part this section is a reminder of features of Mythic understanding mentioned in somewhat different contexts in the first two chapters. I am collecting them together under the sub-heading "Imagination" to stress what seems to me a centrally important feature of Mythic understanding.

Imagination, the word suggests, has to do with the capacity to form mental images. It is particularly associated with the capacity to form images of what is not present or does not exist. This is the capacity, in its many forms (Sutton-Smith, 1988), which seems to differentiate human mentality from that of animals and computers. ("Seems" because we do not know what animals' mental lives are like nor what will become possible with computers.) Imagination is not something extra to be added to, say, basic skills in mathematics or language. Rather, it is properly a constituent of our skills. That is, to be deficient in imagination in mathematics is to be deficient in mathematics in an important sense, as to have some computational block is to be deficient in mathematics in an important sense. Imagination is, increasingly clearly, of crucial educational importance in all intellectual activity as the automatic "skills" work is increasingly taken over by machines. To stress "basic skills" at the expense of imagination today is like stressing muscular development at the expense of imagination to produce manual laborers in an age of machines or physical recklessness at the expense of imagination to produce warriors. It is not that we will instead begin to develop imagination at the expense of basic skills, or muscles or courage, but "skills" of, say, numeracy and literacy, and strength and courage are useful to the degree that they are infused with imagination. (The shift from "recklessness" to "courage" is a hint of the different quality of activity that the presence of imagination creates. Similar differences in quality are evident in imaginative literacy and numeracy, though we do not have separate words for the different conditions.)

I am not trying to define imagination here, but rather to trade on the common meaning of the term, point out its place in this foundational layer of education, and also indicate some of its important stimulants – all in order to clarify it sufficiently so that it is possible to specify curriculum content and educational activities that will stimulate and develop it in children. It might be useful, though, to refine the common meaning a little, in order to differentiate imagination from some thing it tends to be confused with at present. This can be done by using some of the criteria Robin Barrow adduces: "To be imaginative is to have the inclination and ability consciously to conceive the unusual and effective in particular contexts" (Barrow, 1988).

While Barrow has elaborated on each of the points made compactly in this sentence, along with making a number of other acute observations, I would like to note in particular two of his criteria of imaginativeness. First, one cannot be imaginative in the abstract; it is the particular contexts that are important. One can be imaginative in mathematics, language use, science, running, playing, or whatever, but one cannot be contextlessly imaginative. Second, it is the *combination* of the unusual and the effective that marks imaginative activity. This is in part an extension of the first point. One cannot be effective in the abstract either. One is effective at something. This criterion cuts away from imagination the kind of aimless novelty that seems to surround some common notions of "creativity," and which seems tied into much of what passes for "creativity" tests (Barrow and Wood, 1975; Barrow, 1984).

The foundational layer of education is not the only place for imaginative development, of course – something we plug into Mythic understanding and can then forget about. Indeed I think the forms of imaginative development change somewhat, layer by layer, in ways I will try to characterize. In this foundational layer, however, it seems to me crucial that the initial grasping of the subject matter of science, mathematics, or whatever, be achieved imaginatively. This is, that knowledge be absorbed into the vivid, living, oral, mythic imaginative mental activity of the child. This is the Rousseauian problem – how we can make knowledge personally meaningful to the individual learner. It is the problem to which Dewey was most keenly sensitive. He pointed out with great clarity that traditional educational practices, even those which we tend complacently to consider successful, fail most children most of the time. And this remains true. Dewey – for reasons I have sketched earlier – saw the problem as a dissociation of disciplined knowledge from the everyday experience of the student, and thus prescribed solutions in terms of a curriculum and teaching practices that tried to tie disciplined knowledge to the everyday experience of the child. I think he was precise in identifying the problem – that dissociation from meaning – but his way of formulating it, in terms of a dichotomy between "everyday experience" and "disciplines," was less useful and led slightly to the side of the nub of the problem (Floden, Buchmann, and Schwille, 1987). The nub, I am suggesting, is the association of knowledge with the individual's imagination. Disciplines, after all, are an extension of our everyday experience, and our everyday experience is equally amenable to being dissociated from imaginative development. Perhaps one might say that both academic disciplines and everyday experience are equally subject to imaginative impoverishment; each can equally become alienated from "our true selves." The educational task is to ensure that imagination develops along with our everyday experience and academic disciplines.

While the briefest look at imagination, this does provide us with a way of stating the problem to be dealt with later: how can we design a curriculum and teaching methods that will ensure that the early engagement with disciplined knowledge will be of a kind that fuses that knowledge with the individual's imaginative life and serves to further stimulate and develop the imagination. The latter part invites the borrowing of another of Piaget's enriched terms:

the task is to ensure that knowledge must serve as an *aliment* to imaginative development.

We have a number of hints from Chapter Two about how this might be achieved. It seems clear that certain kinds of activity, experience, and knowledge can more forcefully stimulate the imagination, or perhaps rather we might note that their potential to achieve this end is enhanced by their acting within certain contexts. We saw that the need to remember gave birth to a range of techniques that make knowledge vivid and so, memorable, and in that process stimulated and developed certain potentials of the mind, which we rather vaguely call imagination. Among these techniques we have identified rhythm, rhyme, and meter, and various other forms of what I will call narrative classification and explanation. Classification and explanation (i.e. sense-making or meaning-establishing) of knowledge in narratives is achieved, not exclusively according to rational logical principles, but in some necessary degree according to affective and metaphoric connections. (These are not mutually exclusive forms of classification, but when affectivity and metaphor are dominant we, who tend to rely so heavily on rational logics, are so bemused by superficial "irrationality" that we fail to recognize even those features of rational classification that are there.) The techniques that ensure the communicative efficacy of narrative classification and explanation in myths, folk-tales, and children's fairy stories can help us towards solving our major educational problem of making systematic knowledge about the world and experience engaging and meaningful to young children. Brian Sutton-Smith sums up the situation well:

> Imagination is a relative newcomer on the stage of history. Its *lineage* is an inheritance of irrationality, mimicry and dissimulation. Its *currency* is childishness, freedom and uniqueness. Its *future* might be megagenerative. It has cut enormous ice in the arts these past 200 years, but it has had, as yet, meagre influence in education. (Sutton-Smith, 1988, p. 3)

Throughout the previous chapters I have jumbled rhythm, rhyme, and meter together, as techniques that can help to make knowledge vivid and memorable, particularly in oral cultures. I do not want to examine each of these in detail, but I do want to point out that they are not at all trivial matters of only ornamental value. I will try to indicate briefly why we might sensibly pay deeper attention to them in education than is common. I will take rhythm for example here, and discuss the others later in terms of their influence on the curriculum or teaching.

Attention has been drawn to rhythm because of its role in oral cultures and because of its prominence in the oral culture of young children today, suggestive of its resulting from a mental predisposition. Rhythm is not solely or simply concerned with beating out patterns of sound, though the sound rhythms, in music, song, and voice, that we absorb somatically during our earliest years clearly have complex shaping effects on our patterns of expectations. Later verbal rhythms set up conventional patterns that influence both the structures and meanings available and accessible in any particular culture. We might go further, I think, and see that the rhythms of action and response and of associated emotions that are basic to a culture's stories are tied in with, or at least not dissociated from, the structuring of the sense of justice and morality. People's sense of justice and morality change, for sure, and the harbingers of change, if not the cause, are to be located in the rhythmic patterns of action and emotion in what we recognize as great literature (MacIntyre, 1981).

We tend to be more readily able to see this in cultures other than our own. The Greek sense of justice, for example, can be seen changing in, and through the influence of, ancient myths, the Homeric epics, the lyric poets, the great tragedians of the fifth century BCE and the great philosophers of the fourth (Lloyd-Jones, 1971). The causal rhythms in the events represented – who was punished for what action – embody assertions about what is just and proper. It was not without good reason that Plato was so insistent on censoring the rhythms that would be allowed in the musical education of his Republic. A new rhythm, he noted, can bring down the state. Similarly, T. S. Eliot identified that immense change in consciousness that we call Romanticism as a new rhythm to be found particularly in the works of Wordsworth and Coleridge (Eliot, 1936). Well, one can easily slip into rather ethereal realms here, but consider, closer to home, the battles in the Soviet Union about permissible forms of music and art. The problem does not lie at the superficial level of overt messages counter to the dominant ideology of the state; that is relatively easily dealt with. More subtly, insidiously, and powerfully the artist constructs images or sounds that embody claims about the nature of reality. The underlying rhythms, accessible at a relatively explicit level in patterns of expectation and satisfaction, hopes, fears, and realizable intentions, jar at a profound level against the totalitarian state whose very structure asserts a different conception of reality.

Rhythm, reflected at a superficial level in music, song, narrative patterns, linguistic conventions, and at a deeper level in patterns of expectation and satisfaction, hopes and gratification, fears and nemesis. The rhythm of emotions associated with particular patterns of events – such as those which produce in us guilt, anxiety, delight, and so on – represent reality in very basic human terms. Reflecting on the role of rhythm in education leads us – perhaps too precipitously here – to the representation of that reality we feel in our bones, in our "true selves." ("Know thyself,"/"To thine own self be true.") And the poet, again, is the person who is best able to remember and express that original, unique, and isolated consciousness of a pure reality – that bundle of rhythms – that existed for each of us before language came to disturb it and make its recapture and representation so complicated. Arthur O'Shaughnessy's romantic image of the poet as the dreamer of dreams that can bring empires down is not without its, limited, sense. Even Auden did not really believe that "poetry makes nothing happen."

Not surprisingly, perhaps, even so condensed a discussion of one of the techniques generated by the need to remember in oral cultures returns us to a conclusion of Chapter Two: that the foundational layer of education is in complicated ways tied up with poetry. Not poetry in the conventional sense of what is packed away in anthologies, some of which we might prefer as a matter of taste, or indeed as something we do not have much taste for at all. Rather, poetry as a set of techniques that shape consciousness – poetry as a set of intellectual capacities. The foundational layer of education is, it seems to follow from the arguments of the previous chapters, a matter of becoming a poet. The task then is to see how we can introduce science and mathematics, history and literature, in ways that will make sense to and engage the poet within, and that will allow the poet within to expand into and through mathematics and science, history and literature.

I realize that this will appear an odd, perhaps a perverse, way of putting it. Poetry, imagination, orality, metaphoric thinking, Mythic understanding – are heavily overlapping terms in the discussion so far. None of them is very precise, but my aim has been to get a sufficient sense of the general area they refer to and a sufficient sense of some of its structural characteristics to be able to derive some implications for teaching and curriculum.

Towards Romantic Understanding

The major concern so far has been what I called earlier, rather simplistically, Rousseauian: focusing on the nature of children's understanding, or at least on some characteristics of it, with the intention of discovering how we might best bring childhood to ripeness within each child. The Platonic determining sense of direction has only sporadically been brought to bear. Time to attend to the rough-hewing of our ends so that the shaping of our curriculum makes a sound preparation. In this scheme, however, the sense of direction is not a simple one made up of some precise image of mature educated adulthood. There are many ways of being and becoming educated, but they are not infinitely varied. The coalescence of the layers as a whole represents the end, so the ripening of childhood is itself a part of it. But more precisely the set of characteristics to be stimulated and developed during the next more or less distinct layer provides a more proximate objective. It is the move into Romantic understanding, then, that will exert appreciable constraints on how the characteristics of Mythic understanding will be shaped and developed, if that transition is to be most successfully made.

Characterizing Romantic understanding is the task of the next volume, but it should be useful here to outline a few prominent features that will influence curriculum and teaching, particularly as children approach the transition from one form of understanding to the next. (This is not, of course, some total transformation, but more a matter of emphases, qualities, ways of organizing and engaging knowledge, and so on.) In the next volume I will designate year four as a transition year, with its own distinctive curriculum for enabling and encouraging the development of some major capacities of Romantic understanding. But the nature of Romantic understanding will properly exert an influence through the Mythic layer, so that, for example, the ways in which we introduce literacy and numeracy, while primarily attending to the characteristics of Mythic understanding, need also to bear in mind the directions in which those capacities will be developed.

A first characteristic of Romantic understanding is its fascination with 'reality' and its manner of grasping it. In the Mythic layer the limits of reality tend not to be matters of great importance to the child. One can detect the change I am referring to here in the kinds of stories that are found most engaging before and after the transition. During the Mythic layer important stories can casually disregard the constraints of reality – one does not need to know where the fairy godmother comes from nor what physical laws underly her powers of transforming pumpkins into coaches or mice into footman. During the Romantic layer, while one may indeed have supernatural events and characters, such as, say, Superman, it is clearly important that an explanation, however implausible, be given for his powers. So we know about the dying planet Krypton and the baby's escape during the last hours and how the molecular structure of our sun, etc., etc., etc. Similarly plastic man's curious abilities cannot simply be asserted, they have to be fitted within the constraints of some conception of reality. So we learn about his accidental exposure to radiation during some disastrous experiment. (I may be getting my superheroes mixed up. The detailed factuality of the accounts does not matter, however – so I shouldn't be too perturbed. It is the suggestion of a realistic cause that matters.) That is, a sense of the constraints of reality – for reasons I will discuss in the next volume – becomes very important in the intellectual life of students after about seven or eight years in our culture.

The early moves children make in conceptualizing reality do not seem so discontinuous as might be expected with the processes we may observe in their fantasy. Their everyday experience is not something they systematically deal with *conceptually*; rather, like fish in water, it is the taken-for-granted medium in which they exist. Their conceptual grasp on reality seems to make more eager contact first with things very far from the mundane everyday world.

If we look around for the kind of real-world content that first and most engages children, it is the kind that one finds in *The Guinness*

Book of Records. That is, children seem eager to learn, not any longer that a giant can be two miles high, thrilled by that sense of massiveness C. S. Lewis recalls, but rather how tall *really* was the tallest person. They seem most engaged in learning who and what is the fastest and slowest, the fattest and thinnest, the strongest and weakest, and so on. They become fascinated by the romantic gladiatorial simplified real-world conflicts of football teams and their histories, and by heroes and heroines, or by kings, queens, and princesses. This early energetic engagement with reality seems structurally similar to the way that young children make sense of their fantasy worlds, except that the content that bodies forth the binary opposites is real, not fantastic. The change, that is, is not so apparent at the level of underlying structure; the crucial change has been the move to learn about the real world while still using the conceptual tools developed in making sense of fantasy worlds. It is a move analogous to Cornford's account of the Greeks' move from cosmologies full of gods and goddesses to godless speculation. The change is very evident at the level of content, but much less so if we observe the persistence of underlying structures.

It would appear, then, that children's strongest conceptual grasp on reality begins at its extremes, sniffs about the borders as it were, delights in the exotic, in what is distant from their experience, engages in the kind of undisciplined romantic mind-wandering so regretted, and suppressed where possible, by so many educationalists who have urgent religious, social, or academic ends to which children need hurrying. The fact that such an initial engagement with reality seems common does not of course justify it as appropriate. There is, however, an obvious logic in approaching the exploration of reality by beginning with the discovery of limits. Only when we have secured the borders can we feel confident at turning in to explore the details more closely – confident, that is, that we have a sense of the context within which the details are made meaningful.

Indeed, such a metaphor seems closer to our experience of education than does that of gradually expanding horizons. Our conceptual path seems better represented as beginning at the borders and then winding slowly inward until, echoing T. S. Eliot again, at the end of all our exploring we may arrive at the immediate and local and finally get a conceptual grasp over these things that are in a profound sense the most distant and difficult things to make sense of. Human learning seems not a matter of moving from a known to an associated unknown along gradually expanding lines of content. Meaning is established within contexts. We plot things. We see parts as parts of some greater context, some whole. Whatever the validity of such general observations, they suggest that the way children seem to delight most in first engaging reality is not a regrettable intellectual defect, to be cured by initiation into disciplined forms of knowledge or by socially constructive active doing.

So our Mythic layer curriculum need not feel constrained to begin some logical and gradual expansion of knowledge "outwards" from the child. Indeed, the quality of engagement with knowledge, and the general objects of that engagement, will be going through a quite significant shift. The constraint on Mythic understanding is more at the underlying structural level than on the overt content of the curriculum. The content can be selected to best stimulate and develop the capacities that make up Mythic understanding with no looking forward to preparing some particular knowledge base for Romantic understanding. What is important for the Romantic layer is the development of flexibility and control of the underlying conceptual apparatus that is to provide the grappling hooks onto reality. It is that realm of powerful abstract organizers, first elaborated in narratives, in making sense of stories, that we must focus on.

This first constraint, then, is really not much of a constraint at all: it enjoins us to focus on the stimulation and development of capacities that seem also central to Mythic understanding.

A second characteristic or Romantic understanding can be seen in the typical development of obsessive hobbies. As Coe observed, "The first intellectual preoccupation of the child is to establish its inventory" (Coe, 1984, p. 239). What we see become of urgent intellectual importance is the need to grasp exhaustively some aspect of reality. There are many ramifications of this, but I will here focus on just one of them. We have seen the importance of narrative classification and explanation in the Mythic layer; on top of that we will be increasingly concerned with non-narrative forms of classification and explanation. The implication of this direction for our Mythic layer curriculum and teaching is that while narrative forms need to be developed, we must also prepare for the non-narrative.

The non-narrative forms of classification and explanation clearly overlap considerably with what Piaget calls concrete operations and what others have designated as the beginnings of "abstract" thought. I think "non-narrative" is a useful, and in some ways a more accurate, term; it directs us to consider what intellectual changes are occurring in a context which potentially allows us a more technical grasp. "Non-narrative" clearly is tied in with the development of literacy, and I will consider ways in which some of Jack Goody's observations about the use of lists, formulae, recipes, and other non-narrative classification schemes can be incorporated into a Mythic level curriculum directed towards preparing for Romantic understanding. I will tie these observations in with recommendations for "Mythic" uses of computers and the kinds of data-processing that are appropriate in preparing for Romantic understanding.

Our grasp on the world and on experience in the Mythic layer is predominantly contextualized, story-shaped. Obsessive hobbies, exhaustive explorations of some detailed area of knowledge, list-making and list-manipulating, all require and stimulate what has been called "decontextualised" thinking. Paradoxically perhaps, decontextualized thinking, in Goody's words, "gives the mind a special kind of lever on 'reality'. I mean by this that it is not simply a matter of an added 'skill' . . . but of a change in 'capacity'" (Goody, 1977, p. 109). So our direction, once we have grasped the world with, or absorbed the world into, our stories, is towards forms of thought that try to shape themselves to reality. Simply listing bits of the world and inspecting and manipulating our lists can help this process along.

A third feature of Romantic understanding concerns a mechanism whereby students have access to and are engaged by knowledge. That is, while we are moving away from the most basic contexts, and towards concepts that mirror the world, we are not leaving all contexts behind. This third feature is the use of transcendent human qualities in making knowledge accessible, engaging, and meaningful. That is, it is by discovering knowledge in terms of human power, nobility, courage, fear, and so on that the Romantic layer best can grasp it. Physics or geography, say, will be meaningful, less as logically organized bodies of information, and more as seen through the human qualities of the discoverers or inventors of the knowledge, through their hopes, fears, and intentions. Again, this point must wait till the next volume for elaboration, but its constraint on the Mythic layer curriculum and teaching is to direct us towards making sense of events through the agency of transcedent human qualities – particularly those we associate with heroes and heroines. This, rather like the first point above, does not represent a very great constraint, because it reflects developments already decided on as a part of Mythic understanding. But it should serve to heighten our awareness of these, to support the constant use of folk-tales on the one hand, and on the other, to explore the great story of human history through the intentions, hopes, fears, and actions of real people.

Conclusion

The first point I have tried to establish in this chapter is relatively simple, compared with some of the stratospherically complex claims about phonological and mythic systems that I have touched on to suggest plausibility for it. The reason for touching, however fleetingly, such stratospheric complexities is to point out that while my central point is accessible from fairly common observation and quite low-level analysis it also is coherent with a body of sophisticated empirical and conceptual research. This research does not, of course, *directly* support my point, but it does protect it somewhat from casual rejection by people who might want to claim that they do not think binary oppositions are very common: i.e. that if my point rests solely on observation, it can be rejected by people who say they do not observe what I observe. Against such an objection I can place first the analysis of fantasy, and then the logical plausibility of the process, and then the coherence with a body of sophisticated research. But finally it comes back to the surely not so easily dismissed observations. I have considered these areas of research also to attach this polarizing/mediating process to empirical observations, and so not have my claim confused with those that derive directly from some Hegelian metaphysical scheme.

My point concerns the process whereby young children first grasp the world conceptually in terms of binary opposites and then mediate between these binary discriminations until they generate a set of concepts that mirror with varying degrees of precision the contents of their environment and of their experience. This process provides a simple model of an important, fundamental, and commonly ignored process in young children's learning. Of course, much of this process remains to be clarified, elaborated, and detailed by empirical research. Standing back, however, and drawing on some methodological help rarely drawn on in educational studies, we may see its broad pattern in constant operation during learning.

This process is unlikely to be equally prominent in all areas of learning and what kinds of learning it best furthers remains an empirical question. But from its general prominence in children's thinking and learning, we would be sensible to explore its development into a clear model and consider how it might best be utilized in organizing lessons and units of study for young children.

And of course the process is not always as clear and simple as in the example of the temperature discriminations and mediations. In complex ways it seems to go on all the time. Listen to the mediating category of irony being elaborated here between what is said and what is meant (outside the study door as I write):

Three-year-old from the bottom of the stairs: "Mummy, where are you?" Mother from upstairs: "I don't know. I got lost."
A pause. You can almost hear him thinking. Laughing aloud as he scampers up the stairs:
"Here you are!"
"Thank you for finding me."
"You knew where you were all along!"

I mentioned in the Introduction that an important focus for this essay was the losses involved in becoming educated. It may seem a little premature to be considering losses when the process is just beginning. But we have already noted what is lost in the development of Mythic understanding – that participation in nature which Lévi-Bruhl saw myth itself as an attempt to recreate, or for whose loss myth was an attempt to compensate. "Participation in nature" is a concept so remote from the normal range of educational discourse today that it might seem both too vague and too exotic to be worth worrying about when Johnny and Jane can't read or add. And yet if we want to be more successful at educating, including teaching initial literacy and numeracy, we need to get a better grasp on what the process properly entails. Learning to read and to add are very easy for all but the brain damaged, and we spend massive resources on instruction. If we are in considerable degree failing to do something easy with massive resources it is a good bet that we are going about it wrongly. Where we are going wrong, I think, is in seeing things like literacy and numeracy in so narrow a context that we cannot adequately see what they are and consequently cannot adequately plan to teach them.

Before we internalize language we are conscious. There is, one might say, a pre-Mythic understanding, whose characteristics - perceptual and cognitive – are the subject of intense research at present. We also have glimpses of that consciousness through the testimony of those whose memories seem able to penetrate furthest back. Seemingly invariably these are poets and artists. All art, as Picasso noted, is a lie that takes us closer to the truth. I need not rehearse here all those claims from poets and artists that words or any other medium let them at best only approximate the truth or reality they seek to represent. The intolerable wrestle with words and meanings is part of our endless raid on the inarticulate and the realization that the end of art is to capture a truth, a reality, that we had in the beginning. In our end is our beginning; in our beginning is our end – a reciprocity T. S. Eliot was sensitive to.

Again, trying to compress this point – which has been the focus of endless discussion by artists, critics, and philosophers – runs the danger of seeming to escape from everyday educational practice. But my argument is that teaching reading, writing, and arithmetic involves two parts. First, to enable us to be articulate in the conventional forms of the languages of words and numbers and, second, to enable us to use those languages to represent our first selves, our true selves, to make articulate the fundamental truth and reality we had access to in our pre-Mythic consciousness. Because we then lacked words we could not lie; there was a precision and purity to our emotional responses that we find immensely hard to recapture in words. But becoming educated means carrying forward whatever sense-making capacities we can develop and that early participation is basic to an educated consciousness. It is our sense of the fundamental reality and truth that we may never be able to express adequately in words, theories, music, paint, or whatever but which we can try to keep vivid within us, can struggle to be honest to, can keep alive as the criterion against which the adequacy of our words, theories, and other activities can be measured. The common danger is that this pre-Mythic understanding is suppressed and replaced by conventional language and forms of thought, by socialization without education. This replacement is the first, and irreparable, large-scale loss we can suffer in our education. That we must lose the early vividness of this participation is inevitable, but our educational task is to reduce the amount lost as much as possible.

Whatever remains now is to try to work these observations, and those about imagination and the *bonnes à penser* of Mythic understanding generally, into a curriculum and teaching practice. Because this scheme is a little odd in the context of current educational theory and research, it is perhaps useful at this point to take a break for a chapter and reflect on the nature of the scheme.

5

Cultural Recapitulation: Some Comments on Theory

Introduction

In this chapter I will try both to make clear in what sense this scheme is recapitulationary and to justify such a scheme. I will try to show *what* is being recapitulated, on what the scheme rests, and how it respects logical and psychological constraints. I need to show in addition, or as part of achieving the above, how a recapitulation scheme can coalesce the Platonic end-focused and Rousseauian present-ripening insights. So this chapter will, as it were, withdraw a little from the particular concerns of early childhood and consider some aspects of the scheme in general.

The Platonic and Rousseauian insights have also implied distinctive ideas about what one needs to do in order to study education effectively. The Platonic tradition in the main has assumed that conceptual clarity about the aims and meaning of education, the nature of knowledge, and the language of pedagogical discourse will take us a considerable way. The Rousseauian emphasis on the child and on nature as our guide has supported the assumption that the more we can discover about the nature of the child, about how children learn, are motivated and develop, and so on, the better able we will be to educate more effectively. That is, the two major educational ideas have each encouraged somewhat distinct approaches to dealing with educational problems. These ideas are realized in the structure of typical departments of education in colleges and universities across the world. That education is full of conceptual and empirical problems seems self-evident. By and large the former have tended to be the domain of philosophers of education and the latter the domain of psychologists of education. The research of these two groups should complement each other, the former providing the conceptual clarity that permits the latter to conduct more precise empirical investigations. But the products of these two branches of research have had as much difficulty in coming easily together as have the two great educational insights from which they have sprung.

I mention current research because this scheme is going to run somewhat aslant of prevailing assumptions about how one can support an educational program. The distinction between conceptual and empirical questions is a very easy one to hold theoretically, and it is also much exercised as a kind of demarcation line between philosophers' and psychologists' areas of expertise. The trouble with education as an area of study is that empirical and conceptual issues are knotted up in ways that make it very difficult to get anywhere by addressing one or the other separately and, for reasons I will discuss below, they have difficulty coming together. This scheme involves an attempt to bring together the Platonic and Rousseauian insights in some coherent way, and so will involve bringing together, in at least one important sense, conceptual and empirical considerations.

Consider, for example, how A. V. Kelly in one of the clearest general curriculum textbooks discusses how aspects of the Platonic and Rousseauian insights are to interact:

> While it is true that understanding cannot be developed in isolation from bodies of knowledge, it does not follow that decisions about the knowledge content of the curriculum should or must be made first. On the contrary, it suggests rather that they are secondary considerations. We need first to be aware of the kinds of intellectual capacity we are concerned to promote in pupils and, only then, to make decisions about the kinds of content they must be initiated into in order to develop these capacities. (Kelly, 1982, p. 58)[1]

The problem with Kelly's formulation, I think, is that it pre-supposes that there are educationally meaningful ways of characterizing intellectual capacities apart from the kinds of contents that can evoke and realize them. The scheme I am elaborating in this essay attempts to overcome the dichotomy, and bring together intellectual capacities and knowledge by focusing on the sense-making capacities available in our culture.

Some radical distinction between mind and knowledge is presupposed if one is doing psychological or philosophical research, as it is if one is considering education from a predominantly Rousseauian or Platonic perspective. Or rather, one might say, because education is so pervasively thought about in terms of those perspectives, that distinction is taken for granted in the way educational problems, and research on them, are conceptualized. If one wants to bring those perspectives together, an instrument and effect will be to suppress the importance of the distinction between minds and knowledge, and to focus instead on cultural capacities. So I am not, on the one hand, trying to characterize some "natural psychological reality, in terms of which we must understand the development of knowledge," as the most Rousseauian of psychologists puts it (Piaget, 1964, p. 9). Nor am I, on the other hand, trying to describe how knowledge is structured and accumulates in logical sequences. Rather I am concerned with how the sense-making capacities of a particular culture can be stimulated and developed in the individual within the constraints of what is logically and psychologically possible. Another, hardly innocent, way of putting it is to say that my focus is on the "interlacement" of knowledge, psychological development, and cultural history.[2]

The apparent oddity of trying to coalesce considerations of mind and knowledge might be mitigated a little by reflecting on how difficult that distinction is to sustain in practice anyway. We might recall the problems involved in the various attempts to characterize minds and knowledge separately. We know minds almost entirely by what they do with knowledge – the mind is like a transparent organism whose structures only become visible when it ingests the dye of knowledge, but then it has proven immensely difficult to establish whether whatever structures we can make out are a function or property of the mind or of the knowledge. Similarly we need to remember that we store data, not knowledge, in books and computers – the only proper home of knowledge is a human mind and its forms in there are tied up with emotions, imagination, intentions, and all kinds of things that make it much less accessible to precise analysis than are external data. So my attempt to bring considerations of mind and knowledge, empirical and conceptual concerns, together is not necessarily an exotic straining to overcome some invariably fruitful distinction. It is enormously complicated to distinguish between them in practice. This is not to argue that such a distinction cannot be usefully made, just that from an educational perspective it is not so important a distinction as the polarizing of the Platonic and Rousseauian insights have encouraged us to accept. What I am trying to show is that one can get a better grasp on education by coalescing considerations of mind and knowledge in terms of sense-making capacities than one can by approaching education as involving more or less distinct sets of empirical and conceptual questions.

A neat metaphor used by some cognitive psychologists is that the brain is a computer and the mind is the program it is running. It might clarify one part of my point – though, as is the common case with metaphors, run the risk of confusing others – to suggest that the brain is a computer and our culture is the program it is running.

Recapitulating Recapitulationism

The superficial attraction of recapitulation theories for educationalists is fairly obvious. We can readily characterize the history of our cultural development and individual educational development in similar terms. Becoming educated is in significant part a matter of accumulating the most valuable capacities whose initial creation is our cultural history. Also there is evident in, or interpretable in, our cultural history a causal sequence. Certain things are discovered, invented, or made possible as a result of prior things having been discovered, invented, or made possible.[3] There is a semblance at least of logical progression, from a Ptolemaic to an Einsteinian universe, from crude ethnocentric self-glorifying stories about one's ancestors to sophisticated modern historiography, and so on. These developmental sequences seem logical in perhaps a loose sense, but it is a sense that has constantly suggested some imprecise guidance to the curriculum designer.

Alternatively, or perhaps additionally, one can see in these sequences of discovery and invention the product of certain psychological predispositions. Given the nature of human cognition we have of necessity had to construct human culture in these general sequences. It is psychologically necessary that we begin writing history from an ego-centric view, progress to an ethnocentric view, and then, maturing historiographically, try to describe things as they were. (This kind of argument, using Piaget's theory as its basis, has been made by Hallpike, 1979.)

That is, whenever we describe our cultural history as some kind of causal sequence, which one can hardly avoid, we are asserting a logical and/or psychological underpinning to the scheme. If there are logical entailments or psychological predispositions or both underlying the process of our cultural development, then a curriculum sequence recapitulating cultural history will be based on that logical sequence or those psychological predispositions or both. And as logic and/or nature are attractive bases for a curriculum, so recapitulation schemes have an obvious attraction. Aristotle makes the basic point simply: "What has not happened we do not at once feel sure to be possible, but what has happened is manifestly possible" (*Poetics*, Ch.IX).

Some of the problems with this generally plausible principle become quickly apparent when we try to work out detailed curricula from it. Also, despite its general plausibility, reca-pitulation ideas tend to be little regarded today because of the particular and, so it seems at this remove, obtuse interpretations of them that were implemented towards the end of the last century and early in this one. Most commonly a marriage of Rousseauian and Darwinian ideas led to the belief that evolutionary theory provided nature's guidance for the curriculum. G. Stanley Hall claimed that the study of evolution for education "when explored and utilized to its full extent will reveal pedagogic possibilities now undreamed of" (Hall, 1904, vol. 2, p. 221). The development of civilization was seen, analogously to the evolution of species, as a natural growth whose shape should thus, naturally, dictate the shape of the individual's development, and so the curriculum.

The most highly developed recapitulationist curricula were implemented in Germany. All of them made rather literal trans-lations from cultural history to curricula, producing a variety of "culture-epoch" proposals. These curricula seem now oddly content-tied and epoch-tied (DeGarmo, 1895; Seeley, 1906). In North America, apart from the best-known advocacy of recapitulationist ideas in Hall (1904), John Dewey was initially attracted by the ideas. He tried

> a modified system of culture epochs in his Chicago experi-
> mental school during the early 1890s. But he could not
> interest children in all aspects of supposedly appropriate
> material for their age: they loved the Roman heroes, for
> example, but yawned through the study of Roman laws.
> (Gould, 1977, p. 154)

But Dewey, also, did not shake off the focus on content: "There is a sort of natural recurrence in the child mind to the typical activities of primitive people; witness the hut which the boy likes to build in the yard, playing hunt, with bows, arrows, spears and so on" (Dewey, cited in Gould, 1977, p. 154).

Dewey came to deride the cruder kind of culture-epoch curricula, and their disrepute lasts even to the present. Reca-pitulation foundered in the early decades of this century under a two-pronged attack. The less influential came as a simple extension of the attack on recapitulation ideas in biology. It was suggested that educators "who base their work upon recapitulation . . . may well ask themselves whether they are not building on shifting soil" (Bovet, 1923, p. 150).

The more influential attack came from the growing present-mindedness of progressivism. Recapitulation curricula become

> absurd when tested by common sense. Although the develop-
> ment of the child may parallel the development of the race in
> certain respects, it does not follow that the curriculum should
> parallel the cultural development of the race. Obviously a
> child living in the 20th century would pursue a 20th century
> curriculum. There is no justification for delaying the study
> of current events and our present community, state, and
> national life until the child has completed his study of the
> preceding periods of racial development. (Monroe *et al.*,
> 1930, pp. 408–9).

The notion of recapitulation I am developing here is – I hope it is already apparent – significantly unlike those that enjoyed a vogue about a century ago. What is recapitulated in this scheme is sets of sense-making capacities, *bonnes à penser*, forms of understanding – the constituents of the general layers I am calling Mythic, Romantic, Philosophic, and Ironic. The *bonnes à penser* of orality, for example, together constitute what I mean by a form of understanding. I am calling them sense-making capacities because they are not simply mental characteristics nor simply forms of knowledge; they are capacities that are evoked, stimulated, and developed in becoming initiated into the forms of sense-making available in a particular culture.

Education in this scheme, then, is the sequential accumulation of the sense-making capacities, and associated capacities to communicate, available in our culture. This is a recapitulationary scheme because it embodies an argument that the sequence in which these capacities can be accumulated by the individual reflects the sequence in which they were generated in our cultural history. The tie between the two – cultural history and individual development – is located in the logical and psychological constraints which have influenced the historical generation of these capacities and which also constrain the sequence in which the individual can accumulate them. The dynamic of the process of educational development is not located in either of the constraints, however, but in their complex interaction with the range of sense-making capacities available as a result of our particular cultural history.

This scheme has been arrived at by analysing modern educated consciousness into constituent forms of understanding, identifying the logical and psychological constraints that determine the sequence in which those forms of understanding can be accumulated and that determine how they coalesce layer by layer, and by empirically establishing grounds for associating each layer with a particular age range. The analysis of modern educated consciousness has not relied on identifying the characteristics of those conventionally considered best educated, not on inferences from studies of the nature and forms of knowledge or of psychological development, but has been arrived at by identifying the major achievements in our cultural history that have extended our capacity to make sense of the world and of experience. I have tried to interpret these major achievements neither in terms of changing mental structures nor in terms of the contents of the particular achievements themselves, but rather, again, to fuse these into a way of characterizing sense-making capacities in a form that is equally useful in discussing cultural history and individual development.

One result of identifying the dynamic of the educational process in cultural recapitulation may be seen in the way the curriculum is determined. The presently dominant traditions of research remain unclear about how one can move from their results to specifying a curriculum. In psychology of education, research aims to establish facts about learning, development, motivation, teaching, and so on, and whatever implications seem relevant may be drawn from these facts. While much of this research may offer more direct implications for instructional methods and conditions, one can, for example, infer from Piaget's theories what kinds of concepts are likely to be comprehensible at particular ages. Analyses of the nature of knowledge may provide criteria for distinguishing forms of knowledge and lead to implications for the structure of the curriculum, as in Paul Hirst's interesting studies, for example (Hirst, 1974). But each kind of study separately runs into areas of opaqueness such that no precise and comprehensive implications for the curriculum can be securely established. It might seem, again, that we need only bring the results of these two traditions of research together to be able to design a truly effective curriculum – articulating the facts about learners and their development and about conditions of learning with the analyses of knowledge and criteria of education. But, again, they have not and do not come easily together. The problem, as I have argued in the more general context of the Platonic and Rousseauian insights which these distinct traditions seek to elaborate, is that each identifies the dynamic of the educational process differently. This prevents their results coming easily together and tends instead to make them pass one another by or seem even to conflict. Nor is this some contingent matter, to be overcome by collaborative research teams or by some "give" as on a demarcation dispute. The difficulty seems to lie rather at the level of the methodological presuppositions which enable each tradition of research to go forward separately. Each presupposes that one *can* study knowledge independently of what minds do to it or that one *can* study minds, or behaviors, independently of the cultural contexts and contents which give them form and meaning. Each reifies knowledge or mind/behavior as some independent entity. This ascribing to the topic of research an independent existence leads in turn to seeing it as an appropriate source for the dynamic of education; knowledge in-forms minds or minds' changing structures requires knowledge to conform to them.

This is perhaps to overstate and oversimplify matters, or perhaps to state the condition of the more extreme practitioners of each tradition, or, perhaps better yet, to state the past condition of those traditions from which both have moved. The overstatement, or historical statement, is useful, however, to emphasize in what way cultural recapitulation avoids being tied to a presupposition that the dynamic of education resides either in knowledge or in minds and so scanting to some degree either the Platonic or Rousseauian insight. It gives due attention to both by focusing on the cultural development of the individual, by finding a way of characterizing – to put it tendentiously – mind in society.

Easy for me to casually assert a "right" position on matters of intense debate, but it is worth noting that these two traditions of educational research mentioned above are increasingly nudging into each other's territories, acknowledging the necessity for more comprehensive perspectives. I earlier indicated some skepticism about the continuing fruitfulness of these traditions of research if they remained independent of each other and neglected to take into full account the influence of cultural history in shaping their phenomena of interest. Easy, too, to offer such lordly advice, but I am here not trying to engage these methodological debates so much as to indicate that cultural recapitulation is not some exotic sport. It avoids precisely the presuppositions that seem at the root of the practical problems faced by the more established research traditions in education.

If cultural history is going to provide guidance for the curriculum does this not mean that astrology must precede astronomy, alchemy precede chemistry, magic precede physics and medicine, and myth precede philosophy and literature? Such a conclusion might be encouraged by nineteenth-century recapitulation schemes. And perhaps my constant references to oral cultures and the Greek beginnings of our rational inquiries suggests that Mythic understanding requires "prerational" forms of understanding. Also there is my insistence on putting knowledge into story shapes for young children. The point about our rational forms of inquiry is that their first great achievement was to escape from stories. Theories and logic are determinedly not story-shaped, but they are precisely the tools that have enabled us to make sense of the world and of experience in ways that have given us greater control over them.

Will this scheme, then, for example, require that astrology, or something like it, be introduced to children before knowledge of astronomy? No. The particular knowledge content of our cultural history is not what is to be recapitulated. What we see in the move from astrology is indeed an accumulation of knowledge and, crucially, theory replacing story. If, however, we consider astrology in the kind of terms I have been using in the previous chapters we will focus on the *bonnes à penser,* the sense-making capacities, at work. We will focus on the cultural achievements embedded in astrology and their contribution to enhancing our sense-making grasp over the world. We tend to dismiss astrology as nonsense, as the irrational predecessor whose displacement made astronomy possible. But, again, the move from astrology to astronomy cannot be understood if seen simply as a displacement; astronomy grew out of astrology. Our focus is on what survived in that transition. The cultural achievement of astrology was, to put it generally, the imaginative search for meaning in the stars, the consequent observation of order and pattern in complex phenomena, and the attempt to report that order in a memorable and personally meaningful form. It is this that we will try to recapitulate in providing an engaging and meaningful access to astronomy. Identifying the cultural achievement that preceded and gave early shape to astronomy enables us to formulate a principle for the construction of an early curriculum in astronomy. Evoking, stimulating, and developing the imaginative search for meaning in the stars does not require that we begin with astrological stories from Greek, Norse, African, or other mythologies – though we would be a bit obtuse to overlook their possible educational uses in encouraging an initial engagement with astronomy. But we might equally well begin with the most recent findings about the Big Bang, quasars, pulsars, black holes, and so on – if presented in the appropriate form.

What this scheme provides for determining the curriculum, then, is not historically sequenced bodies of knowledge but rather historically sequenced layers of sense-making capacities. The historical sequence is determining not simply because of its historicity but because it embodies and reflects the logical and psychological constraints on the development of sense-making capacities. From the definition of these capacities we can identify appropriate curriculum content and methods of teaching that can best evoke, stimulate, and develop them. Astrology shows us sense-making capacities that are historically foundational to astronomy; astrology embodies, we may say, the cultural foundations of astronomy. It embodies in complex ways, to be discussed below, the logical and psychological foundations of astronomy. However sophisticated might become an individual's understanding of astronomy, the foundational capacities evident in astrology will ideally remain as constituents of that understanding. The imaginative search for meaning, that is to say, is as much a proper part of the most advanced astronomical research as it is the foundational access to the subject. Its absence or repression might indeed permit the accumulation of knowledge and refinement of theory, but the resulting research would likely be characterized by an inability to find imaginative engagement in the work and an absence of the energetic imagination that can break through and refashion theory. (For an examination of the role of imagination in scientific research and in major theoretical breakthroughs see Shepard, 1978, 1988.)

But astrological stories were replaced by astronomical theories, and if we are to recapitulate this cultural enhancement of our sense-making capacities, then stories must surely give way to theories? And as one seems incompatible with the other, surely this involves straightforward displacement? If our initial exploration of the stars is to be dominated by our storying capacities, and these are somehow to persist throughout our education in astronomy, then surely the development of theory will be prevented? Stories cannot "coalesce" into theories. Is this not a fundamental objection to a scheme of recapitulating an historical sequence of sense-making capacities? I think not. In the chapter on stories I stressed the separation between fictional stories and the characteristics of the story form. The story form can be used to make a particular kind of sense of any phenomena. It is a foundational form of meaning-making. The development of theory involves attempts at a more precise, literal, objective grasp on phenomena. The kind of meaning or sense that theories try to make takes place, as it were, within contexts shaped by our storying capacities. An imaginative search for meaning in the cosmos need not interfere with our development of increasingly sophisticated theories about black holes.

Indeed, we constantly coordinate the two kinds of sense-making, and coordinate them with the further layers of understanding to be discussed in later volumes of this essay. Our storying capacities do not go away with the development of theories; they provide the contexts of meaning in which theories make more precise sense of their limited phenomena of interest; they provide the ties between theoretically informed knowledge and our lives; they enable the absorption of accumulating knowledge to our imaginations and ever-active memories.

I should perhaps mention that I have used this astrology/astronomy example to make a couple of points about the recapitulation scheme, not to make a particular curriculum proposal. How we might move from historically derived sense-making capacities to curriculum principles and thence to a particular curriculum is the topic of the next chapter.

This scheme, then, identifies the dynamic of education in the recapitulation of the cultural capacities that enhance our power to make sense of the world and of experience. There are logical and psychological constraints, complexly intermingled, on the historical and on the individual's development of those capacities, but the dynamic of the process does not lie in its constraints. Mythic understanding is not achieved by mastery of any particular body of knowledge – as would be the case if the dynamic of the educational process were to be located in knowledge. Nor is it a product of psychological development; it is not a necessary stage we pass through in reaching maturity. Mythic understanding is a cultural artefact, brought about by teaching particular kinds of things in particular ways during a particular time of life.

"Interlacing" psychological and logical constraints with cultural history makes it difficult to identify the dynamic of education precisely as distinct from the kinds of psychological or epistemological theories that have long held sway. My argument is that identifying the dynamic in cultural recapitulation does not make it distinct from psychological and logical considerations; their constraining forces are felt in different ways in both cultural history and individual development. Cultural history is made up of the invention and discovery of an array of techniques for making sense of the world and of experience. The sequence of those inventions and discoveries was constrained by logic - certain inventions required other knowledge to be in place to make them possible – and by human psychology – certain directions are followed rather than others because of the nature of our hopes, fears, intentions, and so on. But to describe these shaping constraints in the fullest detail is still not to catch the dynamic of the process of cultural development. There is in it a creative, playful, imaginative element, something that slides sideways along metaphors rather than climbs methodically and literally. We can try to impose a causal order on the history of cultural achievements in retrospect, and that causal order depends on some logical or psychological scheme. The order, that is, can characterize something of the constraints on the process. What we cannot do adequately, or have not done adequately, is characterize the creative dynamic of the process.

As our cultural history is constrained by logical entailments and psychological predispositions so is individual educational development constrained. Cultural history is an expression of the creative dynamic of the human spirit working within the constraints of logical entailments and psychological predispositions. The term "constraints" perhaps suggests some sluggish logic and psychology chaining down some wonderful free dynamic human spirit. This would be to miss the meaning of their interlacement. The joint constraints on cultural development are also its conditions. So, understanding cultural development requires our attending to the logical and psychological conditions/constraints of the process, but also requires our attending to the less easily grasped way in which their interlacement with the conditions of human societies in particular environments leads to new ways of making sense of the world and of experience. Similarly, understanding education requires our attending to the logical and psychological conditions/constraints on the process, but also requires our attending to the particular cultural conditions which the individual is to recapitulate. The logical and psychological constraints, and the range of sense-making capacities available in any culture, are given a graspable form in the history of the culture's development of those capacities. The logical and psychological constraints also operate on each individual but, by themselves, are inadequate to characterize the process of education. The process of education can, however, be characterized in a graspable way by seeing it as the recapitulation of the culture's historical development of those sense-making capacities.

Even if it is possible to characterize education adequately this way, and to identify its dynamic in a way that overcomes the dichotomy that has presented an *impasse* for educational theory and practice for so long, there remain some problems. We need to know whether such a scheme is possible and desirable, whether it is better than other schemes presently in place, why the set of capacities characterized earlier should provide the basis for early childhood education; we need to know, in short, how to go about evaluating such a scheme. We have well-developed methods for evaluating empirical and conceptual claims in education, but how are these to be deployed to deal with a scheme that has tied empirical and conceptual questions in a complicated way with cultural history?

Possibility, Desirability, and Evaluation

Because this scheme is not like the kind of psychological theory one commonly sees in educational literature nor like the product of epistemological research, it might be worth pausing to consider ways in which it seems not amenable to the normal array of evaluation procedures. This is not so much a defensive move as an attempt towards clearer definition of the scheme.

If we were to consider the empirical supports for the scheme we might find it difficult to locate straightforward empirical claims that are contentious. That it is possible to evoke, stimulate, and develop the constituents of Mythic understanding in young children is an empirical claim, but hardly a contentious one that merits careful testing. This scheme is not a psychological theory to be tested against empirical observations; it is composed in significant part from empirical observations – of historical phenomena and young children's behavior. It is a product, not of some novel empirical findings, but of exploring implications of some empirically uncontentious observations, of putting what was already known together in a new way. What is open to evaluation, of course, is the adequacy and accuracy of the observations. This scheme is not an attempt to make claims that are cross-culturally valid nor developmentally invariant, nor even necessarily the case; it is a characterization of a cultural process that *can* be brought about. That it *can* be brought about, that young children can be taught the *bonnes à penser* of Mythic understanding, seems quite uncontentious.

The empirical connection of this layer and its constituents with early childhood is also, it seems to me, not particularly contentious. (I have discussed this in Chapter Two.) The characterization of Mythic understanding is built in part from systematic observation and analysis of young children's oral and written behavior, of fantasy stories and singing games, of their early grasp of metaphor and uses of binary opposites, and so on. This connection, however, begins to impinge on a more general apparently empirical claim made by this scheme. This is that in the process of becoming educated in our culture there is a predisposition to proceed through these layers in the sequence I am describing. For this initial layer, this means that we are predisposed to acquire the characteristics of Mythic understanding first. This scheme, that is to say, is not an arbitrary prescription. It reflects a predisposition. The task is to locate the source and dynamic of the predisposition in order that the scheme be appropriately evaluated.

This is not, again, a psychological claim that Mythic understanding is a necessary first stage in cognitive development. A crucial difference is that Mythic understanding is a cultural artefact, not a reflection of some supposed underlying psychological reality. It is a layer of an educational process that need not go forward, of a particular initiation that need not take place. It is necessary, however, if one is to become educated in our culture. The problem with this claim, at least from the point of view of our traditional methods for testing empirical claims, is that it has already slid over into the murky realm where the empirical and conceptual are conjoined. The predisposition, that is to say, is not based only on the nature of human psychology – which would yield straightforward empirically testable claims. Nor again is it based only on logical entailment.

We know, for example, that young children cannot understand some things that adults or adolescents can understand. In some cases we can adequately explain such failures as due to prerequisite knowledge not yet having been mastered. That is, we look to logic for the explanation. The alternative explanation for failures of young children to learn certain things is psychological. It is claimed, say, that the development of certain mental structures must take place before certain things can be understood. There is a problem distinguishing these two kinds of explanations, reflecting the difficulty described earlier in distinguishing mind and knowledge. One may see an aspect of their confusion in arguments about whether Piaget's general stages are psychological structures empirically supported or whether they are guaranteed by logic (Hamlyn, 1978). In the case of this scheme, the problem is compounded by locating the dynamic of the predisposition in cultural recapitulation. This does not obviate the logical and psychological influences, as I argued in the previous section. These together have constrained and shaped the sequence whereby the sets of capacities have been invented or discovered in our culture and they shape and constrain how any individual can acquire them. But we cannot neatly separate out the logical from the psychological constraints as they operate on sense-making capacities, nor can we feel confident that doing so would exhaust what we have to deal with in accounting for either cultural history or individual development within a culture. There remains that imaginative element we glimpse sliding around on mercurial metaphor; which may indeed be simply a feature of the conjointness of logic and psychology operating within cultural stuff, but we would be unwise, I think, to make any firm conclusion about this.

This ambivalence has the effect that it is possible to amass logical and psychological supports for this scheme but they remain somewhat circumstantial to the central claim about developing Mythic understanding. For example, it is possible to locate considerable psychological support for the priority of metaphoric over literal or logico-mathematical forms of thought. Not a little can be found in those studies designed to locate the beginnings of particular logical procedures, wherein we see easy grasp of metaphors – though these are not commonly the focus of researchers' attention – before the ability to grasp even the simplest logical techniques such as the syllogism (see, for example, Piaget, 1951; Luria, 1979). One can see this primacy most vividly in children's own narratives (Paley, 1981). On the other hand one can make a logical case for the necessary primacy of metaphor, as the conceptual grounding which logical procedures need in order to be able to work. The most dramatic assertion of this view as plain common sense is Nietszche's, whose views are presented along with a series of much more systematic arguments in Cooper

(1986; see especially the section on "The primacy of metaphor," pp. 257-79).

When I say these kinds of support are circumstantial, I mean that they provide plausibility for the scheme but do not directly support it. That is, my argument for the primacy of metaphor in early education is based on its primacy in cultural development. Its primacy in cultural development is constrained by logical and psychological forces acting together in terms of the cultural content. What psychological and logical supports for the claims about the primacy of metaphor provide is some definition of the constraints that shape cultural development and individual development in that culture. These are not universal constraints, not universal principles of cultural development, but simply principles that operate in the development of the particular set of cultural capacities that have been evoked, stimulated, and developed in our culture. Because the range of human capacities for sense-making are indeterminate, it does not make sense to assert for the set we are familiar with any more generality than our culture allows. Partly this is sensible because past guesses about "the nature" of human capacities have always been ethnocentric in one way or another, and partly because the occasional bizarre achievements of some individuals suggest we have sense-making potentials as yet largely un-evoked, un-stimulated, and un-developed.

It would be possible to take each of the characteristics of Mythic understanding and try to provide the kind of empirical and/or conceptual support considered appropriate for traditional educational claims. The first odd feature of pursuing such a strategy is that in the case of each characteristic it becomes clear that we can turn either way for support, building a logical or psychological case. Binary opposites, for example, are empirically supported as fundamental structuring devices in psycholinguistics (Jakobson and Halle, 1956), in anthropology (Leach, 1967; Lévi-Strauss, 1966a), and in psychotherapy (Bettelheim, 1976), and in other research cited earlier. But one might prefer to construct an argument about the logical necessity of first grasping certain kinds of phenomena by means of binary opposites and then mediating between the poles, as do the people, beginning with Aristotle, cited in Ogden (1967). Similarly, our storying capacity appears surprisingly early, suggesting a psychological predisposition, for which I cited some evidence above. On the other hand we can argue, as do some other of the authorities I cited, that the story is one of the most prominent of our contextualizing forms, which are logically prerequisite to establishing the meaning of any particular knowledge.

If I am hastily passing over these kinds of arguments, it is not because I do not think they are important, or worthy of research. Nor is it because I think the psychological or logical cases are obviously true or not in need of much more elaborate support. It is because I do not think either kind of argument is convincing by itself nor can it be conclusive.

This set of considerations has grown from my wanting to support the claim that there is in our individual educational development a predisposition to first acquire the capacities of Mythic understanding before those of subsequent layers. This is not, I am suggesting, a conceptual truth-something we can show to be the case by logical analysis. Nor is it a matter of empirical necessity – something we can show to be the case by amassing appropriate empirical support. The major empirical claim – which I take to be uncontentious, though potentially falsifiable – is that one can acquire the capacities of Mythic understanding before those of subsequent layers. The potentially more contentious claim, that we are predisposed to do so, *if we are to become educated*, is complicated by the emphasized conditional clause. (Nor is this simply circular: I am not defining education simply as whatever this scheme characterizes in the sequence in which it is characterized. I have committed it to satisfying the requirements of the general conceptions of education held both in the Platonic tradition and the Rousseauian progressivist tradition.) The source of the predisposition operating in the educational process lies in the interactive force of psychology and logic working within particular cultural environments, possibly along with an imaginative element which seems necessary to account for the contingent nature of our cultural development and the play of children's imagination. If I could characterize this in detail I obviously would. What I am doing, in the hope of being able to be more explicit as this essay proceeds, is pointing at the set of interactive elements from which the dynamic of the educational process is composed, and partially exposing it by charting its effects and how it works itself out in education. Its effects are being charted by finding a level of the phenomena of education which reflects the set of interactive elements that conjointly constitute the dynamic of education – that level I am characterizing as culturally constrained sense-making capacities.

The predisposition seems to work something like this. I am identifying as crucially important, and in large part definitive of cultures, the set of techniques or *bonnes à penser*, each culture has developed for making sense of the world and of its experience. This encompasses in our case our technology, arts, and sciences. To borrow some useful jargon, the set of techniques, or *bonnes à penser*, or sense-making capacities, exist in the present in our culture in a complex synchronicity. They were generated diachronically. Education is the process whereby the individual acquires these techniques, these *bonnes à penser*, these capacities, diachronically. As they are acquired they coalesce into an analogous synchronicity to their existence in the culture. The dynamic that has determined the diachronic sequence of their invention and discovery in our culture is constrained by the interaction of logic and human psychology. The sequence in which knowledge can be elaborated in human minds is constrained by the logic of the various forms of knowledge acting together with the predispositions of human psychology. These same forces whose action we see in human cultural development shape and constrain the individual's acquisitions of the sense-making capacities available in the culture. In becoming educated, then, we are constrained to recapitulate the sequence whereby in our cultural history these sense-making capacities were invented and discovered. Now, we do not need to recapitulate this sequence if we are not to acquire the fullest range of these capacities – if we are not going to become educated. But if we are to become educated, if we want to maximize our acquisition of the range of sense-making capacities available to us – which *is* our culture – then we need to recapitulate the sequence of their historical development. To fail to recapitulate some of the foundational capacities, for example, is to fail to acquire prerequisites for later capacities. To fail to develop metaphoric fluency of imaginative capacities undercuts the degree to which later capacities can be developed. The predisposition derives from or resides in, the shaping given to the dynamic of both cultural development and the individual's acquisition of the culture by logic and human psychology.

In general I am arguing that there are distinct ways that human beings are predisposed to become educated in particular cultures.

Each culture may be seen as a conditioning context which evokes, stimulates, and develops particular human potentials in particular ways. Human nature is plastic, but is so within limits. It exhibits preferences for the sequence in which capacities are developed – even though any particular culture will select, shape, and embody these capacities in distinctive ways. The plasticity means that logic and nature seem not to lay completely determining constraints on culture, but rather their constraining force is evident in general preferences or predispositions. My claim, then, is that this scheme is describing the forms and sequences of certain of the predispositions in optimally initiating people into our culture.

While I am clearly unable to characterize the nature of this predisposition precisely, my point here is to demonstrate why this claim is not straightforwardly empirical, open to straightforward empirical testing. This is not due to my wish to avoid such testing, but rather to indicate that this is not like a psychological theory, and that while circumstantial empirical and conceptual support can be amassed behind it, that support by itself is not its basis. Clearly if any of my claims contravenes what we can show is logically or psychologically the case, then this would count as adequate disconfirmation. Logic and psychology define the constraints within which the scheme is composed. But there is considerable freedom within those constraints. It is in that area of freedom that the detailed specification of the layers is described, and those descriptions are derived from our cultural history and from empirical observations of children.

Before we come to the question of why this scheme should be considered desirable, it might be worth mentioning a further source of circumstantial empirical support for it. This is that the scheme incorporates coherently a number of phenomena that have hitherto tended to be anomalies to commonly held principles that guide educational practice. For example, trainee teachers still learn that children's understanding moves from the concrete to the abstract, from the simple to the complex, and from the known to the unknown. The problem with these principles is that there are some clear exceptions to them; there are, that is to say, a range of phenomena that are anomalies if we accept these as some kind of explanation of the direction of children's understanding. We clearly attain some very simple insights only after long study, and we learn some very complex and abstract things very early. Mastery of language is such a formidably complex task, requiring mastery of abstract rules, that some people, most notably Chomsky, argue that we must have a special Language Acquisition Device to make it possible. The call for a special explanatory device is in part a result of the careful examination of what is learned early, so confounding expectations that follow from the principle of human learning proceeding from the simple to the complex, the concrete to the abstract.

In education we have long settled for the *ad hoc* explanation of some common observations that the simple and concrete must precede the complex and abstract. The logical analysis of subjects, of structures of knowledge, has also taken us surprisingly little way in either elaborating on or refuting these simple *ad hoc* principles. As explanations, however, these principles have left a number of major educational puzzles. There are constant anomalies, language learning being only one of the more general and dramatic. If we look at children through these kinds of explanations we face constant puzzlement about what they can and cannot understand at different stages. They sometimes are bewildered by what seem like very simple tasks, as Piaget has brought out so dramatically, and then show remarkable ease and insight with what seem enormously complex forms of understanding (Donaldson, 1978).

My claim for further circumstantial empirical support for this scheme lies in its offering a quite different explanation for why people at different ages find things easy or difficult to learn. It is different from the explanations presently most commonly accepted and it goes a long way towards accounting for what are anomalies to those explanations. It dispenses with simplicity–complexity/concrete–abstract as adequate explanatory terms. They are obviously not irrelevant, or they would not have held sway for so long. But they simply focus on the wrong level or range of phenomena. What makes material easy to learn during the Mythic layer of education is that it has the qualities I have outlined as Mythic; what makes material difficult to learn during the Mythic layer is that it is organized in what I call Romantic, Philosophic, or Ironic ways.

The achievement of this scheme in accounting for such anomalies as the apparently near-illiterate and dull student being outside class a fertilely imaginative Dungeon Master or gang or fashion leader need not be considered so wonderful, of course.

The scheme was in part composed from the study of precisely such anomalies. But nevertheless its circumstantial empirical support must include the range of significant anomalies that are accounted for within it. And, it should be noted, these are not casual or marginal phenomena, but matters of crucial educational importance.

While the basis of the scheme itself is a complex fusion of the empirical, conceptual, and historical, it does nevertheless yield a whole range of straightforward empirical claims when it is worked out in practice. In general it yields the claim that when material is selected and organized according to the characteristics of the Mythic layer, young children will be more readily engaged by it, and find it more meaningful and comprehensible. When, for example, historical material about the Vikings is organized in a story form, using powerful abstract binary opposites, and having other characteristics described earlier, it will be more easily learned and better understood than similar material organized and presented in ways that exclude the characteristics of the Mythic layer.

The other straightforward empirical claim is the association of this layer with a particular age range. This I take, as I mentioned above, to be fairly uncontentious for this layer, though the association of the layer with ages will become more complicated as the scheme is elaborated. In the earlier chapters, and particularly Chapter Two, I have presented a range of observations supporting the connection of this layer in our culture with the early education years, up to about age seven – allowing a year or so either way for individual differences.

And how do we evaluate the desirability of this scheme so far? What does one say to the person who does not want the character of primary education to be the stimulation of the poet in us? If one's notion of education is the production of people skilled in the various ways required by the economy, then elaborating metaphoric capacities, stimulating imagination, and so on, may be useful for some people but not for most. Indeed, some features of imagination are seen as positively threatening to social and economic stability. This uncomfortably common position is just one of many whose conception of education, or of schooling, devalues certain of the capacities I am describing as fundamental to education. My arguments on behalf of the desirability of evoking, stimulating, and developing the capacities of Mythic understanding are made extensively throughout the book. In general they support the principle that one ought to acquire as many sense-making capacities as possible. The scheme is an attempt to describe how one can do that, an important part being that one first acquire those which are prerequisite to fullest development of other capacities. ("Prerequisite," again, in an educational sense; constrained by psychological predispositions and logical entailments acting through cultural recapitulation.)

The justification for following the path being laid down in this scheme, then, is that it characterizes the way to making fullest sense of the world and of experience in the terms available in our culture. The desirability of the scheme is tied to the desirability of making sense. "Making sense" is that combination of acquiring knowledge, psychological development, and imaginative fluency I have been trying to characterize.

And why – if we do not like "our" culture and its set of sense-making capacities – can we not choose another culture? And what does "culture" entail anyway? What are its limits and extent, especially in "multi-cultural" societies? Some of these questions raise issues that will have to wait for more of this scheme to be described before they can adequately be addressed. Some I will touch on in the next section. The option to choose another culture is, of course, not one that is open to us casually after we have been initiated into a particular language and society. To a large degree fate commits us, but it is not absolute imprisonment. I will return to this in later volumes.

Characterizing education in terms of the acquisition of culturally constrained sense-making capacities allows us to focus on the ripening of childhood in the child while in no way losing sight of the ideal end. The capacities of Mythic understanding are not steps to some distinct goal; they are constituents of the goal. Evaluating the desirability of this scheme will in part include assessing how adequately the aims both of traditional Platonic education into the forms of knowledge and of the Rousseauian progressive ripening of each distinctive period of growth are accommodated. I think it is clear that discussing early education in terms of the *bonnes à penser* or sense-making capacities I have focused on in this book does not obviate considering children's minds or knowledge. That great dichotomy of the traditionalist/progressivist debates is coalesced in sense-making capacities.

Whose Culture?

Most of the issues touched on in this chapter, concerning the nature and evaluation of this scheme, will become increasingly pointed as later layers are described. This is true also of what will be to some the most contentious feature of this scheme. Already those with highly developed ideological sensors will be detecting whiffs of the kind of "cultural imperialism" that has been identified by some (e.g. Street, 1984) in the work of Havelock, Ong, and Goody. Goody, for example, who set out to break down the ethnocentric distinction between primitive and advanced cultures in the end, it is claimed, only entrenches the distinction deeper under the labels oral and literate. He universilizes the particulars of our cultural history, to make the move from orality to literacy seem a necessary progressive move, and so more elaborately rationalizes the same old ideological viewpoint. This is an issue that belongs with questions about the desirability of this scheme.

The claim that an educational program is being designed to recapitulate "the" culture raises a number of ideologically loaded questions. "Whose culture?" comes first. Then we might want to ask about the value of that culture and, indeed, what it comprises. If "our" culture is to be understood to include the whole panoply of largely middle-class WASP ideological assumptions, then this would be adequate grounds for some to reject the scheme out of hand. Defining cultures largely in terms of their sense-making techniques avoids obvious ideological pitfalls only to the point where some kinds of sense are identified as better than others. I may seem already committed to astronomical theories being better sense-making techniques than astrological stories. The ideologically sensitive will see in this the adumbration of an argument that scientific cultures are better than oral cultures, and so just another culturally imperialistic attempt to use education to represent what are in fact contingent cultural forms as necessary, and to represent the difference between oral and literate cultures as hierarchical.

Cultural imperialism and cultural relativism are not exhaustive of the possibilities open to us nor is either desirable or particularly coherent. One is not committed to believe that astronomy is absolutely better than astrology nor that they are, in their cultural contexts, equivalents. Both positions can be held only by refusing to observe a number of perfectly sensible distinctions between the social functions they perform and the kinds of sense astronomy and astrology make. The route I will take to undermining the vacuousness of the relativist position is hinted at in the distinction made earlier between astronomy and astrology and the route to undermining cultural imperialism lies in recognizing, first, that oral cultural *bonnes à penser* are foundational to subsequently developed *bonnes à penser* and, second, that the acquisition of the latter seems to entail losses.

"Our culture," then, is very widely interpreted here. It means the set of sense-making techniques, *bonnes à penser* accessible to us. Some of these are tied up in singing games, some are tied up in Virgil, some are tied up in technology, and so on. Whatever we *can* have access to is "our culture." So I am not using "culture" in a way that would distinguish middle-American culture from French dock-worker culture. For the time being I will continue to use it rather generally and vaguely. We live in a world culture and any individual can get access to a very wide range of the *bonnes à penser* generated throughout the world throughout history. That access in practice, if not entirely in theory, requires literacy, of course, and literacy seems to require some loss of the sense of participation in nature that is possible in oral cultures. The techniques of orality certainly can be extended to absorb *bonnes à penser* whose development has historically relied on literacy – such as systematic scientific inquiry. But without literacy there will likely be severe limits on what can be absorbed. Here is, indeed, a value choice. And it is the value choice basic to this educational scheme; that certain sense-making techniques are worth the losses that accompany them. This is not true for all sense-making techniques – certain forms of religious fanaticism, ideologies, metaphysical schemes, are less valuable than what is lost in acquiring them. So there is no getting away from value decisions in constructing an educational scheme.

Nor is this scheme insensitive to social, class, and "sub-cultural" differences: "Children have to learn to select, hold, and retrieve content from books and other written or printed texts in accordance with their community's rules or 'ways of taking,'and the children's learning follows community paths of language socialization" (Heath, 1982, p. 70). This scheme is not intended as a universal homogenizer. It is sensitive to differences in different community forms of initiation, not to eradicate them, but to ensure that the set of *bonnes à penser* required to develop educationally are accessible to all children. Because different communities evoke, stimulate, and develop various of these *bonnes à penser*, or parts of them, differently, schooling will sensibly focus on attending to those *bonnes à penser* least well developed in particular forms of socialization.

What I have done here is raise a number of issues concerning the ideological implications of any educational scheme, especially one that rather casually refers to recapitulating "our" culture. I want, for now, only to indicate that I am not insensitive to these issues and even think I can avoid at least some of the ideological pitfalls. More than many issues, this cannot adequately be dealt with until more of this scheme is described, so I will put off this discussion to the final volume.

Conclusion

I have used the phrase "evoke, stimulate, and develop" fairly continuously. I think we do at least a little of each when teaching anything successfully. The evoking part is not something the teacher needs to strain at usually, especially during these early years. The striking similarity between the *bonnes à penser* of oral cultures around the world and those of young children in the industrial cities and school play areas of our societies suggest that initiation into cultural life itself evokes those *bonnes à penser*, those sense-making capacities. In part they are a function of acquiring a language and having even marginal mental space to play with it. Thus the capacity for rhyme is evoked. Rhyming games can stimulate this capacity further, and it can be systematically developed by instruction, till it becomes a tool among others for creating certain meanings and communicating them memorably. Some are more complex, like rhythm. Some rhythms are evoked by movement and the regular responses of the world to our actions on it; these may be stimulated by patterns of experience, and are available for development in a wide range of cultural activities, from music to stories to science. The set that constitute imagination is evoked by such linguistic forms as nursery rhymes and fairy stories, is stimulated by increasingly sophisticated poems and stories and accounts of human achievements, and is developed throughout life in making new images with words or wood or stone, or new theories from images of what it might be like to ride on a light wave.

My general argument is that the sequence in which sense-making capacities have been evoked, stimulated, and developed in our cultural history has been constrained by logical entailments and psychological predispositions and that these play an equivalent role in shaping the sequence in which an individual can recapitulate those sense-making capacities. Metaphoric thinking and stories precede literal reflection and theories not as a contingent matter – we can program a computer to deal with the latter first (and the former hardly at all) but we cannot adequately educate human beings that way.

"If one changes the tools of thinking available to the child, his mind will have a radically different structure (Berg, 1970, p. 46). This Vygotskian view suggests a causal relationship between tools of thinking and mental structure. What I am calling *bonnes à penser* or sense-making capacities are properties of minds no less than of knowledge. I have been trying to find a way of characterizing considerations of minds and knowledge together to transcend, not simply avoid, the kinds of dilemmas that have plagued educational discourse this century. That is why the terms of this scheme, with its Mythic, Romantic, Philosphic, and Ironic layers, might seem rather odd, and the focus on stories, metaphor, rhythm, imagination, and so on, in this volume atypical. The oddity, of course, is no guarantee of correctness But it is a necessary condition of generating a scheme that can bring together the great insights of the traditionalist and progressivist/modernist schools of educational thought.

6

A Curriculum for Primary Education

Introduction

What, then, will a curriculum look like that is designed to bring childhood to ripeness within the child while at the same time moving children from an oral towards a literate and scientific culture? How can we evoke, stimulate, and develop the largely oral capacities of Mythic understanding while at the same time teaching children to read and write and introducing them to the disciplined forms of knowledge in which our culture is in large part coded? How, in short, do we bring together in educational practice the Platonic and Rousseauian insights that have tended to diverge?

In general this foundational layer is concerned with elaborating contexts that can make subsequent knowledge meaningful. What has been sometimes seen as a tension in early childhood education between stimulating freedom of the imagination or developing the basics of rational disciplines is resolved in this scheme in the recognition that the proper use of reason requires a properly educated imagination – an insight early propounded by Wordsworth, Coleridge, and Blake – and that this in turn requires the evocation, stimulation, and development of imagination in a manner hospitable to the accumulation of disciplined knowledge. (Imagination + Method = Reason, is Coleridge's way of seeing it.) While at this rhetorical level the concerns of "traditionalists" and "progressivists" are both responded to, what remains to be shown is how the rhetoric can take satisfactory form in curriculum and teaching practice.

In trying to show how this can be done, I will have to raise what might be considered issues to do with teaching as well as more straightforward curriculum matters. I will not strain, then, as the titles of this and the following chapter might suggest I have, to keep teaching and curriculum considerations apart. I will discuss teaching pervasively in this chapter and will focus more narrowly in the next on exemplifying how one can move from some of the principles established in the earlier chapters to a practical technique or framework for teaching.

What I will do in this chapter, then, is begin with some rather general issues concerning the curriculum and teaching which seem to follow from the previous chapters, then focus on more particular implications for the curriculum, and then outline the constituents of a curriculum that can bring about Mythic understanding. I am uncomfortably aware that many people are much more expert than am I about the curriculum areas I will be discussing. I do not want even to appear to suggest that what I have to say about mathematics or history are all or even the most important things that need to be said. Rather, my concerns with the curriculum and particular areas of it are focused on what seem to me the implications of the previous chapters.

The achievements towards which this curriculum and teaching must aim are those expressed in the conclusion to Chapter Two. The development of literacy, and of knowledge in general, must take place in such a way that its forms and conventions do not obliterate the child's earliest sense of his or her unique consciousness. Rather, accumulating knowledge and capacities must become agencies for articulation and expression of that sense of consciousness. (This does not mean encouraging narcissistic self-reflection; or having units on "Who I am." We discover ourselves, paradoxically, by focusing outward on the world and on others.) In addition, literacy and the various forms of disciplined knowledge must be introduced so that they can be seen to have a dynamic life of their own which can extend and enhance the child's experience. And, further, we must be sensitive to the losses that may, and to those that must, accompany these gains.

Importance, Feeling, and Seriousness in Early Education

Becoming educated is a kind of adventure. It has its difficulties, dangers, losses, and it has rewards. The educational adventure involves the search for knowledge and truth about the world and about experience. Its difficulties involve our various resistances to learning, its dangers involve acquiring a little knowledge and thinking we know the whole truth, its losses involve the range of incompatible forms of understanding and experience with those we elect, and its rewards are a range of peculiar pleasures. They are the pleasures that come from being able to make increasingly fuller sense of the world and of experience. The search for knowledge, that notion of truth, and consequently what making sense entails, are problematic in our culture. And so are the pleasures that properly accompany educational achievements. But as the hologram contains within each part some image of the whole, the nature of the educational pleasures we associate with the finest and most sophisticated achievements must be made accessible to young children in their first educational activities. Early in our cultural history the exploration of the world and of experience evoked, stimulated, and developed the senses of magic and ecstasy in people. We miss the point of education, and of the cultural adventure we are engaged in, when we dissociate it at any point from those senses of magic and ecstasy. Again, we will not try to recapitulate the particular knowledge and experiences that evoked the senses of magic and ecstasy early in our cultural history, but we will want to ensure that those foundational constituents of our culture are made vivid and accessible to young children by means of whatever knowledge and experience seem now most appropriate.

I realize, given the current state of educational discourse, that talking about the senses of magic and ecstasy as primary objectives for early education may seem just a little nutty. But by ecstasy I mean that kind of engagement we see in children's responses to good stories and in Einstein's commentaries on his work or in the commentaries of many recent scientist who are at the forefront of their disciplines (e.g. James Watson (1981) and Richard Feyneman (1986)). It is a joy-filled engagement, that does not ask the point or purpose of the activity; one is wholly caught up in it and, while one is engaged, one is enchanted.

By magic I mean something different from our sense of wonder. Wonder works within the given world, magic concerns its existence, its boundaries. The sense of magic comes from confronting mysteries, not problems, and most basically the mystery of why there is existence rather than non-existence, and if that is explained by God, why there is God rather than no-God. This sense that the most taken-for-granted aspects of our experience are ultimately the most mysterious – not even open to any kind of explanation – is the source of our sense of magic. In our culture a prominent enemy of education is the taking of the conventional for granted. This is not to suggest that we need to spend intellectual energy in confronting the mysteries of our existence: they are not puzzles or problems that we might hope to solve. What matters is that we recognize them as mysteries, that we have a sense of the magic of existence. While we can hope to explain the workings of the natural world in the most detailed way, such knowledge resides within a context that is itself wholly mysterious. The educational successor to this sense of magic and mystery is our sense of wonder, which I will discuss in the next volume (recapitulating the succession in our cultural history from magic to wonder, also constrained by logical entailments acting with psychological predispositions). But some readers might find this point a little more comprehensible if they think of the senses of magic and wonder as clearly related, and increasingly during the primary years the sense of wonder is becoming important.

Perhaps I can state the main points of this section as overriding principles that will guide the more detailed curriculum later:

—   Children should be given early some appreciable sense of
        the educational adventure on which they are embarking
        and of its rewards and difficulties.
—   The appropriate rewards of this adventure in the early
        years are the senses of magic and ecstasy it can provide.
—   The appropriate difficulties involve accommodating to the
        disciplines which provide the rules to the adventurous game
        of education.

Something further might be said about this third principle. The term "discipline" has unhappy associations for some, especially as a hangover from 1960s arguments about, say, "relevance" vs "disciplines" as guiding the choice of content for the curriculum. Disciplines provide some of the rules of the adventurous game that education is about; they are some of the main ways in which our sense-making capacities are enhanced. These disciplines are not abstract skills that can be learned by themselves, as is suggested in the phrase "learning how to learn." They are tied up in content. You cannot teach in the abstract "how to avoid danger"; rather you have to teach what particular things to do in particular circumstances to avoid particular dangers. Similarly, the disciplines of education are tied up in particular subjects, and so we must organize our curriculum with specific content and its rules clearly in mind. In education, knowledge is not a means to the end of some cognitive skill; knowledge and skills are inextricably tied up together. "Discipline" conveys precisely this sense of knowledge of a particular kind and the rules that operate within it and the conjoined intellectual skills that come from knowing that area of knowledge and understanding the rules that operate within it. But initiation into these disciplines will be guided by the recapitulation scheme, wherein the logic of the disciplines themselves provides only one of the constraints that must be accommodated to. That is, "making sense" is not a direct product of mastering particular bodies of knowledge, but we cannot do it without them.

How are we to convey a sense of the educational adventure to children through our choice of curriculum content? What is the content of this adventure? It can be encapsulated in the great stories of the development of our civilization, of which the children are a part. One aspect may be represented as people's struggle for freedom against oppression; another as the struggle for knowledge against ignorance; another as the search for security against pitiless nature; another as the will to power over the forces that threaten to overwhelm us; another as the struggle for kindness against cruelty, for love against hate, for humility against pride, for generosity against selfishness; another as the urge to understand and explore the world, the planets, the galaxy; another as the desire to make the body perform the near-impossible with grace and strength; and so on. These all involve great adventures, and children can take part in any and all of them. The present condition of these adventures and how they got to be the way they are provide the stories that make up our civilization. Our culture is made up of things like this, whether in their finest forms or in others that are more debased. Whether one drinks beer while admiring an athlete on television or wonder how the hell our cities got into the mess they're in, or is thrilled by pictures of people in space with the Earth as backdrop, or just wants to be left alone and not be pushed around by "the man" – whatever urges or desires or sparks of interest we may feel are formed by and giving meaning in this culture by the form and meaning of these adventures, or we can become involved more fully. Education is the process for involving children as fully as possible in these adventures.

This is a way of seeing our culture; it is not the only way, but it is a useful way when considering educational curricula. It involves no falsification and brings to the fore the inherently dramatic form of what we want to teach. A further general principle may be expressed this way:

— Early initiation must bring to the fore the inherently dramatic form of the things we wish to teach.

This principle of emphasizing the dramatic core of any topic does not lead to education as entertainment. Rather it entails getting at the most powerful underlying structural features of the content. If we want to teach about the mailman in the early grades, this principle requires that we must excavate from under the routine of the mail plopping through the mail-box that which is exciting in the efforts to keep contacts across distances, the heroic efforts by people to make today's routine possible – the pony express, the Universal Postage Union, etc., must all be brought out. Whether or not we will want to include the mailman in our curriculum will be decided by other principles to follow. How we can excavate the dramatic form of content is discussed in the next chapter.

An important guide provided by this principle might be put in the form of suggesting that a curriculum full of things of little intrinsic interest to an educated adult is an insult to children and will likely undermine the possibilities for their further education. Young children may know less than the typical adult, but they are no less intelligent. Our tendency to measure intelligence in terms of accumulated knowledge leads to much confusion. But if we think in terms of recapitulation we can perhaps better focus on the parts of our culture that are engaging both to children and to adults. What we tend to do is consider either what children need to know in the end and begin with the logical prerequisites, which are simple and dull to adults, or try to take aspects of our culture of interest to adults and simplify those for children, which tend to be near-meaningless to children.

Perhaps I can more clearly make this point by reference to R. G. Collingwood's argument that all history is the history of thought (Collingwood, 1946). That is, the meaning we can derive from any historical event, or document, or ruin, or artefact, or whatever, is limited to, and tied up in, the degree to which we can infer the human thoughts that brought it about or that were involved with it. It is our ability to recreate or reenact in our minds the thoughts, the intentions, the hopes, the fears of other people in other places and times that allows us to derive meaning from history, and that limits the kind and extent of the meaning we can draw. History is not facts and battles, it is human motives, struggles, fears, experience, and the records or traces these leave behind them. We can talk about someone studying a forest in order to write the history of the forest, but we might more properly talk about describing the past of the forest and its changes; it is merely a series of *events*. History is made up of a series of *acts* – what Collingwood calls "the outward expression of thoughts" (Collingwood, 1946, p. 115). (In passing one might note the pedagogical disaster that so often follows from teaching history as though it were made up of events rather than acts. Collingwood notes that when human actions are mere events we cannot understand them; they are truly meaningless. History teaching that focuses on events rather than acts guarantees meaninglessness.)

I think that Collingwood's idea is as important in designing a curriculum for young children as it is for understanding how historical knowledge is possible. *Meaning* must be foremost in our minds when we design a curriculum for young children. Differences in assumptions and presuppositions among adults ensure that communications constantly become mangled. The problem is greatly exacerbated in communicating with young children; they share with typical adults even fewer assumptions, and we tend to suppress our memories of the forms of our own consciousness in childhood, for one reason or another. So while binary opposites are one important means of making content meaningful to young children, we might usefully draw on Collingwood's idea, and ensure that these opposites are framed in terms of human intentions, hopes, fears, joys, and so on. It is human emotion, and human thought, that can vivify the concrete content we want children to learn.

If, then, we want to teach them about early medieval monasteries and the Vikings, we need to see that conflict in terms of the emotions and the human qualities of courage, humility, energy, and make these vividly accessible in representative monks and Vikings. What did they want? What did they fear? If we want to explain why manuscripts were considered so important in the struggle for knowledge against ignorance we can *show* this in the horror people felt at their destruction. If we want to teach a unit on "Where I live" and we want to study the role of the mailman, we need to put him in the context of binary opposites – as an agent of the security offered by a community, perhaps – and to see his role through what he thinks, feels, fears, and hopes. It may be becoming clearer why I think monasteries and Vikings offer more accessible meaning to young children than the everyday world around them. And for those who might think that the idea of an early medieval monk would be meaningless to a young child, I should repeat that virtually nothing is ever meaning*ful*, and there are infinite degrees of meaning in any idea. We know that young children can begin to form an idea of the monk; for a rather gross example, look at their easy acceptance of the idea of Jedi Knights and Obi-Wan Kenobi in *Star Wars*. These are not the same as the Christian idea of the monk, of course, but I mention them to indicate the great ease with which children have access to new concepts if they are fitted meaningfully within a story. From the fantastic we may move towards the real, but the world of fantasy has already provided the template of a person dedicated to a sort of spiritual ideal. (If the fantasy template is well chosen it can do much towards showing something profound about the reality. From the fantastic monk one might more readily move to a Chestertonian romantic image of monks as being full of fire within, not flashy without, and from there we can move to a richer realistic concept of what monasticism was all about.)

— Initial access to knowledge can come most vividly through the thoughts, hopes, fears, and feelings of people, and through the acts which follow from these.

— The early curriculum is to be composed of the most important features of human experience and of the world.

Our early curriculum, then, is to be made up of *important* content that is rich in meaning for children. Its meaning will derive from its being articulated on concepts they know from their experience – love/hate, fear/security, good/bad, courage/cowardice, and so on – and our curriculum concern will be to get at what is of human importance to our social and cultural lives. If we focus on these we need be less concerned to simplify new concepts, reducing them constantly to conform with already known content. If we interpret the known in terms of fundamental concepts, the new content – the idea of a monk, say – can be put in its full strangeness.

Before leaving these principles, I would like to elaborate them by introducing another related concept that leads towards the kind of curriculum that seems most appropriate for early childhood. This is the concept of *seriousness*. Education is an adventure, but it is a *serious* adventure. It matters. Important things turn on whether the adventure is engaged or not.

Much of the present activity in the early years of schooling is not serious. It is not about things that can spark intellectual excitement or emotional engagement in the teachers. It too rarely has significant intellectual or emotional content. The titles of units for the early years may sound most portentous – "Who I am" – but the answers given and the activities engaged in are too frequently intellectually trivial and superficial. Trivial, and often sentimental, stories, programmed reading schemes, and the absence of powerful emotional, dramatic, and intellectual content typify too many primary classrooms.[1]

I should note before passing on that this idea of seriousness refers not just to intellectual content but to emotional content. These principles require that we cannot approach emotion only as sentiment. Disney-esque sentimentality is the exact emotional equivalent to intellectual contempt.[2] It suggests that children's emotions are trivial, that they should be patronized as not serious or powerful. (Children can, of course, seem to prefer Disney-esque sentimentality to more profoundly meaningful stories. They also tend to prefer candy to vegetables. Providing sentimental stories is the educational equivalent of prescribing a diet of candy.) This insult to children's emotional lives – the norm on public media – will produce emotionally stunted adults, as a trivial intellectual curriculum will produce ignorant adults. Emotional education requires taking children's emotions seriously, and providing the kind of stories that do that. (This does not mean that we will provide only "serious" stories, but rather stories that treat the world and their content honestly. Such stories can be funny or tragic.)

What disappears if we implement this first set of principles is the familiar content of the early childhood curriculum in much of the English-speaking world. We remove that emphasis on the local and immediate, we remove the focus on the *content* of children's experience and instead work from the conceptual substratum which that experience has provided, and we remove the relative triviality of so much of the emotional and intellectual material dealt with.

I should perhaps indicate here that I am aware that this kind of abstract discussion may sound very idealistic, in the worst sense of wholly unrealistic, to those whose imagination of early childhood education is caught up in the detailed reality of present classroom experience. I would ask such people to try to remember that early education has been quite different at different times and places, and that the products of our schools at present should not convince us that our present curriculum and methods are so wonderful that alternatives should not be considered. Very different practices are possible and the children who would be working within those would present to the observer very different realities. What I am sketching here, then, is not an unrealistic ideal, but some principles that will lead us towards a quite different but no less practical reality from the one teachers face day by day at present. It may seem that I do not understand the daily struggle to achieve even marginal literacy in huge numbers of children, and the problems of trying to teach emotionally and psychologically troubled children. Of course I do not think the curriculum I recommend here will solve, or even perhaps address, the problems of children who are not loved and are beaten at home. But it will not make their problems worse, and it may even help them to gain access to a world that does not merely offer them a rather meaningless and sentimental image of a reality they cannot recognize, nor provide an emotional and intellectual escape, but rather that provides the small solace that beyond their experience there is a world of wonder, brutality, hope, fear that *really* can mirror and *really* expand their experience and perhaps allow them some real access to some small hope and wonder that will make life seem more worth living. (A reader of an earlier draft felt that I could be more positive here: "serious imaginative literature takes pain seriously and provides some kind of pattern and parallel which is not provided by the mild babysafe school" (June Sturrock).) The common illiteracy is another, and smaller, problem. Becoming literate is, intellectually, very easy for nearly all children. The problem is schools and homes that cannot show why it is worthwhile. The curriculum we are working towards here will show children why literacy is worthwhile.

The Direction of Education

I have argued insistently against the common interpretation of the progressivist principle of moving from the known to the unknown and its product in the "expanding horizons" curriculum. Typical early childhood curricula suggest that education moves from the child and the here and now "outward," from local, simple, and relatively trivial matters towards complexity and importance.

Let me first repeat a theme of the previous section: education cannot move from the trivial to the important because we must begin with the important. And while of necessity we proceed in learning from the known to the unknown, by interpreting the known in terms of fundamental abstract concepts we will see additional and more complex content not providing new and different underlying concepts but rather elaborating and refining the concepts with which we started. What we should focus on when we consider the direction of education, then, is neither a linear accumulation of content nor the development of sets of thinking skills. Rather, we will focus on the elaboration of children's sense-making capacities. As far as curriculum content goes, the discussion of the earlier chapters suggests that the "direction" might better be represented as quite the opposite to that implied in the "expanding environments/horizons" curricula. In early childhood the more important and, I have given reasons to believe, the logically and psychologically prerequisite move is from fantasy to the extremes and limits of reality. So we move from giants and gnomes to the biggest and smallest people, from gods to heroes, from monsters to dinosaurs, from heaven and hell to galaxies, stars, black holes, and planets; and so on. At the very least, we may feel confident that the content of children's experience need not dictate the content of our curriculum.

— We begin by establishing contexts and then move to grasp the limits of reality.

More particularly we are moving in the direction of the *bonnes à penser* of literacy and those intellectual capacities associated with rationality – such as being able to correctly conclude a simple syllogism. This is a capacity rare in the embedded or "empiric" (Tulviste, 1979) thinking of oral cultures but routine in literate and schooled cultures. The orality/literacy divide has, as I indicated earlier, become considerably complicated by recent studies. Literacy is increasingly recognized as too limited a term for the range of capacities it has been used in earlier research to account for. Perhaps more generally useful might be the term "literal." This refers to the constraining force that the forms of reality can impose on the metaphoric exuberance and fluidity of myth and fantasy. Literal thinking is that kind which tries to mirror reality as closely as possible, with the intention of getting control over it. Metaphoric thinking uses bits of reality to mirror the mind's rather than the world's lineaments.[3] Of course, this is a crude distinction – Ockham's chainsaw – but it serves to mark off something central to the array of forms of thought and *bonnes à penser* we are moving towards in this scheme; they are all bound up with making thought conform to the shapes of external reality. "Hot," "cold," and "warm" are terms which refer to temperature relative to its effects on our bodies. Literal thinking seeks to refer to temperature in terms that better reflect its nature – for which an arbitrary and abstracted (from our bodies' point of view) set of numbers are well suited. Mathematics is the language of science because of its ability to refer to minute differences and reflect sequences that are more akin to the nature of most physical phenomena than are words. Words refer better, relatively, to great galumphing, discrete, slabs of things. This scheme aims in the direction of forms of thought and of languages that are better able to reflect reality. We have a considerable menagerie of terms that try to catch some aspect of the change in sense-making capacities to follow this Mythic layer – disembedded thinking, thinking in concepts, theoretic syllogistic reasoning, scientific thinking, rationality, literacy, abstractions, reflective thought, operational thought, and so on. (The next volume, perhaps seemingly oddly called *Romantic Understanding*, will try to be precise about some of the sense-making capacities these terms hint at.)

What is to be borne in mind in designing the Mythic layer curriculum, then, is not only the Mythic capacities that are to be evoked, stimulated, and developed, but also the general form of the capacities of the next layer that have to be prepared for. This need not strain ingenuity greatly. For example, I have earlier referred to those studies which show that reading and writing do not *cause* what I am calling literal thinking, though clearly they are at least hospitable to such thinking. When we teach young children to read and write, then, we can do so in such a way that we stimulate oral *bonnes à penser* while at the same time developing those skills which, gradually internalized and coalesced with others, are important for evoking, stimulating, and developing the *bonnes à penser* of literal thought. In designing the Mythic layer curriculum, then, these dual considerations need constantly to be brought together.

Under this heading I might usefully consider an aspect of the role of memorizing in the Mythic layer curriculum. I will be advocating the importance of learning a range of things by heart and, while this may appear consistent with some of the principles established earlier about oral cultures, it may seem to conflict with the direction children are to take into literal thinking. I raise this because of the practical implications that have followed from a number of educationalists' conclusions that memorizing knowledge is less important than knowing where to find it, and learning considerable amounts of particular knowledge is less important than "learning how to learn." Now clearly this is not a radical divide, but rather a matter of emphasis. Those educationalists who stress the importance of "learning how to learn" or where to find required knowledge encourage practices that somewhat depreciate the value of "rote-learning" and memorizing significant bodies of knowledge. Generally their position follows from the observation that literacy, and efficient means of storing and accessing data in libraries and increasingly via computer terminals, make the data-sorting functions of the human memory – which are not particularly good anyway – largely unnecessary. Priority, in this view, must be given to teaching children and students how to find knowledge when needed and how to "process" it (using "thinking skills").

I discussed in Chapter Two the inappropriateness of the analogy commonly made between human memory and computer memory, or human memory and library, as a storage place for information. Clearly the human memory can be made to function like an external data-storage system – as when we memorize a shopping-list or an appointment. All we want in such cases is an accurate replication of what we "input." The reason the human memory is not particularly good at this kind of storage and retrieval is that it seems designed to do other, much more complex things, with knowledge – such that the medieval rhetoricians' erosion of the distinction between memory and reason seems appropriate. The value of holding some distinction between the stored data of a book or a computer and the memorized knowledge of a human mind is to stress that the vast piles of data accumulating all round us do not contribute anything to our sense-making capacities. The memorization of knowledge, learning content, is a necessary condition for the development and elaboration of sense-making capacities. So what people know, as distinct from what data they have access to, remains no less important educationally than it ever was.

As I noted, nobody holds that we should teach nothing but how to "access" data. What is in question is a matter of emphasis. Nor will I argue for massive amounts of meaningless rote-learning. The problem, as I see it, is that a number of educationalists have been distressed at the amount of memorizing of facts that children and students have been required to do. Much of what may have been successfully memorized remains effectively meaningless. This use of the memory seems idle, and additionally seems to stunt the use of "thinking skills" or critical faculties that should go to work on the facts memorized. This restricted conception of the memory – as data storage – is then taken as the whole, and used in arguments about the relative unimportance of memorizing. By distinguishing between data storage and memorizing knowledge, however, we can undercut such easy depreciation.

In an oral culture memorization is vital. And we have seen that the need to memorize stimulated the development of such techniques as rhyme, rhythm, meter, the story, and, through a complex of these, the development of imagination. Forced memorization in schools has tended to be seen as an inhibitor of imagination in children. Here, having pointed to their close historical relationship, I want to stress also the ways in which they can support each other in children's education. Memorization seems to me important during this Mythic layer because of its potential role in developing the *bonnes à penser* of orality, which are foundational to all further sense-making capacities. And I think this importance is not diminished because the direction of education is towards literal thinking and literacy. Memorization seems equally important once literacy is internalized because access to data is irrelevant to the development of sense-making capacities. The acquisition and memorization of knowledge, on the other hand, are necessary conditions of their development. The kind of content whose memorization will encourage sense-making, as distinct from being idle rote-learning, will be discussed in the section on curriculum content below.

It seems to be commonly assumed that one of the losses that accompanies literacy is the capacity for the precise and extensive memorization evident in oral cultures. This seems to me, if it is true, a contingent matter. Certainly, as literate but book-poor medieval scholars showed, systematic memorizing techniques of considerable power are not inconsistent with literacy (Spence, 1984; Yates, 1966) (but on the other hand those techniques hardly seem to stimulate and encourage critical reflection on what one memorizes). I am not, however, proposing to teach young children medieval memorizing techniques nor to make early education revert to massive rote-learning. Rather I am concerned only to redress what seems to me an excessive depreciation of the educational uses of memorization, by recalling the complexity of the human memory and arguing for a more balanced recognition of its ever-active and generative functions. The task, then, is to decide on a Mythic layer curriculum that will stimulate the memory and its generative functions in ways that set appropriate patterns for future sense-making. It will be necessary to ensure that what children are required to learn by heart and remember will stimulate the capacities of orality and also play a proformative role for those of literal thinking. So when young children are living largely in their oral culture – while literacy and literal thinking are in formation but are not functionally internalized – a significant part of their knowledge is made up of what they can remember. This knowledge is one of the necessary conditions for the adequate development of the sense-making capacities that constitute Mythic understanding. Thus:

  —   Learning by heart plays an important role in early
      education.

The Great Stories

Because the nature of knowledge is one of the constrainers of
our cultural development, its influence must also be felt on the
structure of the curriculum in this recapitulation scheme. But in this
scheme psychological predispositions also play an influential role,
so the nature of knowledge will not play the kind of determining
role it tends to in Platonic schemes. Cultural history, containing
the results of these dual influences or constraints, is to provide the
more overt guidance in structuring the Mythic layer curriculum.
Perhaps for purposes of dividing up the curriculum I can compare
our culture to a rather messy crumbling pie; any attempt to cut it
into slices is going to leave crumbs all over the place. My divisions
of curriculum content, then, do not pretend to be the product of
some precise analysis of the nature of knowledge. Indeed, I have
already made clear that I think any such attempts at definitive
analyses of knowledge or culture are will-o'-the-wisps. We can
analyze and categorize knowledge for particular purposes, but
there are no cut-lines etched into the universe of knowledge that we
may find and slice down with sharpened epistemological knives.

For the present purpose of designing a Mythic layer curriculum,
headed in the direction of literacy and literal thinking, I will
divide the curriculum into five main sections: History – Language
and Literature – Science – Mathematics and Logic – Arts (in no
particular order). These are not tight compartments. They are in
part organizational conveniences, but in important part divisions
useful in clarifying something of the kinds of sense we can make
of the world and of experience.

But is is important, too, to see the overlaps among these
sections. I mean not so much the kinds of thematic overlaps
that form the basis of interdisciplinary studies, but the important
identities of capacities that are equally foundational to different
areas. Focusing, as is common, on the modern condition rather
than the cultural history of, say, Science and the Arts, we tend
to emphasize the features that differentiate one from the other.

If we think in terms of recapitulation, however, we will recall that through the Renaissance, even up until the Romantic period, our sense of the artist and the scientist having different interests and different tools did not exist. Leonardo and Goethe exhibited as much the qualities of the scientist as of the artist. Close observation, and precise description and representation, of nature was as basic to the development of the sciences as it was to the further development of the arts. Their common foundations are more to the point here, while we remain sensitive to the different potential developments that can follow from those foundations. Similarly we will focus on the common foundations of Mathematics and Music, while remaining sensitive to the different capacities that their later developments can stimulate (Langer, 1982).

The guiding question I will address to each section of the curriculum will be something like "What constitutes the oral foundation of Science/History/etc.?" In the case of Language or Arts it might seem that we have some intuitive sense of what such a question might direct us towards. But in the case of, say, Science, this intuitive sense may seem to have less to grasp. In the case of Science, its mature forms are quite clearly defined and are articulated into familiar curriculum sequences, and this is even more true of Mathematics. To ask what their oral foundations consist of invites an unfamiliar perspective. Even so, I will use this as the directing question for each curriculum area, conscious – let me add again – that there are many better equipped than I am to answer the question for each of the areas I shall fearfully tread into. I am conscious, too, that what I am offering below are notes that focus on only one aspect of curriculum design. Spinning a full curriculum from these notes for the first three years of schooling would require a lot of further work, but my aim here is to outline the bases for a curriculum in sufficient detail that such spinning could go forward.

History

The oral foundation of history is in myth. Is our primary History curriculum then to be made up of myths? No. We excavate below the level of myths in oral cultures to consider what *bonnes à penser* they stimulated and developed, and then we consider how we can use history to stimulate and develop those *bonnes à penser* in children today. Those aspects of myth that seem the precursors of history establish the place and roles of individuals in the present in the context of some wider story. In all oral cultures there are traditional tales that perform this function in a more or less familiar linear time frame, though somewhat unreliably and over a relatively short period. But in myths the context is more commonly made up of a sacred world of gods and original ancestors with which the individual and the present are connected directly. While the traditional tales might exemplify particular virtues or follies, it is the myths that do the more serious job of establishing the individual's place and sense of identity in the natural and social worlds. What such myths do is enhance the significance of the conditions in which one finds oneself by relating one's daily activities to a cosmic story, thereby providing a kind of explanation of present circumstances and so making sense of them in a wider context. The sense-making capacities developed by such myths are what we are after. In our case, conscious that we are moving towards history, we can aim to establish these foundational sense-making capacities but by using the stuff of history rather than of myth. (For elaboration of this paragraph, see Egan, 1973, 1978a, 1978b.)

We can do this by telling children the dramatic stories of human cultures, and particularly of the one of which they are a part and partial product. We can begin with the cosmological context for those cultures, as recounted in a source such as Virginia Lee Burton's *Life Story* (1962). Within that context history is made up of the great stories of human struggles for freedom against oppression, for security against danger, for knowledge against ignorance, for hope against despair, and so on. For each of the first three years we can tell the history of the world, from the beginning to the present, as, in the first year perhaps, the dramatic story of the struggle for freedom against oppression. There is no shortage of dramatic material for such a story. It can readily be organized as a developing story, with each segment being a dramatic story within the overarching theme. It would include topics such as slavery in the ancient world, the building of the pyramids, the revolt of Spartacus, the Greek city-states against the Persian Empire, the Roman Republic and the spread of the Empire, Feudal protection systems after the fall of the Empire, Robin Hood, Jews in medieval

Europe, the expansion of European empires and slavery, the French and American revolutions, the independence movements of modern times, Ghandi, and so on. Using the principles of good story-telling appropriate to this age, it would be possible to plan a year-long dramatic and coherent story of our civilization seen in terms of the struggle for freedom against oppression. One would have to select the most vivid and dramatic material and one would have to simplify history. But even the most sophisticated historical narratives require selection and simplification. This great story does not require the falsification of anything; it is a true and important story.

For the second year we might tell the story of the struggle for security against fear and danger. This would likely include such topics as the needs for food and shelter in early times and the threats against these, the importance of the family, aggression as one response to a lack of security, the first villages and towns, the cooperation and mutual benefits of trade in early times, the beginnings of massive empires and their armies, the Roman army and its engineers, building a Roman town, the medieval castle and its village, nation-states and their armies, the need for money to pay them and the consequences of taxation, diplomacy and attempts to balance powers, modern wars and the League of Nations and the United Nations, the attempts at security by balanced arms today.

The third year could retell the story, but this time as a struggle for knowledge against ignorance; dealing with the early human communities and the knowledge that kept them together and enabled them to thrive, the value of myth, the forging of new forms of thought in the ancient Near East, Socrates and Plato, Roman order and organization, monks, monasteries and Vikings, the cathedrals and their schools, Alfred the Great and Charlemagne, Peter Abelard and the first universities, culture-heroes of the Renaissance, the development of modern science, and so on.

Put so starkly I realize such a curriculum outline raises many questions. An obvious one, which seems nevertheless easy to answer, is whether such a curriculum could be comprehensible to five-, six-, and seven-year-olds. The easy answer is yes. The grounds for that answer are given in the earlier chapters of this book. Of course, one could easily make this content inaccessible to young children, but we could also easily make it accessible, by drawing on the principles discussed earlier. In the next chapter I will discuss one way of adapting those principles to organizing such content in an accessible way.

Another immediate objection is based on on the implicit ethnocentrism and ideological imperialism of a curriculum made up of the Western tradition presented as progressive stories. We can dispense with the last point easily by pointing out that they need not be told simply as progressive stories. What is required in this scheme, though, is that they be told as dramatic stories. In fact they are potentially terrific stories – whose dramatic power has tended to be undermined by the typical old-fashioned History curriculum and by the more modern relevant-activities History curriculum which engages older children in "discovering" things. But what about the ethnocentrism? This is a difficult problem, especially in classes made up of children of many cultural backgrounds. In what sense are these the appropriate stories that help secure the historical and social identities of Indian children in British schools or Vietnamese children in North American schools or even Anglo-Saxon children in Australian schools? What I have outlined are some of the elements that help account for some significant features of the Western societies such children find themselves growing up in. What might usefully be added are related themes from other cultures and their contact with and impact on the traditional European and English-speaking cultures. That is, while the sketches I have given to exemplify what I mean by teaching history as great true stories may indeed suggest a certain "mainstream" ethnocentrism, an elaborated curriculum based on the principles outlined earlier need not be ethnocentric in this way. What I am concerned to establish here are the basic principles for a recapitulation curriculum and to indicate what it could look like.

A further potential benefit of such a dramatic stories History curriculum would overlap a little with the benefits Bettelheim has claimed for the classic folk-tales (Bettelheim, 1976). In such a curriculum, in contrast to the typical Social Studies curriculum in North America and Australia, children are introduced to their world in its powerful and dramatic forms rather than through the ordered routine of their local customs. Children's early lives, we may forget, are full of titanic struggles and accommodations. What they see in the great stories History curriculum is that their own struggles have an analog in human history. If the world is represented through the order of local routines, children may be led to conclude that the storms of their psyches are anomalous wild elements in the play of dramatic forces. And this is not so; their world has gone through struggles and accommodations that are comprehensible in terms that can also help to make sense of their own struggles. Young children, too, are engaged in struggles for freedom against oppression, for security against danger, for knowledge against ignorance, and so on. The historical dimension of these struggles can provide a valuable context for making sense of one's own struggles, and for enlarging the sense one can make of them. The young child, reciprocally, can make sense of the historical struggles initially in terms given by the experience of families, playgrounds, and daily social interactions.

One other element of the great stories curriculum that I may as well add here, though it would not be a part of the History curriculum, concerns the shapes imposed on the year by festivals. This too might respond to concerns about ethnocentrism. Festivals put a pattern into the otherwise uniform linearity of time. The main festivals of the various cultures represented in the class and the surrounding society can be taught about as they arise during the year. What needs to be brought out are the story behind the festival, its emotional meaning, and its place in that culture's shaping of time. Many festivals can also be related to the great stories of history. Hanukkah, for example, can be tied into the dramatic story of Judas Maccabeus and his struggles for freedom against oppression.

Language and Literature

Educational writing in this curriculum area seems to be richest in proposals that are consistent with the principles I have supported earlier. So I will just briefly outline what seems to me implied by the earlier discussion for the primary Language and Literature curriculum, confident that a large body of writing can provide many and varied suggestions for detailed implementation. The starting question about the oral foundations of each curriculum area is less of a challenge to conventional practice here than in some areas. Literature, we saw, is not an invention of literate people; its most powerful techniques for conveying messages with emotional, almost somatic, force are still in daily use. Our objective for the primary years is to empower children to express and communicate their unique sense of their experience and of their world by shaping sound and meanings and to develop the capacities for ecstatic response and enlargement of experience through the shaped sound and meanings of others.

The shaping techniques that we considered included rhyme, rhythm, meter, and the story form. We see these used most obviously in poems and stories, though of course these techniques can be found in a wide range of language uses and narratives that do not easily fit into these categories. We will, then, include in our primary curriculum lots of poems and stories, and we will encourage children to tell and write lots of poems and stories. One aim is to enable children to become sufficiently fluent in the use of these techniques that they can express their unique perceptions through them. This will be doubly difficult if teaching is tightly controlled to achieve particular conventional "skills." That is, a significant amount of time, and encouragement, should be given to *playing* with these techniques. This might be seen as analogous to the babbling of the two-year-old in the crib – that period of life when babies explore the range of possible sounds they can produce. They play with a huge range of phonemes, gradually settling on the distinctive forms of those used in their environment. So we might encourage children simply to play with rhymes, play with meter, play with stories, and so on. The school yard and the street will provide stimulus for much of this kind of activity: rhyming slang, rhyming abuse, chants, jokes, ghost stories, riddles, and so on, are instantiations of the predisposition to engage in this development of oral techniques. Classroom encouragement of them can be more self-consciously systematic, building on and extending, and disciplining, the kinds of *bonnes à penser* already in development.

While we are encouraging children to be makers and shapers of sounds and meaning, we will also give them many examples of other people's shapes. Particularly we will tell stories and recite poems. I need add nothing to the persuasive literature on the value of telling stories at this period, some which I have quoted earlier. Though it might be worth reiterating the observation about the considerable enhancement of their enchanting effects if stories are told rather than read. In telling a story one puts the narrative in some degree under the somatic control of the audience, as the teller responds to the responses of the listeners. Prominent among the stories young children should become familiar with in our culture are those of the Bible and of Homer. Also we will include folk-tales and myth stories from around the world, particularly the most powerful and vivid sets that have played formative roles in our cultural history, such as the Greek and Roman, and more recently the Norse and various African corpuses of myth stories. We are fortunate to have available a number of suitable versions of biblical and Homeric stories for young children.

I realize that use of the biblical stories for purely secular educational purposes may present a problem for those, on the one hand, who do not want their children becoming familiar with the Judeo-Christian Bible, and those on the other who see it simply as the word of God and not appropriately treated as "literature." My reasons for considering the Bible stories so important for this primary layer of language and literary development can be indicated by two quotations:

Of all the raw deals meted out in the Bible – not excluding Job's or that blighted fig tree's – Moses surely suffered the meanest. After all he had gone through for Yaweh and the Chosen People, his exclusion from the Promised Land within sight of it was cruelly unfair. Or so it seemed to my child's mind, as repeatedly in Scripture classes and Sunday school we rehearsed the story of the Exodus, the 40 years wandering in the wilderness and the entry of the Children of Israel into the Land of Canaan. My sense of solidarity with the patriarch, in which I am sure I was not alone, was mixed with awe that this sort of thing could happen to grown-ups too, and behind that a dim perception that perhaps it was in the nature of promised lands and the bid to reach them that they should entail a high vulnerability to disappointment and dashed hopes. Clearly, growing up was no solution, unless growing up meant putting by such longings altogether. (Spice, 1985, p. 27)

If we don't know the Bible and the central stories of Greek and Roman literature we can still read books and see plays, but our knowledge of literature can't grow, just as our knowledge of mathematics can't grow if we don't learn the multiplication table. (Frye, 1963, p. 28)

I think that Frye perhaps exaggerates a little, but he does point to the centrality of the Bible in the formation of consciousness in our culture. The Bible stories have the enchanting power required to stimulate and develop the Mythic layer of understanding and they contribute a basis for understanding much of the literature to follow that stimulates and develops subsequent layers of understanding. They give a frame for a particular moral and emotional grasp on the world that may indeed be too simple for some and inappropriate for others if the stories are taken as conveying a dogma, but which helps to make meaningful the moral and emotional categories built into our culture. This is not the place to engage in a detailed argument for the value of the Bible stories in education (but see, for example, Frye, 1982). My primary concern is with stories that, on the one hand, embody the qualities that stimulate the ecstatic response in children and, on the other, contain material that is significant for the development of subsequent capacities. For those with objections to the Bible, perhaps greater emphasis may be placed on the Homeric tales. They have played a similar role in shaping the moral and emotional categories of our cultural consciousness; they are also vivid and dramatic stories that are foundational to the development of subsequent capacities. They are foundational in the sense that the kind of literature that stimulates and develops subsequent capacities is less accessible to those lacking familiarity with the Bible and with Homer.

During the primary years children's grasp of various rhythms of language, their fluency with meter and rhyme, their ease in developing metaphors, will all be enhanced by learning a lot of verse by heart.[4] One would expect the seven-year-old, then, not just to have heard Mother Goose rhymes, but to know a large number of them by heart. One would also expect the seven-year-old to be able to tell a wide range of stories. We will not expect master story-telling, but rather the beginnings of the compositional/repetitional skills we see at work in the Homeric poet and the Balkan singer of heroic tales. Among the best material for initial practice of these skills is the joke. Another form of "oral literature" that will stimulate children's development of Mythic *bonnes à penser* in the proverb. By age seven we will expect children who follow this curriculum to know a large range of proverbs by heart. Increasingly as we move towards the next layer we will ask children to reflect on the proverbs. We can do this by bringing into justaposition those which with equal wisdom seem to counsel opposite or conflicting actions ("Too many cooks spoil the broth": "Two heads are better than one").

During this period most children will be learning to read and write. There is a vast amount of educational writing and research on this topic, to which I have nothing much to add. What is clear is that if we treat literacy as a set of coding and decoding skills children can learn them by any of a wide range of procedures, some children learn them only marginally, and some seem unable to grasp what the whole business is about (Hall, 1987). Literacy seems to me better thought of in terms of a change in sense-making capacities rather than as the mastery of specific skills. It is a part of what I am calling the development of literal thinking on top of the predominantly metaphoric thinking of this Mythic layer of understanding.

Given this, in a Mythic layer curriculum reading and writing will be encouraged in all areas of the curriculum. The kinds of engagement in History and Science that are to be encouraged will employ oral techniques prominently but will continually introduce symbols and require decoding and coding skills in contexts where meaning is clear and engaging. Systematic work dealing with reading and writing can be best accommodated within this Language and Literature area, and there is no escaping the need for some hard work by children to internalize literacy. Sensitivity to individual differences in learning and to individual difficulties is required at this important transition. I have nothing to add about methodologies for instruction, apart from the common point about avoiding dogmatism about the best method that every child is to follow. The implication of the earlier principles concerns the contexts in which literacy is to be learned. These are spelled out throughout the book; in general they support introducing the basic skills of literacy in contexts that are engaging and providing a lot of practice in using them in enhancing "oral" capacities – their use in rhyming, making stories and verses, inventing metrical patterns, playing with sounds and symbols, and so on.

The other concern we have is with the direction of the process towards literal thinking. What kinds of activities will continue to

215

stimulate initial developments of literacy while shaping them in the direction of literal thought? We might again look for guidance from the beginnings of literacy, and see what activities seemed most to enhance new sense-making capacities. Drawing on Goody (1977) we might consider the potency of list-making. It has an evident engaging quality for many young children. It is a crucial tool for "establishing their inventory," as Coe put it. Making and manipulating lists provides a use of early literacy that stimulates meaningful non-story shaped ways of organizing and classifying the world and experience. (List of rivers. List of musical instruments. List of emotions. List of favorite people. List of foods, and so on. Then one can take the lists and sub-divide them: of musical instruments, say – those we scrape, those we hit, those we pluck, those we blow, and so on.) Similarly the use of the recipe, flowchart, table, etc., can be introduced and developed. These and numerous other non-narrative or non-story forms of language use can stimulate the internalizing of literacy – that is, can stimulate the use of literacy for literal thinking.

I should perhaps say more or nothing about foreign languages at this point, but may perhaps be excused a note based on the Canadian experience with French immersion. In immersion programs children at five enter a school environment in which only the new language is spoken. English-speaking children are expected, and helped, to pick up French in much the way that they earlier picked up English. There are various disputes surrounding these programs – some social, as they tend to create an elitist stream within the state school system, some pedagogical. What is of interest here is the, to some, unexpected achievements of these programs. By age nine most children are quite fluent in French, though commonly inaccurate in ways that then can be systematically corrected, but their abilities in English seem no less than those of similar children in normal English-language schools, and perhaps somewhat better (Cummins and Swain, 1986). The immersion provided in many of these schools is not simply in the grammar and lexicon of French but, to a significant degree, in French culture. An informal observation, that has been nevertheless very striking to me, is that children in these programs seem much less ethnocentric than their English-language-school companions. (Again, I suspect there is a degree of analystic truth in this: what we mean by ethnocentrism is tied in with the lack of the cultural initiation that goes with a good

French immersion program.) To recommend, on the basis of the Canadian experience, that all primary education be conducted in a second language would be reckless, of course. It would also not allow for the difficulties of children whose schooling is already in a language different from that of their homes, and it would casually ignore the practical impossibility of finding bilingual teachers, and so on. I mention it here only because, under the heading of "Language and Literature," the value of early becoming fluent in a foreign language should not be ignored.[5]

Science

The oral foundations of science are magical. But isn't science the enemy of magic, the destroyer of mysteries? Here more than in any other area of the curriculum our inherited, and unmediated, binary opposites tend to undermine education into scientific understanding. How can we sensibly introduce science to young children if we take seriously the need to recapitulate its origins in magic? Again, the oddity of such a proposal is so apparent only when we make the mistake of assuming that the recapitulation is of the knowledge content. If we instead focus on the sense-making capacities that underlie the content we might be able to find ways of introducing science that are both meaningful and potent for developing more sophisticated understanding.

As I noted in the previous chapter while discussing astronomy and astrology, we can see in the "oral" precursors of scientific inquiry, a range of sense-making capacities at work. We see an imaginative search for meaning, observation of patterns and order in complex phenomena, classification and categorization of the results of observations, and the representation of the results in a memorable form that makes clear the importance of the organized categories for the individual lives of each member of the culture. Put this way, of course, we can make magic sound like science. What this suppresses are those prominent features of oral cultural representations of the natural world and of experience that seem to run completely in opposite directions to science. Put in this way, however, we can at least see that mythic and scientific approaches to nature are not entirely mutually exclusive; they have some very important features in common, and it is these common features that will form the basis of our Mythic layer curriculum. What are they?

Most basic is careful observation and categorization of what is observed. Some element of categorization seems indistinguishable from observation – we do not observe "raw data"; we structure and categorize what is perceived as a part of the process of perception. Other forms of categorization can be conducted subsequently, particularly those that result from reflection on the adequacy or appropriateness of our original categories. This latter form of categorization seems very rare in oral cultures, and seems culturally subsequent (in the sense of involving the joint action of logical entailments and psychological predispositions) to the former kind. In our primary curriculum, then, it is the former kind of categorization that will concern us. Observation, too, has a number of forms. In oral cultures various kinds of categorizations of natural phenomena give evidence of enormously acute and discriminating observation. Commonly, however, that observation seems to be significantly different from our scientific ideal of objectivity and seems to lack very largely the kind of observation of causal processes that accompanies experimental procedures. It seems to be "embedded" and participatory in the sense outlined in Chapter Two. This kind of participatory observation seems to be one of the "oral" foundations of scientific understanding, and we need to work out how we might recapitulate it – evoke, stimulate, and develop the capacities embodied in it – in young children.

We can know *about* nature – about trees and spiders and stars – but there is also a sense in which we can *know* them more directly. That is, we can be sensitive to our shared existence and sensitive to the uniqueness of each thing. We might begin our science curriculum, then, not by introducing children to categories of things but by encouraging sensitive observation of some individual thing. We might encourage each child to "adopt" some natural thing – a particular tree, patch of grass, kind of weather, constellation, vegetable, spider, horse, or whatever is convenient. Time will then be given regularly and quite extensively for children simply to be with and observe their adopted bit of nature. If a particular tree is chosen, the child might be encouraged to notice the patterns of its branches, the way different kinds of rain run down the leaves, the movement of the branches in different winds.

It might be no bad thing if it became a commonplace of our society to see children silently observing trees or spiders or patches of tall grass or clouds, or standing in and watching carefully at every opportunity how rain falls.

This kind of observation is not initially intended to lead to some systematic product – a "report on my tree" – or to answering questions about it. Rather it is more nearly to be a kind of dream-like absorption into the thing observed, leading to reverence for the uniqueness of "their" piece of nature. Imagining some of the wilder, "culturally deprived" children whose major delight seems to involve destruction, this may seem a "pie-in-the-sky" ideal. I suspect rather that much of the distressing disregard of nature that we see in many young children is caused by the fact that the human potential for feeling a part of – rather than set off from – nature is too rarely evoked, stimulated, and developed in children. It may be that the social and environmental odds are stacked against easy achievement of this kind of sensitivity but it is clearly possible, so our ingenuity should go to working out how to realize it routinely in schools.

(I should perhaps stress that what I advocate here is quite different from the common textbook recommendations on Observation in elementary science programs. Nearly all such texts have a section on The Child as Observer, or some such, in which proposed activities such as careful observation of some feature of the natural environment. In all the textbooks I have consulted, however, these activities are not designed to stimulate and develop the kind of participation I describe above – indeed, almost the reverse. They are designed to engage the child directly in simplified scientific inquiry. In all the textbooks there are suggestions for activities that either prepare for or follow on, or both, the periods of observation. Most commonly they recommend that the child begin by observing the tree, flower, spider's web, or whatever. Thereafter the child is encouraged to describe to a partner or to the class, just what was observed, notes or drawings might be made and compared, the names of parts of the tree, flower, or spider and web might be learned, and so on. This is what I have characterized as attempting to *replace* the skills of orality with those of literate rationality. There is little flavor in such recommendations of stimulating the participation in nature as the foundation on which the later skills can be built.)

The recapitulation principle leads us here to try to recreate the sense of magic and mystery out of which science has developed historically and, I am arguing, can best develop in individual children. The initial participatory observations, requiring no systematic reporting, does not mean that the mind is disengaged. The mind rather is free to play on what is being carefully observed. Illusions and peculiar patterns will flit to and fro. It is not only the observed that will be the source of changing perceptions but also the observer. The child gazing at heavy rainfall or snow will suddenly feel that the rain or snow is no longer falling but that they are rising swiftly upwards through it; the tree's branches are no longer swaying idly in the wind but it is the child's many branching arms that feel the wind; the spider's web is being spun out of their body; the grass is whispering to them; and so on. This engagement in nature must not be sentimental. We might learn a lot about how to educate young children in this regard from the greatest teachers of such skills – the Plains Indians of North America (Merkel, 1985).

If this is one of the oral foundations of science, how are we to tell young children the great story of science? What is that story and how can we convey it to primary school children? This can be tied into the History curriculum, as a part of the struggle for knowledge against ignorance. (Not, note, the progressive move towards knowledge *from* ignorance, but the constant struggle in which knowledge is attained and valued throughout history.) It can also be elaborated in smaller-scale stories – of flight, from Daedalus to space probes; of the discovery of the universe; of locomotion on land, from the wheel to the hovercraft; of the exploration of Earth, from African beginnings to satellite mapping; of the variety of animals, plants, and insects, focusing on the most dramatic and strange life-cycles; of measuring time, from sun and stars to quartz crystals.

I realize that to primary school teachers dealing with large numbers of immigrant children, this might all seem weirdly remote. Such teachers spend enormous energy trying to teach the basics of English and familiarize the children with their local environment. When they have study topics they may focus on "Who I am" to give the children some clearer sense of identity. To such teachers facing enormous practical difficulties, telling the stories of science and technology may seem a luxury for which they cannot afford the time, even if they had the resources. This is not the place for extended arguments, beyond those I have given earlier in this book, but I think learning the story of flight and spiders' behavior contributes much more to an understanding of "Who I am" and contributes much more to making sense of one's environment than does the practical involvement with that environment or with units of work focused on one's self. Such a primary curriculum also prepares for further layers of understanding in a way the local and self-focused curriculum cannot adequately do.

As one moves towards the next layer of understanding it is appropriate to introduce those less narrative forms of exploration of the natural world, those forms in which the empirical world is encouraged to impact on children's forms of thought. The most common and most powerful of these is the experiment. During the primary years, however, experiments can be fitted into the great stories to exemplify unexpected discoveries or dramatic inventions. Their role in stimulating literal thinking will become more prominent in the year four transition to the next layer of understanding science.

Mathematics and Logic

Mathematics tends to be introduced to young children these days by procedures that have resulted from a series of ideas each of which has left some residue; that active manipulation needs to precede conceptual grasp, that socially relevant activities should determine curriculum content, that basic "skills" must be ensured as early as possible, that the "structure" of the subject should be made apparent to young children, and so on. What kind of early Mathematics curriculum will we get from applying the question about the oral foundations of the subject?

Logic, in as far as it appears at all in primary curricula, has occasionally been introduced in experimental programs teaching formal logic. This thrust was seen particularly in the USA during the late 1960s and early 1970s as a part of the diversification of programmed learning from texts and electro-mechanical devices to computers. Its other source is in the quiet different and, to me at least, much more interesting programs of Philosophy for

Children associated with the work of Matthew Lipman and the journal *Thinking*, and illustrated also in Gareth Matthew's books (1980, 1985). Why do I think the principles developed earlier lead to including logic in the early childhood curriculum, and what form might it take? And why associate it with mathematics? It might be useful to begin with logic and then move on to mathematics.

Earlier I discussed the primacy of metaphor in our thinking, and suggested that the logic of literal thinking grew out of the logic of metaphor. Given the starting question for determining our curriculum, then, the Logic curriculum seems to require some initial involvement with metaphor. Logic involves establishing connections and relationships among the propositions we talk or think with. The first task is to notice the kinds of connections and relationships that can be formed. We need to recall here Max Black's point which I stressed in Chapter Two: that metaphor creates connections rather than catches and reflects some already existing connection. We need to sensitize children to the way language builds its meanings, and to enable them to find this kind of inquiry engaging. The foundation of logic that we find in oral cultures, then, focuses us towards the play with metaphor, and the building of linguistic structures by a complex logic of metaphoric connections. Where can we find an appropriate form accessible to children that can expose to conscious observation this kind of metaphoric play? Metaphoric exuberance finds outlets in silly rhymes, word-play riddles, and – one of the prominent forms we can draw on to stimulate this first step in the study of logic – the joke. Of particular interest for this purpose are those jokes that rely on word-play; those that create deliberate confusion, one of whose results is to establish greater clarity; those that assert an identity between things that are different, usually by confusing meanings of homonyms. The point of such jokes lies in our putting into the same category things that are different in ways that makes the assertion of identity threaten to explode the category. The result is usually to underline the difference the joke momentarily eradicated, and our typical response is to explode with laughter – at the mix of the threatening madness of the crazy category with surprise and the relief of its rejection. Jokes threaten to undermine all sense but in a way that draws attention to the importance of the sense they playfully threaten. Lewis Carroll, of course, is a classic player with such jokes. His curriculum is made up of things like Reeling and

Writhing, and, in Mathematics, Ambition, Distraction, Uglifica-
tion and Derision, with dollops of Mystery, ancient and modern,
and such Art work as Drawling, Stretching and Fainting in Coils,
and, of course, the classics, Laughing and Grief. His timetable for
the different lessons required:

> "Ten hours the first day," said the mock Turtle: "nine the
> next, and so on."
> "What a curious plan!" exclaimed Alice.
> "That's the reason they're called lessons," the Gryphon
> remarked: "because they lessen from day to day."

Such jokes call attention to the way meaning is constructed, and
may be deconstructed. Observing how meaning is constructed is
an important foundation of logic. At a more general level the logic
of conventional expectations can be reinforced by their threatened
explosion in a joke, Consider this Hungarian joke which my
mother-in-law told me yesterday: The fattest man in the village
leaned over the well pulling the bucket up. He overbalanced and
fell in. He was so fat that he stuck half way down. A few friends
threw him a rope and pulled and pulled, but couldn't get him out.
They got more and more help, until the whole village was pulling
on the rope. Then slowly he was dragged up. When he came near
the top they could hear him laughing. They got him out, and he
sat on the edge of the well with tears streaming down his face,
holding his sides as he shook with laughter. The villagers asked
what he was laughing at. "I kept imagining what would happen to
you," he said, "if I'd let go of the rope." (My mother-in-law did
say it was a peculiarly Hungarian joke.) While the joke depends
on the incongruity of the behavior, given normal expectations,
it also enlarges our sense of incongruities. The pompous person
slipping on a banana skin satisfied, with great brevity, a story
convention and disrupts a conventional expectation; the category
of over-confident control is shown to be disrupted by something
trivial not taken into account. Such jokes enlarge our repertoire
of expectations, and make more complex and fluid the categories
we use in making sense of the world and of experience.

The contribution such jokes can make to logic may be more
evident if we consider one of the major defects that literal thinking
or "rationality" is prone to. Literal thinking involves forging

concepts and categories that reflect reality as far as possible. We commonly – indeed, seem predisposed nearly always to – reify in some degree the concepts and categories we forge; we tend to see them as themselves real like the things they are supposed to reflect, or at least as having a firmness and clarity that is rarely warranted. This confusion is evident in gross ways in the adherence to ideological schemes which people take to be *the* truth. In less gross ways, a rigidity of categories is one of the main hindrances to efficient literal thinking. An important constituent of rational or literal thinking, then, is that capacity which enables us constantly to keep our concepts and categories fluid and enables us constantly to reassess the relationships we establish among them with the reality they are intended to represent. This capacity in part at least can be evoked, stimulated, and developed by jokes.

While joking will become a part of our primary Logic curriculum, the development of the capacities it can stimulate will need appropriately changing aliments as the individual moves from layer to layer, some of these aliments being more sophisticated kinds of jokes. I am arguing for what is sometimes called a "sense of humor" as an important constituent of the educated person, but arguing also that this should be seen not simply as a pleasant but somewhat irrelevant piece of equipment but rather as crucially important to the subsequent development of literal thinking – of a whole range of sense-making capacities – and as something necessary to civilized life in mass societies. Now clearly by a "sense of humor" I mean something more, or more precise, than this term is often casually used to mean. My meaning will become clearer as the layers of its development are discussed in subsequent volumes of this essay, culminating in its elaboration into what I will call a sophisticated sense of irony. During the primary school years, however, we need to set in place the foundational constituents of this sense of irony, and, I am suggesting, we can begin this by building certain kinds of jokes into the Logic curriculum.

Directed by the question about the oral foundations of each subject area, I am led to conclude, then, not just that we should use the occasional Lewis Carroll-style joke in our early Logic curriculum, but rather that joking – stimulating each child to become a jokester – is fundamental to the later development of logical thinking; that, put more generally, a sense of humor is a necessary constituent of any adequate conception of rationality.

So while we might, on implementing a Mythic layer curriculum, begin to find it unexceptionable to see children standing in silence observing a tree in the wind, so we may expect to hear regular bouts of belly-laughs from primary school classrooms, as a product of a deliberate curriculum objective. In this curriculum area children are not to be merely the audience for jokes, as they are not to merely the audience for stories. They will spend time and energy making up jokes as well, and with deliberate seriousness we need to construct activities that can help children to make jokes.

Such joking, like storying, ties in with the oral culture of the school yard and the neighborhood street. The classroom task is to make it more systematic (not solemn!) and move it in the direction of literal thinking. From jokes to Zeno's paradoxes, as it were. That is, while one part of this curriculum will continue to involve certain kinds of jokes, it will increasingly include also riddles and verbal puzzles. The puzzles can include the everyday kind familiar from Christmas crackers and those fashions for, say, elephant jokes, and so on, including regularly, and increasingly as children move towards literal thinking, the kinds of philosophical puzzles that Gareth Matthews discusses so engagingly with young children. I think a carefully constructed curriculum of such verbal jokes and philosophical puzzles will make vivid the "space" between what can be said about the world and experience and the reality that always confounds being captured in our propositions. In cases where the jokes themselves do not make this clear perhaps the teacher might explicitly draw attention to it. The danger here, as with stories, is that exegesis and testing to see that children understand the point of the joke or story get in the way of and tend to usurp their educational possibilities.

Foundational to mathematical understanding is our number-sense. This we share with many animals. Ours is about as good as that of the blackbird, but rather worse than that of some species of wasp (Danzig, 1967). The extent of our number-sense is evident in our ability to distinguish at a glance up to a certain number of things, and our inability to distinguish precisely once the number exceeds six or seven. To overcome the limits imposed by our number-sense some enormously creative people long ago invented counting systems. Being clear about the difference between number-sense and counting systems seems to me important. By keeping that difference in mind we will appreciate the artificiality of counting systems and see them as the product of enormous ingenuity. They are not obvious, nor to be taken almost as natural. On the other hand, this does not mean that they are very difficult to learn. It means simply that they are artificial. Their clever artificiality, however, is in part the source of their potential engaging power for children. Historically the first abstract counting systems and other mathematical inventions and discoveries were considered magical, tied in with mystery religions and peculiar sects, such as that of the golden-thighed Pythagoras.

So it is the sense of magic that mathematics once evoked and can evoke for each child that is to be the focus for our primary curriculum. It is the peculiar, magical way in which numbers work and spin patterns and structure out of their essence that we must try first to show to children. It is too easy to see mathematics as a set of "skills" that have to be learned mechanically. This approach simply obliterates the nature, and fun and magic, of the subject. Alternatively one can try to move too directly to exposing the "structure" of the subject in some abstract way that makes it incomprehensible to all but the cleverest. What we want to achieve is competence in dealing with numbers within a context that conveys a sense of the magic of the subject.

The first counting systems were embedded in the activities they helped with, e.g. the counting of herd animals, and some echoes of these are to be found in the number rhymes that still exist. The rhythmic base of many of these persists in the tunes that accompany them. So one part of our primary mathematics curriculum can include singing such rhymes. From this one can elaborate the common foundational constituents of mathematics and music by playing games in which numbers and sounds interact.

Overlapping with the Logic part of the curriculum, we can include simple number-based puzzles, magic-number games, number tricks, and so on. These can all help the transition from reliance on a number-sense to a grasp of counting systems. Moving gradually towards literal thinking will be stimulated by the introduction of various counting systems; teaching some of the old finger systems to do addition, subtraction, multiplication, and division problems also may be fun and useful here. Such skills also can be made vivid in stories and games – which will form a significant part of the primary Mathematics curriculum. With stories particularly the magical power of counting systems can be made vivid in contexts of human intentions, hopes, fears, and so on (see Egan, 1986, for examples). Within games, played in groups (cooperating within one's team, competing with others'), particular mathematical functions can find clear formulations that have both "concrete" and "abstract" features. The "skill" level, becoming proficient in addition, subtraction, multiplication, and division, for example, can be achieved meaningfully within curriculum activities that focus constantly on the magical aspects of mathematics. But, as with mastery of the "skill" level of literacy, we cannot escape the need for a period of quite hard work by children and a need for continuous practice to ensure fluent mastery. As with the early development of literacy, the development of numeracy also requires for young children a transition that is not intrinsically difficult but can be made so if we are confused and confusing about what it entails, and can be made even more so perhaps if we are unaware that it exists.

Arts

The Arts comprise the curriculum area most devoted to keeping alive elements of our oral *bonnes à penser*. That is, in their distinctive forms in adult culture the Arts stimulate and develop further capacities that are in significant degree present in the oral culture of childhood. I have referred to the losses that commonly go with educational progress. One educational function of the Arts is to minimize the losses that can easily accompany our development of literal forms of thought. For one thing, they keep alive metaphoric thinking. To overstate my point for the sake of making clear what may seem a peculiar approach to the primary Arts curriculum: Arts are for adults to recapture or retain what is potentially a normal constituent of childhood experience. The *recognition* we experience as adults, for example, in that mixture of pity and fear generated by a great tragedy is a memory of the purity of childhood sensation. Victor Shklovsky puts it well: "Art exists to help us recover the sensation of life, it exists to make us feel things, to make the stone *stony*" (in Webb, 1986, p. 24). For the young child the task is not to recover the sensations so much as to become immersed in them; during early childhood the stoniness of stones has not yet been smothered under layers of perceiving them only in utilitarian terms. If we see trees as lumber, conservationists will seem crazy. The Arts help us to hear and see afresh, to force our perceptions and sensations to experience again the immediacy and vividness of earliest experience. We tell stories of golden apples, Chesterton reminds us, only to recall the wonder of discovering their greenness or redness.

Perhaps we can bring to mind the vastly greater vividness of childhood sensation by recalling simple physical things. Try to remember the degree of loathing felt for your least favorite food – prunes, stilton cheese, or whatever. Overcoming these distastes as adults is not so much a development of character as a decay of taste buds. In Chapter Two I cited Traherne and others as witnesses to what we can all remember, if only we forget the overlay of the years. So the Arts curriculum in the primary years will be less concerned with teaching the basic skills of music, painting, drawing, dance, and so on, as exploring the range of possible sensations available to ear, eye, taste, touch, movement, and so on.

Our Arts curriculum, then, overlaps with Science to begin with. Careful observation is foundational to the scientist no less, and fundamentally no differently, than to the artist. We will explore noise and the endless ways it can be shaped, and we will devise techniques for enabling children to control the shaping of various noises (see, for example, Walker, 1988). All girls and boys should be taught to whistle and sing and to explore the range of clicking noises humans can make. Similarly, sensing and shaping color, movement, materials, and so on, will be a major focus for Arts activities. Varied sounds and their shapes can usefully be introduced here – Mozart, Kalahari bushmen, John Cage, whales' song and bird song, should all be available for careful listening. The emphasis here is on the shaping – not with learning conventional shapes but exploring possible shapes while hearing the range developed in various traditions. Music can be combined with History, for example, in listening to the music and songs that can vivify the story of history as a struggle for freedom against oppression. The exuberance of the music of liberation can help to make the historical story more meaningful.

As we move towards the next layer, the shaping exploration of sound and color and various materials can move increasingly towards the patterning organization of these into publicly accessible forms. We are moving towards, that is, the disciplines involved in being able to express patterns of sound, image, or whatever. This, analogously to reading, writing, and mathematics, will require some work. The metaphoric exuberance needs towards the end of this Mythic layer to begin to accommodate increasingly to the structure of available means of expression, such as a piano, or violin, or colored pens and paper, or gymnastic apparatus. The trick here again is to ensure that the structure of the available means of expression does not obliterate the metaphorical exuberance, but rather provides a means for its expression while also enhancing what can be expressed.

Conclusion

Any number of teachers, if they were persuaded that these principles are sound, could probably use them to design a better curriculum than I can. Experts in curriculum development, along with good primary school teachers, could no doubt draw up an elaborate and detailed curriculum, with examples of available materials, with new resources, with unit and lesson plans and descriptions of various strategies, and so on. Such a task for each of the curriculum areas touched on here could easily take up a book twice this size. And, indeed, if enough people with such skills find this initial stab at articulating principles persuasive, perhaps we may produce just such books and materials. Here, however, lacking these skills and resources, I have tried just to sketch an outline of the kind of curriculum I see as following from the earlier discussion.

The central feature of this curriculum is its focus on evoking, stimulating, and developing the sense-making capacities logically and psychologically proper to early childhood and foundational to the other forms of understanding available in our culture. Prominent in this purpose is stimulating children's metaphoric thinking, their storying facilities, and their imagination. These are to be stimulated because their development sets in place precisely the capacities from which can be best engaged the major disciplines in which further sense-making capacities are embedded. I have laid so much stress on the "oral foundations" of education because, it seems to me, initial schooling at present tends sometimes to stimulate children's oral culture but then teaches literal thinking skills as *replacements* for these. Perhaps more commonly the role of the school in teaching literacy, numeracy, and literal thinking skills generally is seen as something quite distinct from the oral culture of the playground and street. And indeed it usually is, to the destruction of educational possibilities.

The piano and mathematics and literacy can be taught as having a nature to which the child has to conform. Educational progress is then measured by the degree of conformity achieved. The trouble with this is that we, too, rarely distinguish between the nature of such instruments and tools and their conventional forms and uses. Learning the conventions of piano, mathematics, and literacy can, and clearly often does, kill the metaphoric exuberance they should be providing both an outlet for and enhancement of. The piano and mathematics and literacy require discipline and accommodations from the child; their fair return to the child is ecstasy and magic. Ecstasy and magic are the general categories for a set of *bonnes à penser* or sense-making capacities proper to early childhood. The piano and mathematics and literacy have to be presented in such a way that they permit the expression of children's metaphorical exuberance and also enhance and transform that exuberance into new sense-making capacities. What I have tried to do in this chapter is point to the kind of curriculum content that might achieve these aims.

7

A Framework for Primary Teaching

Introduction

Education is rich in discussions of teaching methods. There are many excellent books that distill the practical experience of outstanding teachers, some focused on teaching in general, others on particular subjects. There is no point trying to compete with or add to this valuable literature in a single chapter – even if I could. A difficulty with this literature, however, is in the transference of its practical wisdom. Reading accounts of the most inspiring teaching can energize us, and give us some practical ideas to incorporate into our own teaching. But however much we admire the ideas and descriptions of practice of – to choose more or less at random – a Dorothy Heathcote or Frank Smith, their practical guidance can go only so far. Their influence is unquestionably significant and beneficial, but the inspiration which, one feels, ought to affect all teachers and lead to a gradual and general improvement in pedagogy through the years seems to become dissipated in the profession as a whole.

While some teachers might be interested in the general approach that I have recommended so far, they may also wonder about how one can move from the principles of Mythic understanding discussed in the early chapters to distinctive teaching practices. I have mentioned various appropriate teaching practices during discussion of the curriculum, but it might be more useful here to focus on how we can convert such principles into a framework or technique to aid teaching of whatever subject. The value of moving from general principles to a technique or framework is the provision of an immediate practical tool; the danger is that the limited tool can come to replace the more generally useful and flexible principles.

I will take just a few of the principles discussed earlier to show how one can employ them in practice. I will focus on the story form, and binary opposites here. Following the practice of Ralph Tyler (1949), I will make the framework from a series of questions, the answers to which will give one a lesson or unit plan. I will then demonstrate how the framework might be used in a variety of curriculum areas.

The Teacher as Story-Teller

From the earlier chapter on stories it will be clear that the story form is not a trivial thing meriting attention only if we are discussing fiction. Rather it is a fundamental, perhaps *the* fundamental, intellectual tool that enables us to make sense of the world and of experience. In particular, it seems crucially important in early childhood. So use of the sub-heading "the teacher as story-teller" is intended to draw attention to the main principle to be elaborated in this chapter. The task of the teacher who wants to make lessons and units accessible and meaningful to young children is to learn how to use the main features of the story form in planning and teaching. In passing it might be noted that in a well-wrought story there is room for detailed knowledge and for the use of inference and discovery processes together, so we will not ignore these topics. In general, this framework is designed to encourage teachers to think of a lesson or unit as a good story to be told rather than as a set of objectives to be achieved.

I will begin, then, by sketching a set of questions which can guide our preparation of a unit or lesson:

1.   Identifying importance:
     What is most important about this topic? Why does it matter?

     What is affectively engaging about it?

2.   Finding binary opposites:
     What binary opposites best express and articulate the importance of the topic?

3. Organizing content in story form:
   What content most dramatically articulates the binary opposites, in order to provide access to the topic?

   What content best articulates the topic into a developing story form?

4. Conclusions:
   What is the best way of resolving the dramatic conflict inherent in the binary opposites? What degree of mediation of those opposites is it appropriate to seek?

5. Evaluation:
   How can one know whether the topic has been understood, its importance grasped, and the content learned?

Perhaps the best way to show how this framework can be used is to take a number of examples of units and show how applying it would shape the way they would be taught. Let us say we are going to teach "the story of flight," and "our town/city," and subtraction, and the Greeks' wars against the Persian Empire, and about North American Indians. As an introduction it might be useful to select one of these topics and sketch briefly how its treatment by this framework would make it different from the way it would be taught using the common objectives model. This will allow me also to comment on the framework in the context of an example.

If we take the topic of North American Indians I will briefly indicate how that topic is dealt with and taught in the traditional model, then I will show how it would be taught using this model. What is different throughout is a matter of focus; this should be evident even though actual activities may not seem to differ so greatly.

The dominant procedure requires first that the objectives of the unit be stated. These may include a general aim, such as that children will become familiar with an earlier culture and form of life that prevailed before the white man came. Then, depending on how "behaviorally" oriented the teacher's training, there will be a series of objectives stating what new things the students will know, what skills they will acquire, what "concepts" they will understand, and what they will be able to do at the end of the unit. These are typically arranged under headings of clothing, shelter, food, social structure, and so on. Materials and procedures to be used may then be listed. The teaching may go forward in a variety of ways. Some teachers may use didactic procedures based on standard texts, others will include building a model Indian village, fishing using the old Indian methods, having an Indian address the class about past and present details of the life of his or her tribe, and so on. The evaluation will involve methods of testing how well the objectives were achieved. These evaluative procedures can vary from the "behavioral" to "ethnomethodological" surveys; they will seek to test whether and to what degree children have mastered the appropriate knowledge and skills, can use the requisite "concepts," and whether some evidence of enhanced intercultural understanding can be provided.

In contrast, I am recommending that teachers should approach a unit on North American Indians as a story that is to be told. The first task in such a case is to decide on the most important and profound meaning that is to be conveyed. First, we *identify importance*. We will not be concerned with a story in the sense of following a fictional "Little Talker" or "White Cloud" through a cycle of the annual activities of their tribe – though if written using the principles sketched earlier this could form a part of our unit. Rather we are looking for the story in the sense that a newspaper editor asks "What's the story on this?" What is it that is important about it, and – for our next step of *finding binary opposites* – how is that importance brought out in the clearest and most dramatic way? Any complex content will involve many stories, so we must make choices about which to tell.

These first two procedural steps will usually be taken close together. They direct us to think first about what is truly important about this content. Essentially we are justifying the place of this content in our curriculum. If we cannot identify its importance in terms of profound concepts that are meaningful to young children, then we need go no further. Such content has no place in an early childhood curriculum. The related second step of finding binary opposites directs us to try to see the content through the prominent conceptual forms whereby the child can have clearest access to it.

In the case of our unit on North American Indians, then, we must ask first, what is important about this topic for young children? What are we teaching them? Why does it matter to them? How do we deal with Indians of North America in a manner that engages children affectively? What is important is learning something about what a culture is and why there are different cultures. We cannot deal with all aspects of this, nor provide the complexity of answers anthropologists seek to express. We must focus on a part, but it must be a central and important part of the answer. Our choice will be best expressed in the binary opposites we find in order to articulate our story. Let us, then, take as binary opposites "survival/destruction," and tell our story on those. What we are choosing thereby to teach children about cultures, and about a North American Indian culture in particular, is that they are, as it were, machines designed to maximize chances for survival against the various threats of destruction that face them. This is not, of course, all that is to be said about cultures, but it is important and it will allow us to say much else as well. Also our choice of binary opposites provides us with a principle for the selection of relevant contents. (In cases where the range of content is undetermined, any standard technique, such as concept mapping or webbing, can be used.)

Now we need to set about organizing the content in a story form. There are two parts to this. First is the choice of a particularly vivid example of our binary opposites in order to provide direct access to the heart of what we intend to teach. We must look at the range of content that falls within our topic and consider what can be used most dramatically to show the culture of a particular North American Indian tribe as a struggle for survival against destruction. What aspect of the life of the tribe we are teaching about would vividly exemplify the theme of survival against destruction? We could begin with a dramatic account of Plains Indians hunting; they have taken a food supply that could last for three days and it is the third day. The hunters grow weak, the village waits for fresh meat – what will happen? Or we might dramatize the problems of Cree Indians facing a brutal and late winter, waiting to move south. Our beginning, that is, will be designed to engage children's affective response in a struggle between survival and destruction which they understand profoundly.

The second stage of building the story is the longer activity of building the content onto the binary opposites that provide our story line. Even though the general choice of content might be no different from that made using a more traditional model, its organization and focus will be quite different. Also the abstract

235

story line, stretching between our binary opposites, allows us a much more precise principle for determining exactly what aspects and details should be included and what excluded. The key to telling a good story, as Aristotle tells us in *The Poetics*, is that the incidents should be carefully chosen to body forth the plot in a causal sequence. The worst kind of plot is what he calls "episodic"; by this he means stories in which the incidents follow each other as in a more or less random list. They may all be relevant to the plot, but they are not tied to each other in any clear way that enables the reader or hearer to be engaged by them. It is as if in, say, *The Empire Strikes Back* we were to follow the activities of Yoda for ten minutes before Luke Skywalker arrives on the planet. Interest would wane because the hold of the story line would be loosened. Exactly the same principle is important in designing a unit of study or a lesson. Once it becomes episodic, interest will be loosened, engagement will flat.

Having chosen the basic structure of our story as the binary opposites survival/destruction, we must tie the rest of the content to the structural line that they offer. Thus, when we examine "shelter," we will be concerned to see the particular shelters of our chosen tribes as part of the struggle to survive against the particular threats of destruction that the tribe faces. This will constantly focus our attention on the limits of the protection offered. In the case of shelter, we will focus on each feature that protects against particular threats, and so we will see the form of their shelters as a part of a system determined in part by natural threat. We will thus consider, for example, against how many weeks of what winter temperatures such shelters would protect their inhabitants. The teacher might look up weather reports for the area and see if or how often during the period for which we have records lower temperatures prevailed for longer periods. Similarly when discussing food, our focus will not simply be on what was available at what time of year. The typical account of North American Indian life in textbooks at present suggests a harmonious and rhythmic swing through a mostly leisurely year. Our focus will be on what food supplies were available in the context of what is needed for health and survival. The relatively brief normal life-span of North American Indians needs to be tied in to what was usually an insufficiently varied and inadequate diet. (Though often no less so than for the masses of industrial cities or rural laborers of the same period.) We will again focus on the limits of the food supply to provide for survival. What happened when a particular crop was late or diseased or killed by late or early frosts? How often did such weather conditions prevail?

That is, we choose the content that can be fitted to our binary opposites and which the binary opposites in turn wield into a coherent order. Each element is tied to this basic structural feature and we allow no "episodic" elements that fail to further that particular story line. We do not, that is, decide to include a section on, say, the particular designs they weave into mats or baskets just because that is a part of their culture. If we want to include such a topic, we have to tie it into our story line. Perhaps the designs have religious significance, and represent charms to enhance the contributions the baskets or mats make to the survival of the tribe. Perhaps we will focus on the survival function of the baskets, and show the designs incidentally. If we cannot find a plausible and clear relationship between a topic and our organizing binary opposites, then we should leave it out. It will slacken interest and dissipate the lesson we are teaching. If we cannot attach it to our story line structure but nevertheless think it is important that children should learn it, then we should use different binary opposites to organize our unit, binary opposites that would enable us to include such other topics.

We cannot teach everything about any tribe of Indians in North America. Our choice of binary opposites involves a choice of what to include and what to exclude. But it is a choice that provides a clear principle for making decisions about inclusion and exclusion. The traditional model is somewhat weaker in this regard, in that it provides no such principle. Any things that seem relevant may be included, and there are no strong and clear structural relationships built into the array of content to ensure that it is being made meaningful to children. When each element is tied to the same powerful structure, and that structure is made from binary opposites that are affectively engaging, we have an organizing tool that can add clarity and ease of access to the content.

By using the survival/destruction binary opposites, children will learn both that Indian cultures were systematic, interrelated activities all of which were closely tied into survival techniques in particular environments, and also that, for most tribes most of the time, survival was won often tenuously and at the cost of often brutal and unremitting hardship. This particular important lesson is what is brought to the fore by the choice of the survival/destruction organizers. I am not arguing here that this is the most important or the only way of organizing a unit on North American Indians. It is one useful way, however, because it allows us to deal with much of the content of their lives and focuses attention on something very important to learn about a culture. Cultures are not sets of arbitrary differences in human behavior; they are in large part responses, and elaborations of those responses, to particular threats from nature and from other peoples. If any teacher considers other lessons about Indian life as more important, then he or she may focus on these by choosing different binary opposites. Indeed one could use the survival/destruction organizers for one unit and choose, say, cooperation/competition or adventure/conservation or some other binary opposites to exemplify other aspects of a tribe's life or to compare different tribes. My point, here, is about how one needs to tie all the content of a unit onto a powerful binary organizing structure in order to make it most accessible and engaging and meaningful. To ignore this principle is the educational equivalent of including "episodic" elements, like Yoda wandering around his swamp before Luke Skywalker arrives, in a story. This is not a principle concerned with making things entertaining, but with making them meaningful. To ignore it is to dissipate meaning.

Good stories do not just stop; rather they reach some kind of resolution of the conflict that started them off. Similarly our unit should not simply peter out, but must find some way either to resolve or to move towards mediation of the binary opposites that have provided our story line so far. We can conclude the kind of unit I have sketched here in a number of alternative ways.

One way might be to consider what happened to the Indian tribe(s), whose way of life we have been studying, with the coming of the white man. In so many cases this is unrelievedly tragic. Such historical facts, however, fit precisely and meaningfully into the unit as structured so far. The conclusion, then, is an examination of ways in which the survival techniques of particular Indian cultures were unprepared for, and inadequate to, the threats presented by a rapacious, land-hungry, expansive culture with a developing technology. The cultural defenses broke down in the face of the US cavalry, or because of displacement for cultures that were tied closely to particular environments, or because of diseases against which there was no immunity. In some cases, the conclusion is not so unrelievedly tragic. We may reach mediation in some tribes' persistent attempts to survive and to maintain their culture in alien environments. The particular conclusion in the above cases would depend on the history of the particular tribe. An alternative is to reach a mediation by developing the concept of equilibrium – whether one uses that term or not – between culture and environment. It would be an image of the culture accommodating with more or less success to a somewhat unstable environment. The greater the flexibility of the culture, the more able it is to deal with greater environmental threats and instability.

How does one evaluate a unit such as this? Does our principle provide us also with new forms of evaluation? No, I do not think it does. One might, however, pause to consider how one might evaluate whether *The Return of the Jedi* had been properly "learned," understood, or appreciated. One could ask factual questions, record how well narrative themes were understood, seek clues about how much it was enjoyed. Much of that would be idle because we know that a typical child will successfully *follow* a well-crafted story. What is entailed in *following a story* is the use of a variety of intellectual skills, having a sense of what I called earlier "affective causality," understanding relationships and what underlying concepts were embodied in particular characters, and so on. If the meaning is clear and the content is articulated on binary opposites constantly to expose and elaborate that meaning, we feel fairly confident that children are "getting the message." We really do not worry if a detail of *E.T.* is missed because the whole story carries the more profound message forward consistently. This is to suggest that in a well-crafted unit structured on clear binary opposites we might well be less concerned with elaborate evaluation procedures. We may seek evidence in the process of the unit that children are following the unit, that they see aspects of the Indian culture as parts of a machine against destruction, that they are able to make reasonable judgments about what contributed to survival, and so on. From projects within the unit we can assess areas of comprehension or misunderstanding.

(I should acknowledge a personal quirk here, perhaps due to ignorance of the variety of forms of evaluation and the ways in which some of them can positively contribute to teaching. I tend to think that evaluation procedures should be subservient to teaching and not assume such importance that they affect the organization of the unit or its teaching. If the evaluation procedures, for example, are inadequate to provide precise measures of whether children have followed the story, we do not simplify or dilute or degrade our teaching to the level of available evaluation procedures. If we do this, we have no incentive to make evaluation procedures more sophisticated. If I seem to labor an obscure point here, I should explicitly note that one of the constant dangers in eduction seems to be the replacement of ends by means. The means of using certain evaluation procedures to measure the results of teaching, has led in the case of the behavioral objectives and "effective" teaching movements, among others, to the evaluation procedures requiring particular forms of objectives which in turn affect the method of teaching. This is a case of the tail wagging the dog. The more clear is our teaching, the less complex is the task of evaluation. We must recognize that procedures for evaluating learning are, at the moment, vastly more crude than learning itself. We should be ever aware, then, that we will get only the vaguest evaluation of the most important things children can learn, and we should be wary of the temptation to make learning cruder so that we can measure it more securely.)

Identifying Importance and Choosing Binary Opposites

What is important about the story of flight? We need to provide an answer in terms that are meaningful to children. Parts of an appropriate answer might touch on the "outward urge," the drive to do the impossible, the desire to imitate the grace and freedom of birds. How can we capture this in terms of affectively meaningful binary opposites? We may pose the courage, ingenuity, and sense of romance of those who wish to fly in opposition to the conventional refusal to believe that anything other than what is the case is really possible. We might abbreviate this as a conflict between the practical visionary vs. the conventionalist, which is a concretization of the affective pair courage/fear. Children know courage and fear from their earliest experience; by teaching them about Daedalus, Leonardo, the Wrights, Goddard, and so on, in terms of these binary opposites we both provide them with access to the topic and use the topic to refine and elaborate their "concepts" of courage and fear.

What is important about "our town/city" for young children, and how might that be organized on binary opposites? I argued in the previous chapter against topics such as this in the primary curriculum, but I will include it here because teachers in North America and Australia at present are required to teach such unit, and I have also argued that these principles can serve to make any content more meaningful and accessible. I argued for it exclusion from the curriculum on the grounds of the limited sense of the topic that can be conveyed to children. What is important about it, then, includes the idea of a community mutually supportive even while pursuing individuals self-interest. It includes protection and security, and the facts of change and growth and decay. One might decide to present the unit as an extended metaphor, in which the town or city is seen more as an organism than as a machine. As an organism it needs food to grow, which it sucks in through its roads; it eats the surrounding land as it spreads, etc. We might consider as useful binary opposites a town vs. country pairing, which in turn may be presented as a concretization of a dominance/submission pair. In the next section I will discuss how this can allow us to organize significant content.

And subtraction? What is important about subtraction is its ingenuity in simplifying certain counting procedures. Instead of having to re-count from the beginning to discover quantities, subtraction allows us to count backwards by the amount taken away. This saves time and tedium. We will want to convey something of the ingenuity and magic of subtraction, so we might choose the common binary opposites of ingenuity/conventional dullness.

If we ask what is important about the struggle between the Greek city-states and the Persian Empire we can, again, find many answers. We need to make choices, which will highlight some events and personalities at the expense of others. What is important in terms of the fundamental concepts children already have available? Perhaps most easily identified is the struggle between small independent city-states intent on organizing their *poleis* the way they chose and the massive, tyrannous Persian Empire that was intent on destroying their independence. This can be expressed in terms of the binary opposites freedom vs. tyranny. Children by age five know about freedom and tyranny from the experiences in which they are free to pursue something they want, and those experiences in which they have been prevented by parents, siblings or peers from pursuing what they see as some legitimate aim. If they learn about the Greek struggle against the Persian Empire in those terms they will have access to the content and be able to use the content to elaborate and refine their concepts of freedom and oppression. (In teaching, of course, it may often be useful to make such connections between their experience and Athens's experience explicit.)

Organizing the Content into a Story Form

The first part of organizing the content of our unit is to choose an event or an example that brings the binary opposites into most vivid and dramatic focus. The binary opposites are our main structural prop, and children's most clear access to meaning, so we will want to begin by setting them in place as firmly as possible. In the case of the unit on the story of flight we will look through the range of content we want to include in the unit, searching for something that is central to it and most vividly exemplifies the conflict between the practical visionary and the conventionalists. The story of flight is a long one, rich in such examples. One might choose the journalistic account, simply and clearly written, of the Wright brothers' first flight in Europe. We see the French peasants and villagers gathered around the field laughing at the craziness of what has been promised, listening to the banging and clanking coming from inside the barn in which the plane is being readied. Then the howls of derisive hilarity as it is wheeled out; the calmness of the Wright brothers; the shouts as one climbs into the cockpit; the continuing laughter as the plane clumsily jolts down the field and gathers speed; and the sudden silent awe as the lumbering wire and metal and wood leaves the ground and becomes as graceful as any bird turning and wheeling in the sky above them. What is selected to start the unit is the most precise instance of the binary opposites that will carry the meaning forward.

In constructing the rest of the unit one must use these binary opposites in selecting what content is best able to tell *this* story of flight. (There could be many other ways of telling it, many other meanings that could be developed. We must select one, and having selected it, we must be consistent in order to be clear. This does not, as I will argue below, commit us to indoctrinating or oversimplifying.) Thus, when we look at the achievements towards human flight that will form our unit, we should focus on the combination of practical skill and visionary insight together and contrast the instances of these with the derision of the conventionally minded who can imagine nothing other than the conditions with which they are familiar. For the story of flight this is not very difficult.

Our units on "our town/city" may be organized on a dominance/submission theme. The town or city began as a small, peaceful and quiet "organism" and has gradually grown and become increasingly a monster devouring the country – eating it up in its expansion, tearing it apart for metals and chemicals that it wants to feed its factories, which in turn belch their smoke across the land. And so on. The country has been cowed and enslaved by the city. We might best begin this unit, whose organizing structure is, as are they all, very abstract, with a local example. Teachers might search their local newspapers for a particular case in which the needs of the town or city are having a particular impact on the more or less distant countryside. Such cases should not be hard to find. The unit can then begin by laying out the particulars of the case *in terms* of the binary opposites of dominance/submission.

Once such a case is clearly presented, the rest of the content of the unit may be tied to the same binary theme. This will mean, again, that the selection of content will be to some degree determined by what best fits that theme. And this means that much content will be omitted. We cannot teach everything, of course, and what this principle provides us with is not simply a tool for selecting centrally important content but for selecting only that content that we can be sure to make meaningful. Our dominating city can, of course, be presented as a benign monster if desired. But the content of the unit will focus on ways in which the countryside is made to serve the expanding needs of towns and cities – given this choice of binary opposites. (Other binary pairs, to say it again, could be chosen to bring other aspects of "our town/city" into focus.)

In the case of subtraction, we might begin with a story that shows the value of subtraction and indicates something of its magic and ingenuity. We can set it long ago, during the days of Dilmun or the Sumerian Empire, when trade was developing from north-west India around Arabia, touching Egypt and the Levant. We can exemplify ingenuity in a young girl who worked on board one of her father's trading ships. The ship carried stocks of wheat, wine, cedar logs, figs, and whatever else needed taking from one centre of trade to another. Her job was to keep a count of what was on board and what was off-loaded at each port of call. Conventional dullness can be exemplified through her overseer – a pompous manager of her father's business. He taught her to count and how to keep track of all the goods.

When they stopped she was to count out the goods to be off-loaded. She then had to count up the remaining quantities. So if they had 320 sheafs of wheat and they off-loaded 20 at Sidon, as soon as they put to sea, she had to count up to discover that there were 300 still on board. And was kept at it by the pompous oversee. She spent a great deal of her time tediously counting. Using her ingenuity, however, at Tyre, the next port of call, she counted off the 3 barrels of figs as they were carried along the gang plank. When they set off to sea again, instead of counting the remaining barrels, she counted backwards from the 26 there had been before they landed at Tyre. Counting 3 backwards from 26 she concluded that there must be 23 barrels remaining. She invented subtraction, and discomforted the overseer who could not understand why she was spending so little time counting nor how she was, even so, always right in knowing what quantities of goods were on board.

From this illustration of the underlying principle one can move to other examples of the practical value of subtraction. As for many aspects of mathematics, I would turn for help in encouraging a first practical grasp on the mechanics to that other form which embodies structural features similar to those of the story – the game. As in the teaching of most basic mathematical functions, I would seek out games in which the function to be learned will be picked up incidentally in learning the game. For subtraction one might begin with some simple card games which involve a hand of three to seven cards, and involve giving up, or putting down, one to three cards. After the game(s) have been explained, children can be left in groups so that the slower learners will be taught by the others. Dice games can follow, involving addition and subtraction. Scoring games can also be introduced, in which penalties and successes require simple calculations. Such games need not take up a lot of time. Even the slowest learners seem able to pick such games up quite quickly in the context of playing them with their peers.

To begin the unit on the Greek struggle with the Persian Empire we need to select an event that best exemplifies the binary opposites on which we are going to build. We might choose the battle at Thermopylae, where a small band of Greeks held the mighty Persian army at bay while the Greek armies behind them managed to organize themselves to face the onslaught to come. The ingenuity and courage of the small Greek contingent ready to die for their independence is dramatically set against the lumbering brutal giant, which eventually, when wave after wave of its finest soldiers are beaten back by the small band of Greeks, defeats them only by trickery.

Though Thermopylae is not the chronological starting place for an account of Greeks vs. Persians, it is a good causal starting place, not causal in a precise logical sense but causal, rather, in an *affective* sense. The characteristics of courage and ingenuity and love of independence are the causes of Greek success against the Persians. By setting this out most clearly at the beginning one sets up the basic structure and means of access to its content.

The binary opposites then serve to select what content carries the unit forward. We may follow a roughly chronological narrative hereafter but the focus will be always on actions, characters, etc., that best exemplify the binary conflict set up by our beginning at Thermopylae.

Unit Conclusions

To conclude our units we need to seek some kind of resolution of the conflict which the use of binary opposites typically sets up. In some cases we will want to note the clarity and appropriateness of the binary conflict in some example or conclusion of the unit, in other cases our conclusion might more appropriately move towards a mediation between the binary opposites.

In the case of the story of flight we might find examples of the continuing conflict between practical visionaries who foresee colonies in satellites around this and other planets, the restructuring and settlement of Mars, as presented by Carl Sagan, and those conservative elements whose imagination cannot see such things as possible and so will do nothing towards realizing them. Alternatively, or additionally, we might conclude such a unit with mediating examples of impractical visionaries whose crazy ideas have led to waste and failure, in order to stress the values of conservative responses to visionary suggestions.

In concluding the unit on "our town/city" we may choose either to represent the monstrous city as the despoiler of the country, or, perhaps better, to focus on those signs that in the future cities will likely be smaller, that there will be a more harmonious balance between the city and the country, that the days of massive industries focusing populations in centers of supplies is being countered by the microchip and high-tech industries which allow a dispersal of cooperating groups of people.

For the conclusion to the lessons on subtraction we will want to ensure that the principle highlighted in the story and the practices grasped in the context of the games is also understood at the utilitarian level of abstract calculation. This need not involve endless practice at the usual kinds of "sums," but neither should we shy away from ensuring that children can routinely do these. The more simple subtraction calculations can be helped along by some old-fashioned chanting: A harmonious "Nine take away six is three" can be a lot of fun, can involve some instruction in music, and can help to build up a sense of the rhythms whose grasp makes mathematics almost a somatic, intuitive activity.

Our choice of binary opposites focuses our attention on certain aspects of a topic and certain content at the expense of other aspects and content that we might otherwise have considered. It is, that is to say, a way of selecting and limiting and structuring material. But it is a selecting and limiting that focuses on what is most important in the material. Similarly with our choice of conclusion, we highlight some aspects and content at the expense of others. In concluding the unit on the Greeks vs. the Persians we may choose to present an Herodotean image of a victorious free Athens, representing the best of the Greek spirit, and a defeated scattered Persian army, with a final glance forward to Alexander as "fire from heaven" leading the Greeks through the tatters of the Persian Empire. Alternatively we may move a step towards mediation, seeing in the results of Marathon and Salamis the creation in Athens of an empire that inherited some of the less desirable characteristics of the empire it defeated. Other choices are of course possible, and our choice will turn on the age of the children, their stage of educational development, and the lessons we consider valuable for them. Nether one is right or wrong; they are different, legitimate ways of seeing what happened. (Constraints on such choices, and so the content of each unit, are those discussed in the previous chapter. This is not an assertion that "anything goes.")

Evaluation

How does one know after the conclusion of the unit that the theme has been understood and that the content has been grasped as relevantly articulating that theme? Some clues can be gained from traditional kinds of evaluation instruments – which could be informal questions whose answers require that children have learned the basic facts and understand their relationship to the main theme. So the regular kinds of evaluation that go on in schools are appropriate for such units no more nor less than for other units. What one might particularly focus on given this framework is something written, dramatized, drawn, that gives evidence of the affective effect of the unit while drawing on supporting knowledge, skills, and so on. One would request activities illustrative of the topic that would indicate understanding of the material while also making the teacher's intentions and the meaning of the unit more explicit.

Objections to the Use of Binary Opposites

Using binary opposites like good/bad, brave/cowardly, dominance/submission, freedom/tyranny is to teach children that, say, the Persians were bad and tyrannous and the Greeks were good and freedom-loving. This is to falsify the nature of things and lead children to stereotype and crudely categorize groups of people and events. It is a principle that disguises the proper complexity of the world; things are not simply good or bad and the use of binary opposites encourages children to see the world in black and white terms all the time.

What would one say about the fairy stories of the world? The characters are composed of one or two characteristics – poor and brave, rich and mean, strong and stupid, beautiful and wicked – and are either good or bad. But the Greeks and the Persians are history not fairy stories. Why, though, are children so engaged by such fairy stories when, typically, they can make neither head nor tail of a watered-down scholarly account of the struggle between the Greeks and the Persians?

First, I would argue that the proper use of binary opposites requires that we simplify content not that we falsify it. To see the Greeks as brave and ready to die for their freedom to lead their lives the way they wanted and the Persians as a tyrannous empire determined to crush the spirit of freedom which was causing so many political and administrative headaches, and more, in the western parts of the empire is not to falsify, but to simplify. That we select content, and structure it in such a way that we approve of those who fought for their freedom and disapprove of those who tried to end that freedom, is the condition of making the endless complexity of events meaningful to children. Nor is this different in kind from what the most austere historian does. Despite Ranke, it is recognized that the historian cannot record *wie es eigentlich gewesen war*. Exactly what happened, the past reality, cannot be expressed in words. The most austere historian constructs events and selects and organizes them in a narrative which carries affective import beyond the mere fact themselves. The objection to using binary opposites because they carry affective associations is to contrast them with a quite unreal image of what the historian, or any other scholar in the humanities, does. The difference, then, is not one of kind but of degree.

Second, we might note that we constantly use binary opposites to orient ourselves to events and people. When we hear about a particular event our initial response tends to be to say "That's terrible!" or "That's wonderful!"; we begin with the extreme, with the simplified contrast, and then gradually refine it. This process is evident in various forms perhaps a dozen times as we read through the newspaper, from the political news, the sensational events, economic developments, and so on. If we read that there has been fighting in, say, an African state, we first want to know whether the rebels are supplied by the Russians and have Cuban advisors, or are receiving aid from the US administration. We grasp first the information that allows us to fit the event into our binary scheme of good/bad, and then we can refine our responses. So recommending the use of binary opposites to provide initial access to new knowledge is not to suggest something at all odd or unusual.

A third response is to point out that binary opposites are a condition of making complex content accessible to young children. The process of education is one of grasping onto content and making it more complex, sophisticated, and elaborate, attempting to make understanding more nearly mirror the complexity of ineffable reality. We cannot meaningfully begin with complexity. What I have tried to sketch is an outline of a common and useful way of first making contact with knowledge and then elaborating it. It seems pointless to object to the form of the first contact because it is not the same as the most sophisticated achievement. If it could be argued that the form of the first contact prevented movement in the direction of the most sophisticated achievement, then that would be a powerful objection to using binary opposites. Not only does this not seem to happen, however, but, indeed, the use of binary opposites should develop through sequences of mediations towards just the kind of complexity that we find in the best scholarly work. (This in turn is not to argue that we induce children to see the world in terms of binary opposites in order to make little scholars out of them, but simply to point out that there is no inconsistency between starting in this way and making sense of experience in the most sophisticated ways we know.)

I should perhaps point out also that I am not advocating the teaching of binary opposites. When teaching a unit such as that on the Greeks and Persians, the aim is not to teach children about freedom and tyranny. We *use* those underlying concepts to organize the content and to give access to it. The whole point is that we can be sure that young children already have in some form the concepts of freedom and tyranny even if they do not know the words. What we do achieve by teaching about the Greeks and the Persians is an elaboration of their concepts of freedom and tyranny. They begin to see the world in terms of the concepts that make sense of their own experience. By using those concepts to teach them about the distant world we provide them with more elaborate tools to make sense of their own experience. (And we do this without having to teach eviscerated units on "my family," "my neighborhood," etc. Children who are not permitted by the teacher or by the ethos of the classroom to declare – even to themselves – that they hate their father or uncle or mother because they are always bullying, can readily associate with the brave Greeks struggling for independence against the bullying Persians, and see thereby that they are profoundly a part of the world. Children taught this way will never ask what relevance the ancient Greeks have to them.)

The relatively recent study of children's thinking has provided us with a clearer image of childhood as an alien place. The old assumption that children's thinking is no different from adults' except in that children know less has been profoundly challenged. What has emerged in its place in some quarters at least is what is probably an equally extreme assumption about children's thinking being quite different in kind from adults'. Piaget has encouraged this view in stressing the qualitatively different changes in thinking as children mature. It is always useful to remember that Piaget has focused almost exclusively on a small range of logico-mathematical intellectual skills, and that he has not dealt with the huge range of other abilities that are found in human thinking. We might reasonably conclude that there are significant differences between typical children's and adults' thinking but that childhood does not for that reason become for adults an alien place about which we have only hints and guesses. While there are indeed differences, there are also continuities between children's and adults' thinking. The kinds of thinking I have been focusing on here, while they too may go through qualitative shifts as we grow older, are not the kinds of things which are left behind as we go from layer to layer. We add to them, elaborate them, but we do not leave them behind. Thus the most sophisticated historians writing about the Greeks and the Persians do not leave behind a basic orienting use of binary opposite concepts such as freedom and tyranny. They do not give such concepts as much prominence in their texts as the young child would and they will not gather to the one pole all things Greek and to the other all things Persian, but even so we find them there as structural elements of the meaning conveyed by the narratives.

It must be apparent, of course, that the kinds of topics most adequately organizable according to the principles in this chapter are precisely those that make up my curriculum in the previous chapter. So my response to this objection begins with a reiteration of the arguments in support of the curriculum laid out in Chapter Six.

In addition I argue that, binary opposites being keys to accessible meaning for young children, we should select the bulk of an early childhood curriculum in terms of what they can best organize. They point us towards particular kinds of meaning. One value of this at present, I think, is to remind us that the curriculum for young children should be rich in meaning and not a dessicated training in limited skills.

Conclusion

I have focused in this chapter on the organization of units. I should mention that the organization of each lesson within a unit could employ the same principles. It could begin with a vivid example of the binary opposites, elaborate them with content selected to best fit them and conclude with some resolution or mediation of them. This principle is evident in typical soap-operas, where each episode reflects in small scale the story-structure of the entire series. The challenge for each episode of the soap-opera is to keep the viewer engaged and to carry forward the general story. Similarly, the teacher has to use each lesson as an integral part of the unit. To take a lesson to introduce content that cannot be fitted to the theme selected by one's choice of binary opposites is akin to introducing an episode in the soap-opera that is peripheral to the overall story. Interest is lessened because the *meaning* is being gradually dissipated.

I should perhaps conclude by noting that what I am recommending here is a systematization of principles that I observe in good teachers' teaching. They instinctively shape material into a story form as they teach. I am proposing here a framework which should allow us routinely to organize curriculum material for maximum meaningfulness; one which will perhaps assist those instinctively good teachers more consciously and clearly to see how they might further add to the communicative power of their teaching. It is a framework which might be of more value to those intending to be teachers, to allow them routinely to use principles that should enhance the success of their lessons and units.

Initially, organizing units and lessons by these principles may seem quite hard. It is easier to list objectives and line up the content according to some logical principle. These principles require a careful reflection on the whole unit and, as it were, a shaking of it to and fro till it exposes it most basic organizing structure. Of course no one will be able to sustain tight organization all the time, and of course much school work will remain tedious. But use of these principles should ensure that we will be able to show children more frequently why the tedium and work is worthwhile, why learning about flight and the Greeks and subtraction matter, that meaning is there, is real, and is accessible to them.

By occasionally contrasting this framework with the common "objectives" models, I am in danger of suggesting that these represent unmediated binary opposites. Of course I do not mean this, and of course the "objectives" models are significant contributions to teaching. Nor do I want to seem to be suggesting that this framework should be applied, Procrusteanly, to any and all teaching. Rather, it is offered as a way of implementing some of the principles discussed earlier in this book. Describing the framework tends to make it seem a complicated and lumbering piece of machinery. I have put it into a tight form to indicate how the kinds of principles discussed earlier can be used in daily practice. I hope any teachers who consider the framework will adapt it flexibly in ways that make most sense to them.

Conclusion

Education is being characterized here as the process wherein the individual recapitulates the accumulation or development of the sense-making capacities invented and discovered in our cultural history. "Sense-making capacities" are a product of knowledge accumulation and psychological development working together along with a generative element, which may be a product of their joint working or may involve something independent. Cultural history can enlighten our study of education because we can see in it the effects of these forces in shaping the sequence in which sense-making capacities have been and can be generated.

The US space shuttle was possible only after the invention of the vacuum flask, the machine gun similarly required the clock, the representational style of Leonardo required the technical developments of Giotto, the historiography of Thucydides required the forms articulated by Herodotus, Boolean algebra required Pythagorean harmonies, and so on. The causal sequences in these processes are complex and very difficult for us to pin down, but the sequences are not arbitrary or accidental; Thucydides' history could not have preceded Herodotus', nor could Leonardo's style have preceded Giotto's, nor the space shuttle the vacuum flask. In writing histories of technology, or painting, or various forms of inquiry, we try to pin-point necessary prerequisites of later developments and locate the causal dynamic. In some cases, such as mathematics, we tend to rely on a sense of an unfolding logic in the subject, in others, such as technology, we find a logic in the sequence of inventions tied in with social purposes and occasional psychological quirks of inventors, in cases like historiography and the arts, the logical element tends to take a subsidiary place to social environments and the psychological make-up of the writers and artists. In the sciences it is claimed that if Darwin or Rutherford or Einstein had not made the discoveries associated with their names someone else very soon after would have. In the arts if Leonardo or Beethoven or Joyce had not produced the works they did no equivalents would have appeared. There is considerable opaqueness about causal dynamics in cultural history but what is evident is the effects of these shaping dynamic forces; regardless of our ignorance about causes and our imprecision in defining the constituents of these dynamic forces, we can see and describe the sequences in which they permit the sense-making capacities that constitute our culture to develop. These same forces – logical, psychological, and generative – constrain the sequence in which any individual may develop the sense-making capacities available in our culture; the logic of subjects does not let up, nor is the human psyche released from its bounds.

It has long been obvious that education involves in some fashion a recapitulation of cultural history, but it has not been clear how we could find a basis for describing whatever may be common to the two processes nor how we could locate a dynamic that would point up some causal sequence that they share. The bifurcated ramifications of Plato's and Rousseau's insights have encouraged in the study of education separate focuses on knowledge accumulation and on psychological development, assuming that separate advances from philosophical and psychological research will somehow be brought together. Clearly recapitulation does not make much sense in terms of knowledge accumulation or psychological development separately. Even if it were possible, there is no good reason to recommend that the child should recapitulate the accumulation of knowledge as it was invented or discovered in history. How, for example, would one teach geography or history in such a scheme? Similarly, any scheme that sees the individual as recapitulating an historical process of psychological development faces the bizarre need to characterize Euripides and Plato as somehow psychological equivalents of modern children. What I am trying to do in this essay is describe, in terms of sense-making capacities, what cultural history and education share, and so what the latter recapitulates of the former, and locate, if only imprecisely, the dynamic that points up the causal sequence that they have in common. The focus on sense-making capacities enables us to bring concerns with knowledge accumulation coherently together with psychological development and it allows us to transcend the Platonic and Rousseauian, the traditionalist and progressivist conflicts by designing a curriculum that stimulates the ripening of childhood in the child while putting in place the foundations for later layers of education.

The category of "sense-making capacities" is intended to bring together what we have been accustomed to think of as appropriately distinct, or at least as meaningfully distinguishable. The distinct studies of epistemology and psychology have had difficulty coming together in education, I have argued, because we cannot give an adequate account of how they are to interact. Clearly accumulating knowledge and psychological development, if considered separately, have to interact in the process of education. One problem this creates is where the dynamic of the educational process lies. Does accumulating knowledge drive psychological development, or does psychological development drive accumulating knowledge? Or, in terms of the Piagetian/Vygotskian dispute, does learning drive development or development learning? Perhaps they drive each other, dialectically? This last is a convenient but unfortunately vacuous solution, in that it fails to deal with the problem at all. A similar dilemma appears in education when "learning" is separated from what is to be learned. The content to be learned is left to the philosophers or curriculum specialists while "the process of learning" is investigated separately. Again these separate forms of inquiry have not been brought together with any notable success. Once we are engaged with the practical task of helping children to understand mathematics or Chinese or history the promise learning theories offer to enlighten "processes" of learning vanishes away. My argument has been that one cannot meaningfully separate minds and knowledge, "processes" and "content." The category of "sense-making" resists being artificially broken apart; we are not inclined to look for abstract processes of sense-making distinct from what is being made sense of. Nor are we inclined to consider accumulating knowledge apart from the psychological uses it is put to. If we think of education in terms of increasingly elaborate sense-making we will contain the insights that education requires accumulating knowledge on the other hand and requires psychological development on the other; we will transcend the artificial problem of their interaction generated by holding those two separate; and we will avoid the *impasses* into which identifying the dynamic of education in either one or the other runs.

The use of "sense-making capacities" is not itself an ideal term, of course. For one thing, "capacities" suggests some abstract structures of mind or something that can be distinct from particular knowledge. Similarly "techniques of thinking," a phrase I have used occasionally, carries a similar implication of a distinction between abstract techniques and what is thought about. The trouble is that the language we have available has been generated presupposing the value of the distinctions I am suggesting are educationally dysfunctional. And for reasons similar to my resorting to "*bonnes à penser*" previously, I prefer it here again. "Good things to think with" catches both the knowledge and psychological components we need to keep together. If the accumulation of knowledge goes forward with too little concern for psychological development we get, in Michel de Montaigne's rude phrase, "asses loaded with books"; if psychological development is pursued with too little concern for the accumulation of knowledge we get skilled, cheerful, confident ignoramuses.

The area of study that this scheme finds most useful for education, then, is cultural history. Rather less, it follows, should be expected from the presently dominant research traditions, concerned with knowledge and with psychological processes, than their considerable scale seems to promise. Education seems unlikely to be improved by some dramatic new findings about children or learning, development, motivation, or about the nature of knowledge. Education seems likely to benefit more, to echo Wittgenstein, not by getting new information but by rearranging what we have known all along. The sense-making capacities this scheme focuses on were not generated, to use Walter Ong's nice phrase, "in the hollow of men's minds but in the density of history" (Ong, 1971, p. 7). Similarly their recapitulation by children is not a matter of learning abstract "thinking skills" but of making sense of their social and cultural circumstances in the density of their history and of their experience.

I have perhaps dwelt a little too much on oral cultures and the oral foundations of our forms of knowledge for some people's taste. It has seemed useful as a means of emphasizing the central point that rationality, if it is to develop richly, must keep in contact with its oral foundations. Our sophisticated forms of rationality are not the result of "breaking away" from myth and from the forms of thought most evident in oral cultures; the result of breaking away is dessication, sterility, and inhuman(e), technocratic, directionless thinking. Mythic understanding is, I have argued, a foundational constituent of any rich rationality; it is the connection of thinking to life and to our hopes, fears, purposes, and so on. A well-developed Mythic understanding is our grounding. Only if we remain well-grounded can our thinking – Anteus-like – grow strong and effective. To "break away" from these oral foundations leads to the pathological autisms of thought that are unfortunately common in our society. Perhaps the kind of technocratic thinking that invades social and political policy-making and loses sight of the varied purposes of human societies is a common example of such autism (Wilson, 1979).

We see symptoms of this autism in the common and casual use of industrial and technological analogies for educational processes. Use of these analogies inclines their users to think of education in terms of industrial or technological processes and consequently to deform education to fit the categories given by the analogies. Builders of clockwork oranges continue to thrive in education. The hope for a positivist science of society that would guide the social engineer, the felicific calculator, in making precise interventions to produce precise and specifiable outcomes, has faded for society at large. But the school, with its relatively distinct social existence and its relatively distinct social purposes, seems to provide a haven for exotic forms of positivism. A common symptom of positivistic autism is the ability to calculate but not to evaluate, and so the reduction of values to units. We see this in movements associated with such terms as "systems management," "behavioral objectives," "effective teaching" and in other movements which attempt to engineer education to more precisely planned and efficient productivity. Their common feature is the call for more technical precision within the system that can be formulated about the system. (As in, for example, the call for precise educational objectives when only an imprecise conception of education is available.) This has the effect of reducing, as it were, a three-dimensional process to two dimensions. It is hard to tell the difference only if one insists on standing dead still with one eye closed. (These reductive movements have been adequately criticized elsewhere (e.g. Apple, 1979; Callahan, 1962; Pring, 1973; Stenhouse, 1975.)

This essay obviously runs aslant these prominent, reductive movements in education. The insistence on a "poetic" component for any adequate conception of rationality and as a foundational constituent to all areas of rational inquiry is a crucial distinguishing feature of this educational scheme. An image that has cropped up a few times in previous chapters is that of the Homeric poet. I think this is appropriate, as it catches something significant about the conception of primary education sketched here. Homeric poets did not learn their traditional songs as though they were fixed texts, nor did they strive for radical novelty. Rather they learned the underlying rhythms and meters of their tradition and its great stories, and in retelling those they shaped them to their own voice. That is, they constantly recreated or reconstructed their tradition in the process of carrying it on. If we think of the primary school curriculum as the great stories of our culture and our underlying rhythm and constant meter as the disciplined struggle to discover and tell the truth about the world and experience, and we treat children as novice poets who will learn to sing our great stories in their own voices, we have a useful image of one general feature of primary education. In recapitulating a culture in this sense, then, children are not to be expected to "internalize" *the* culture, as a body of fixed knowledge, set criteria for aesthetic appreciation, moral rules, and so on. The child is not to be *initiated* into the culture, so much as taught to recreate it.[1]

The skilled poet in the Homeric tradition is a master of techniques. My use of the image of the poet is not to set up a contrast between the technician or technologist and the poet. Rather it is to stress that an adequate conception of a technician must involve a poetic component, and indeed an adequate conception of a poet must involve a technical component. I have suggested that literacy and rationality can be achieved in a formal, dessicated sense, and that they can be socially and individually destructive if their development comes at the expense of the poet within us. Vico observed that culturally we began as poets. My recapitulation thesis leads to the conclusion that individually we begin as poets, too, and that the first layer of the educational process should be primarily concerned with evoking, stimulating, and developing poetic techniques. These vivify the imagination, stimulate metaphoric fluency, and expand sensitivity and sympathy. The further layers of education must not displace these, rather they coalesce a range of other *bonnes à penser* with them. Our poetic beginnings inform our educational ends.

I recognize that this kind of scheme of primary education will seem odd to some people, but it seems to me more a matter of redressing an imbalance – and, I hope, redressing it in a way that does not simply tip the balance over in an opposite direction. Most state primary education systems seem imbalanced in the degrees of emphasis they place on reproducing the formal conventions of a restricted literacy and rationality, sometimes referred to as "basic skills." Many of the romantic opponents of these systems seem imbalanced in the degree to which they neglect mastery of techniques. This scheme is an attempt to bring together the insights of both positions, to show that the best and fullest development of "skills" and techniques comes through the development of the "poet" in each child.

What I perceive as an imbalance is not simply restricted to education, however. The education system, rather, mirrors certain pervasive trends of thought in society at large. I am hardly the first to reflect on the persistent dominance of what are commonly called technical–rational patterns of thought in social and political affairs. They are technical–rational in the restricted sense discussed earlier, and have tended to be aggressively promoted with very great optimism: an optimism increasingly difficult to sustain. Their limitations are better explored by others (e.g. Simon, 1983), but their general influence on the social consensus concerning the nature and functions of education is my concern in this book.

The dogma that schools cannot change society can be sustained only if one does not bother to analyse it. Schools are not separate from society; they are not wholly distinct institutions. A recommendation from a curriculum committee made up of teachers, professors, and industrialists may affect the school and in turn the revised curriculum may have results that will affect society. Who is changing whom? A recommendation that we quite radically change the curriculum to increase "poetic" productivity is obviously not without its social, and ideological, implications. What happens to social institutions that tend to be calculative and narrowly technical–rational when they are invaded by more imaginative agents? Would we run into conflicts with present assumed goals and images of our nation if members of society are increasingly hospitable to imagination and increasingly hesitant about their, and their society's, claims to rectitude and certainty? While it is easy to *try* to stimulate more imaginative development in young children, it is not clear at all what the social consequences of more imagination in politics, business, bureaucracies, shops, social services, and so on, might be.

These kinds of speculations are obviously a bit starry-eyed, and indulgent, and they assume that the primary school educational scheme sketched here can be adequately elaborated into a full curriculum which will be effective in achieving its aims. But, those considerations aside, it is worth, however briefly, speculating on the impact of more imagination on our social and political institutions. I clearly believe that more "poetry" – more imagination, metaphoric fluency, evaluative sensitivity, and so on – would be socially beneficial. In part this is because I tend to believe that much that is socially and politically destructive can be traced to the lack of these qualities. This is not the place to pursue this more general discussion of society and politics, but I raise it because the kind of education this scheme recommends runs aslant some prominent forms of thought embedded in current social conventions. The educational foundation set in place in this scheme is designed to produce poets with a sense of humor who are fluent in the basic techniques of rationality and knowledgeable about the great stories that constitute their cultural tradition. If we are, by some wonderful chance, successful in educating more people in this direction, then we should be prepared for the consequences.

I have not written much about the losses that go with evoking, stimulating, and developing this Mythic layer of understanding. In part this is because the foundational layer does not threaten to displace a previous form of understanding; though I have referred to the loss of an initial sense of participation in nature that is disrupted by the internalization of language, and the development of the *bonnes à penser* that elaborate the possibilities of oral language. Naming things in classes and categories seems to entail effects on our thinking about things that leads to an objectification of them; it begins to set them off from the living world which we inhabit. "It is a chair" takes something of the individuality away from each chair. The other part of my reason for saying little about the losses entailed by the educational developments during this layer is simply that I remain somewhat ambivalent about the degree to which losses are necessary or contingent. This will come to more focused discussion in the next volume with the internalization of literacy and literal thinking. What seems obvious is that oral *bonnes à penser* are quite commonly ill-developed in schools, and some are positively discouraged or repressed in the drive to induce "basic skills." Metaphoric quickness, imaginative elaboration are seen too often as frills rather than as true bases of education.

So in present practice at least the mastery of literacy does commonly seem to involve losses of oral *bonnes à penser*. The potential developments stimulated by the oral culture of school yard and city street commonly become stifled under the conventional forms of a dessicated literacy. But at the same time one sees what looks like a persistence, not only of oral *bonnes à penser*, but of that vivid sense of participation in nature in many adults. A writer like Richard Jefferies, for example, seems to have seen the natural world as though it had all been freshly made each day for him. My concern is to preserve as fully as possible all the *bonnes à penser* we can develop, all the ways of making sense our culture allows. Perhaps we need to give up very little if we are careful.

Education can be described, like our cultural history and perhaps like the development of life on the planet, as a kind of evolutionary process punctuated with revolutions. Remaining alert to the ideological trouble our metaphors can run us into, I will go on in the next volume to the revolutionary change that can be brought about around age seven or eight by evoking, stimulating, and developing the *bonnes à penser* of Romantic understanding.

Notes

Series editor's introduction

1   Fred Inglis, *The Management of Ignorance: A Political Theory of the Curriculum* (New York and London: Basil Blackwell, 1985), p. 23.
2   These issues are discussed in greater detail in Michael W. Apple, *Ideology and Curriculum* (New York and London: Routledge and Kegan Paul, 1979).
3   Michael W. Apple, *Teachers and Texts: A Political Economy of Class and Gender Relations in Education* (New York and London: Routledge and Kegan Paul, 1986) and Michael W. Apple, *Education and Power* (New York and London: Routledge and Kegan Paul, ARK Edition, 1985).
7   In some ways this is similar to William Walsh's earlier work *The Use of Imagination: Educational Thought and the Literary Mind* (New York: Barnes and Noble, 1959).
5   Inglis, *The Management of Ignorance*, p. 167.
6   See Marcus Raskin, *The Common Good* (New York and London: Routledge and Kegan Paul, 1986).

1   Some educational implications of children's fantasy

1   It is perhaps not simply coincidental that we note, as though to compensate for excessively Apollonian schooling "how exceptionally intense is the Victorian need for fantasy and play like that in *Alice* or Edward Lear or *Goblin Market* or much of Dickens or the excesses of the visual arts of the period" (June Sturrock, comment on this ms).
2   Perhaps I should stress that my concern is not psychoanalytic, but educational. And of course these are not mutually exclusive domains. Rather, one's concern determines one's focus and the kind, and "level," of interest one has in a subject like children's fantasy. My concern being educational I am not much concerned here with

the nature of fantasy, with Freudian or Jungian interpretations or their validity, or with psychotherapy. More reluctantly, I will also pass over ideological, media-created, pathological, and educationally destructive uses of fantasy. My concern is narrowed to what I perceive as its valuable and educationally useful functions.

3   More complex views of the logic of myth, while still a contentious subject, can be found in Lévi-Strauss (1966a; 1969), Jean-Pierre Vernant (1980), especially "The reason of myth," and Vernant (1983), especially "From myth to reason." For a more extensive defence of Cornford's position, see my "Thucydides, tragedian" (Egan, 1978c). A useful "Anglo-Saxon" summary of the study of myth is available in G. S. Kirk (1970). A more "continental" review is available in Blumenberg (1985).

4   And we need to remember that Dionysus without Apollo can be a reckless and destructive force. Plato's decision to ban poets from his Republic should not lead us just to an academic discussion about the role of "fine arts" in eduction. Poetry, in our rather impoverished sense, is only the anaesthetized edge of a vast and asymptotically expanding wedge that has to do with the human passions and their threats to social order. The ancient Greeks seem to have clearly recognized these passions and their inclination to frenzy and tried to socialize, domesticate, them through various festivals and rituals. Unordered frenzy does not build anything for the common good, and a conception of early education that pays too little attention to Apollo's constructive and disciplined order serves neither the child nor society.

3. The Story Form and the Organization of Meaning

1   Throughout I will be dealing with the standard basic form of story that children seem so readily to enjoy. I will ignore those kinds of stories that derive their power from ambivalence, and I will ignore more complex forms of narrative in which the story form is only one of the structuring devices used. This is not because I do not find the complexities of such stories and narratives similarly instructive in reflecting on the mind, but because the points I want to make here are relatively simple and they can be made clearer by focusing on the basic story form as it is found in, for example, the classic fairy-tales.

2   We may apply Chomsky's "paradox of the poverty of the stimulus" to stories as well as, if not better than, to sentences. Children's sense of the story form (and the joke) seems to develop very early even though their environments apparently cannot be providing appropriate information in the requisite quantity and form. Consider how you might program a computer to recognize a story or a joke.

3   In a review of Roald Dahl's enormously successful children's stories,
    Michael Irwin notes of *Charlie and the Chocolate Factory*: "This is a
    very moral story. Dahl has a Manichaean approach that goes down
    very well with children – in other words, he makes his bad characters
    as repellent as possible and then beats the hell out of them" (Irwin,
    1981, p. 22).
4   This means "Sentence is to syntax as story is to plot."
5   In passing, Applebee does an injustice to the diversity of divisions with-
    in psychology. There are indeed schools of psychologists that would
    find this empiricist way of putting it in need of qualification. The system
    of representations that yields schemata and plot structures seems to
    share many features across people and cultures (Mandler *et al.*, 1980),
    so it begs important questions to see them simply as a mental record of
    past experience. Applebee's formulation is akin to claiming that syntax
    is a mental record of language heard. Such an account has difficulty
    explaining the degree and commonality of structuring achieved among
    people and across cultures and it has difficulty explaining the fact that
    children very early can generate original sentences and stories.
6   I realize that much of this research is vulnerable to the criticism that
    it takes as straightforwardly empirical findings what are in fact the
    product of confusing, to use Jan Smedslund's phrase, analytic and
    arbitrary elements (see Smedslund, 1979). That the conclusion I am
    drawing attention to may be a logical rather than empirical truth is
    irrelevant to my point. All I am presently concerned with is the fact
    that contexts are important for meaningful learning.
7   This is obviously too casual a way of putting it. If, as seems likely,
    such stories and nursery rhymes, etc., are crucial constituents of an
    educational program and their stimulating influence is ideally felt in
    the years prior to schooling – along with the physical contact of a
    parent's body and the rhythms of emotion felt through this – then
    clearly a teacher telling or reading such stories to a class of thirty is
    hardly the ideal, but if this is the environment we can control, then we
    do what we can.

4. Some Further Characteristics of Mythic Understanding

1   "Pidgin" is a pidgin form of "business."
2   In passing, it is interesting to note that the beginnings of mathematics
    and proto-scientific speculation in ancient Greece and Asia Minor were
    absorbed with questions about whether time, space, and matter were
    made up of infinite continua or atomic bits. (See Kretzmann, 1982.)
3   This is perhaps an unduly innocent way of putting it. It will be
    evident that William of Ockham's razor might insist in slicing into the
    psychoanalysts' unconscious if we can account for fantasy creatures
    without recourse to that shadowy realm.

5. Cultural Recapitulation: some comments on Theory

1 I use this quotation in part because I used to think it expressed precisely how we should go about determining content (see Egan, 1986, p. x). But increasingly I see it as still carrying an echo of the educationally unfruitful dichotomizing of mind and knowledge.

2 This way of putting it raises the ghost of Vygotsky but acknowledges it only in passing. His insistence on considering cultural history and its present social effects on the child as a necessary element for understanding individual development is clearly in tune with this scheme, though his hostility to recapitulation equally clearly is not. I will leave these issues for a later volume, when there will be more material available to address them. This is hardly innocent also because of the undeveloped undercurrent of skepticism about programs of research that pursue psychological questions independently of epistemology, and vice versa; this explicitly educational scheme attempts a fruitful combination of a kind perhaps more widely interesting than its present educational concerns might suggest.

3 For examples of such an argument see James Burke's popular television series and associated book *Connections* (Burke, 1978). See also *Art and Illusion* (Gombrich, 1960) and *Mimesis* (Auerbach, 1955).

6. A Curriculum for Primary Education

1 Even when important and serious material is introduced, such as a study of different cultures, it tends commonly to remain at the superficial level of differences in clothes, games, food, and so on. In the next chapter I will show how a more meaningful level can be reached routinely.

2 "Perhaps one of the greatest sins against the child of the twentieth century is that committed by Walt Disney, who contrived to present almost *all* living creatures, from grasshoppers to elephants, as assimilable to the human state, as *cuddly*" (Coe, 1984, p. 135). One can overdo criticism of Disney in distress over the sentimentalizing of the natural world and so much children's literature. But it is important to recognize that the Disney style of sentimentality is patronizing and contemptuous of children's emotional lives. The trouble with sentimentality is that it goes nowhere; its total depth is all there on the surface. The myth stories of the world have an engaging power that is accessible in layered depths, each pulling the mind towards richer implications. As earlier, it is easy to become very high-minded about this, but it attracts comment because the commercial success of

Disney-style sentimentality seems to have convinced large numbers of people that the nature of children's minds and emotions are such that they properly should be given access only to the "cuddly" features of the world and of human experience.

3   As Northrop Frye puts it, metaphor is useful when our desire "is not to describe nature, but to show . . . a world completely absorbed and possessed by the human mind . . . .The motive for metaphor, according to Wallace Stephens, is a desire to associate, and finally to identify, the human mind with what goes on outside it, because the only genuine joy you can have is in those rare moments when you feel that although we may know in part, as Paul says, we are also a part of what we know" (Frye, 1963, p. 11).

4   This seems to me more nearly an analytic truth than an empirical claim, though, as with so many significant educational claims, it has the character of a mix of the two. An empirical claim involves the assertion of a relationship between two distinct things. In this case knowing lots of verse by heart in some degree *entails* grasping rhythms of language and fluency with meter; they are not, that is to say, entirely distinct things. The area of distinctness, the area of empirical claim, in this case seems not to be particularly contentious anyway – though it would be interesting to have more empirical knowledge of the kinds and degrees of grasp of rhythm, and so on, that different children gain from learning particular kinds of verse by heart.

5   One of the points I should not ignore, given this example, is that children in, say, the west of Canada learning French are making contact with a minority culture. The political and ideological experience for such children is obviously significantly different from that of a black immigrant child becoming "immersed" in, say, British English or a Vietnamese or Mexican child becoming "immersed" in, say Californian English. In the one case, the children are learning some respect and acceptance for a culture that is simply "other"; in the case of disadvantaged immigrant minorities there has been a complex demand for significant conformity to the majority culture along with a refusal to allow significant integration into it.

Conclusion

1   This may seem to bring to the fore precisely what Plato wanted to banish – the Homeric poets and all they stood for in terms of education. This is no doubt the case, but my argument has been that one cannot adequately reach the end Plato pointed towards by the means he proposed. We must also incorporate Rousseau's insight about the distinctive stages that coalesce to constitute the educated person.

Bibliography

Ames, L. B. (1966), "Children's stories," *Genetical Psychological Monographs,* **73,** 337-96.

Anderson, Charles C., and Travis, L. D. (1983), *Psychology and the Liberal consensus*, Ontario: Wilfrid Laurier University Press.

Anderson, R. C. (1977), "The notion of schemata and the educational enterprise," in R. C. Anderson, R. J. Spiro, and W. E. Montague (eds), *Schooling and the Acquisition of Knowledge*, New Jersey: Erlbaum.

Apple, Michael (1979), *Ideology and Curriculum*, London: Routledge & Kegan Paul.

Applebee, Arthur N. (1978), *The Child's Concept of Story*, Chicago: University of Chicago Press.

Ashton, P. T. (1975), "Cross-cultural Piagetian research: An experimental perspective," *Harvard Educational Review*, **45,** 475-506.

Auerbach, Erich (1955), *Mimesis* (Willard R. Trask, Trans.), Princeton: Princeton University Press.

Augustine, St (1944), *The Confessions* (F. J. Sheed, Trans.), London: Sheed & Ward. (First appeared AD397.)

Bacon, Francis (1905), "De sapientiae veterum (Wisdom of the ancients)" (1609), in John M. Robertson (ed.), *The Philosophical Works of Francis Bacon*, London: Routledge & Kegan Paul.

Banks, M. S., and Salaparek, R. (1983) "Infant visual perception," in M. M. Haith and J. J. Campos (eds), *Handbook of Child Psychology*, vol. 2, New York, Wiley.

Bantock, E. H. (1981), *The Parochialism of the Present*, London: Routledge & Kegan Paul.

Barrow, Robin (1978), *Radical Education*, Oxford: Martin Robertson.

Barrow, Robin (1981), *The Philosophy of Schooling*, Brighton: Wheatsheaf Books.

Barrow, Robin (1984), *Giving Teaching Back to Teachers*, Brighton: Wheatsheaf Books.

Barrow, Robin (1988), "Some observations on the concept of imagination," in K. Egan and D. Nadaner (eds), *Imagination and Education*, New York: Teachers College Press.

Barrow, Robin, and Woods, R. (1975), *Introduction to Philosophy of Education*, London: Methuen.

Barthes, Roland (1966), "Introduction a l'analyse structural des récits," *Communications, 8*.

Bartlett, F. C. (1932), *Remembering: A Study in Experimental and Social Psychology*, Cambridge: Cambridge University Press.

Baumann, Gerd (ed.) (1986), *The Written Word: Literacy in Transition*, Oxford: The Clarendon Press.

Berg, Edward E. (1970), "L. S. Vygotsky's theory of the social and historical origins of consciousness," Ph.D. thesis, University of Wisconsin. Cited in L. S. Vygotsky, *Mind in Society* (ed. Michael Cole *et al.*), Cambridge, Mass.: Harvard University Press, 1978.

Bettelheim, Bruno (1976), *The Uses of Enchantment*, New York: Knopf.

Bettelheim, Bruno, and Zelan, Karen (1982), *On Learning to Read*. New York: Knopf.

Bickerton, Derek (1982), *Roots of Language*, Ann Arbor, Michigan: Karoma.

Black, Max (1962), *Models and Metaphors*, Ithaca, New York: Cornell University Press.

Blumenberg, H. (1985), *Work on Myth*. Cambridge, Mass.: MIT Press.

Boas, F. (1911), *Handbook of American Indian Languages*, part 1. Bulletin 40, Bureau of American Ethnology. Washington DC.

Bossy, J. (1985), *Christianity in the West*, Oxford: Oxford University Press.

Bovet, P. (1923), *The Fighting Instinct*, London: Allen and Unwin.

Brown, Geoffrey, and Desforges, Charles (1979), *Piaget's Theory: A Psychological Critique*, London: Routledge & Kegan Paul.

Buck-Morss, Susan (1982), "Socio-economic bias in Piaget's theory and its implications for cross-cultural studies," in S. & C. Modgil (eds), *Jean Piaget, Consensus and Controversy*, New York: Praeger.

Burke, James (1978), *Connections*, Boston: Little, Brown.

Burke, Peter (1985), *Vico*, Oxford: Oxford University Press.

Burkert, Walter (1979), *Structure and History in Greek Mythology and Ritual*, Berkeley and Los Angeles: University of California Press.

Burkert, Walter (1985), *Greek Religion* (John Raffan, trans.), Cambridge, Mass.: Harvard University Press.

Burton, Virginia Lee (1962), *Life Story*, Boston: Houghton Mifflin.

Callahan, R. (1962), *Education and the Cult of Efficiency*, Chicago: University of Chicago Press.

Cassirer, Ernst (1946), *Language and Mind* (Susanne K. Langer, trans.), New York: Harper.

Chesterton, G. K. (1953), *Selected Essays*, London: Collins.

Chomsky, N. (1968), *Language and Mind*, New York: Harcourt Brace Jovanovich.

Clark, Kenneth (1969), *Civilization*. London: BBC and John Murray.

Coe, Richard (1984), *When the Grass was Taller*, New Haven: Yale University Press.

Collingwood, R. G. (1946), *The Idea of History*, Oxford: The Clarendon Press.

Cooper, David E. (1986), *Metaphor*, Oxford: Blackwell.

Cornford, F. M. (1907), *Thucydides Mythistoricus*, London: Edward Arnold.

Cornford F. M. (1912), *From Religion to Philosophy*, London: Edward Arnold.

Cornford, F. M. (1932), *Before and After Socrates*, Cambridge: Cambridge University Press.

Cornford, F. M. (trans.) (1941), *The Republic of Plato*, London: Oxford University Press.

Cornford, F. M. (1950), *The Unwritten Philosophy and Other Essays* (W. K. C. Guthrie, ed.), Cambridge: Cambridge University Press.

Cornford F. M. (1952), *Principium Sapientiae: The Origins of Greek Philosophical Thought*, Cambridge: Cambridge University Press.

Cummins, J., and Swain, M. (1986), *Bilingualism in Education*, New York: Longman.

Danzig, Tobias (1967), *Number: The Language of Science*,

New York: Free Press (first published New York: Macmillan, 1930).

De Garmo, C. (1895), *Herbart and the Herbartians,* New York: Scribner.

Dearden, R. F. (1968), *The Philosophy of Primary Education,* London: Routledge & Kegan Paul.

Dewey, John (1956), *The Child and the Curriculum,* Chicago: University of Chicago Press. (First published 1902).

Dewey, John (1966), *Democracy and Education,* New York: Free Press. (First published 1916).

Dewey, John (1963), *Education and Experience,* New York: Collier Books. (First published 1938).

Dodds, E. R. (1951), *The Greeks and the Irrational,* Berkeley and Los Angeles: University of California Press.

Donaldson, Margaret (1978), *Children's Minds,* London: Croom Helm.

Douglas, Mary (1966), *Purity and Danger: An Analysis of Concepts of Pollution and Taboo,* London: Routledge & Kegan Paul.

Eakin, Paul John (1985), *Fictions in Autobiography: Studies in the Art of Self-invention,* Princeton: Princeton University Press.

Egan, Kieran (1973), "Mythical and historical reference to the past," *Clio,* June, 291-307.

Egan, Kieran (1978a), "What is a plot?" *New Literary History,* **IX** (3), 455-73.

Egan, Kieran (1978b), "From myth to mythos," *Western Humanities Review,* **XXXII** (2), 99-120.

Egan, Kieran (1978c), "Thucydides, tragedian," in Robert H. Canary and Henry Kozicki (eds), *The Writing of History: Literary Form and Historical Understanding,* Madison: University of Wisconsin Press.

Egan, Kieran (1979), *Educational Development,* New York: Oxford University Press. (Reprinted as *Individual Development and the Curriculum,* London: Hutchinson, 1986.)

Egan, Kieran (1983a), *Education and Psychology: Plato, Piaget, and Scientific Psychology,* New York: Teachers College Press; London: Methuen.

Egan, Kieran (1983b), "Educating and socializing: a proper distinction?" *Teachers College Record,* **85** (1), 27-42.

Egan, Kieran (1986), *Teaching as Story Telling,* London, Ontario: The Althouse Press; London: Methuen; Chicago: University of Chicago Press.

Egan, Kieran and Nadaner, Dan (eds) (1988), *Imagination and Education*, New York: Teachers College Press.

Egan, Susanna (1984), *Patterns of Experience in Autobiography*, Chapel Hill and London: University of North Carolina Press.

Egoff, Sheila (1981), *Thursday's Child*, Chicago: American Library Association.

Eisner, Elliott W. (1984), "Can educational research inform educational practice?" *Phi Delta Kappan*, March, 447-52.

Eliade, Mircea (1959), *Cosmos and History*, New York: Harper & Row.

Eliot, T. S. (1936), "Tradition and the practice of poetry," lecture in Dublin. See *Southern Review*, Autumn 1985.

Elkind, David (1976), *Child Development and Education: A Piagetian Perspective*, New York: Oxford University Press.

Evans-Pritchard, E. E. (1936), *Witchcraft, Oracles and Magic Among the Azande*, Oxford: Oxford University Press.

Finnegan, Ruth (1970), *Oral Literature in Africa*, Oxford: Oxford University Press.

Finnegan, Ruth (1977), *Oral Poetry: Its Nature, Significance, and Social Context*, Cambridge: Cambridge University Press.

Floden, R. E., Buchmann, M., and Schwille, J. R. (1987), "Breaking with everyday experience," *Teachers College Record*, **88** (4), 486-506.

Frankfort, Henri (1961), *Ancient Egyptian Religion*, New York: Harper.

Frankfort, Henri, Wilson, J. A., and Jacobson, T., (1949), *Before Philosophy*. Harmondsworth. Pelican

Frazer, G. (1900), *The Golden Bough* (2nd ed.), London: Macmillan.

Frye, Northrop (1963), *The Educated Imagination*, Toronto: Canadian Broadcasting Corporation.

Frye, Northrop (1982), *The Great Code*, London: Routledge & Kegan Paul.

Fuller, Renée (1974), *Ball-Stick-Bird Reading System*, vols 1–5, Stony Brook, NY: Ball-Stick-Bird Publications.

Fuller, Renée (1975), *Ball-Stick-Bird Reading System*, vols 6–10, Stony Brook, NY: Ball-Stick-Bird Publications.

Fuller, Renée (1979), "Has the construct 'Intelligence' determined our perception of cognitive hierarchy?" Paper presented to the American Psychological Association symposium: "*Is the* construct *'Intelligence' a twentieth century myth?"* New York, September.

Fuller, Renée (1982), "The story as the engram: is it fundamental to thinking?" *Journal of Mind and Behavior*, **3** (2), 127–42.

Gallie, W. B. (1968), *Philosophy and Historical Understanding*, New York: Schocken.

Gardner, Howard, Kirchner, Mary, Winner, Ellen, and Perkins, David (1975), "Children's metaphoric productions and preference," *Journal of Child Language*, **2**, 125-41.

Gesell, A., Halverson, H.M., Thompson, H., Ilg, F. L., Castner, B. M., Ames, L. B., and Amatruda, C. S. (1940), *The First Five Years of Life*, New York: Harper.

Gibson, E. J. (1969), *Principles of perceptual learning and development*, New York: Appleton-Century-Crofts.

Gombrich: E. H. (1960), *Art and Illusion*, Princeton: Princeton University Press.

Goodlad, John. I. (1966), *Changing American School*, Chicago: University of Chicago Press.

Goodlad, John I. (1984), *A Place Called School*, New York: McGraw-Hill.

Goody, Jack (1977), *The Domestication of the Savage Mind*, Cambridge: Cambridge University Press.

Goody, Jack (1982), "Alternative paths to knowledge in oral and literate cultures," in D. Tannen (ed.), *Spoken and Written Language*, Norwood, NJ: Ablex.

Goody, Jack (1986), *The Logic of Writing and the Organization of Society*, Cambridge: Cambridge University Press.

Goody, Jack (1987), *The Interface Between the Written and the Oral*, Cambridge: Cambridge University Press.

Goody, Jack, and Watt, Ian (1968), "The consequences of literacy," in Jack Goody (ed.), *Literacy in Traditional Societies*, Cambridge: Cambridge University Press.

Gould, Stephen Jay (1977), *Ontogeny and Phylogeny*, Cambridge, Mass.: Harvard University Press.

Gould, Stephen Jay (1981), *The Mismeasure of Man*, New York: Norton.

Greene, Graham (1936), *Journey Without Maps*, New York: Viking.

Greimas, A. J. (1966), "Éléments pour une théorie de l'interpretation du récit mythique," *Communications*, **8**.

Griffiths, Ruth (1935), *A Study of Imagination in Early Childhood*, London: Kegan Paul, Trench, & Trubner.

Hallam, Roy (1969), "Piaget and the teaching of history," *Educational Research*, 211–15.

Hall, G. Stanley (1904), *Adolescence*, New York: D. Appleton.

Hall, Nigel (1987), *The Emergence of Literacy*, London: Hodder & Stoughton.

Hallpike, C. R. (1979), *The Foundations of Primitive Thought*, Oxford: Clarendon Press.

Hamlyn, D. W. (1978), *Experience and the Growth of Understanding*, London: Routledge & Kegan Paul.

Hanson, Karen (1986), *The Self Imagined*, London: Routledge & Kegan Paul.

Havelock, Eric A. (1963), *Preface to Plato*, Cambridge, Mass.: Harvard University Press.

Havelock, Eric A. (1976), *Origins of Western Literacy*, Toronto: Ontario Institute for Studies in Education Press.

Havelock, Eric A. (1980), "The coming of literate communication to Western culture," *Journal of Communication*, **30** (1), 90–8.

Havelock, Eric A. (1986), *The Muse Learns to Write*, New Haven: Yale University Press.

Hazlitt, William (1951), "On the ignorance of the learned," in W. E. Williams (ed.), *A Book of English Essays*, Harmondsworth: Penguin.

Heath, Shirley Brice (1982), "What no bedtime story means," *Language in Society*, **11** (1), 49–76.

Heath, Shirley Brice (1983), *Ways with Words*, Cambridge: University of Cambridge Press.

Hilyard, Angela, and Olson, David R. (1982), "On the comprehension and memory of oral vs. written discourse," in Deborah Tannen (ed.), *Spoken and Written Language: Exploring Orality and Literacy*, Norwood, NJ: Ablex.

Hirst, Paul (1974), *Knowledge and the Curriculum*, London: Routledge & Kegan Paul.

Hirst, Paul, and Peters, Richard (1970), *The Logic of Education*, London: Routledge & Kegan Paul.

Hollis, M. and Lukes, S. (eds) (1982), *Rationality and Relativism*, Cambridge Mass: MIT Press.

Horton, Robert (1970), "African traditional thought and Western science," in Bryan Wilson (ed.), *Rationality*, Oxford: Blackwell.

Horton, Robert (1982), "Tradition and modernity revisited," in M. Hollis and S. Lukes (eds), *Rationality and Relativsm*, Cambridge, Mass.: MIT Press.

Hughes, Ted (1988), "Myth and education," in Kieran Egan and Dan Nadaner (eds), *Imagination and Education*, New York: Teachers College Press.

Huizinga, Johan (1949), *Homo ludens: A Study of the Play Element in Culture*, London: Routledge & Kegan Paul.

Hume, Kathryn (1985), *Fantasy and Mimesis: Responses to Reality in Western Literature*, London: Methuen.

Inhelder, B., and Piaget, Jean (1969), *The Early Growth of Logic in the Child* (E. A. Lunzer and D. Papert, trans.), New York: Norton.

Irwin, Michael (1981), "Sweet porn," *London Review of Books*, October.

Isaacs, Susan (1930), *Intellectual Growth in Young Children*, London: Routledge & Kegan Paul.

Isaacs, Susan (1932), *The Children We Teach*, London: University of London Press.

Jakobson, R., and Halle, M. (1956), *Fundamentals of Language*, The Hague: Mouton.

Jenkyns, Richard (1981), *The Victorians and Ancient Greece*, Cambridge, Mass.: Harvard University Press.

Jowett, Benjamin (1953), *The Dialogues of Plato*, Oxford: Oxford University Press.

Kelly, A. V. (1982), *The Curriculum: Theory and Practice*, London: Harper & Row.

Kermode, Frank (1966), *The Sense of an Ending*, Oxford: Oxford University Press.

Kirk, G. S. (1965), *Homer and the Epic*, Cambridge, Cambridge University Press.

Kirk, G. S. (1970), *Myth: Its Meaning and Functions in Ancient and Other Cultures*, London: Cambridge University Press: Berkeley and Los Angeles: California University Press.

Kliebard, Herbert M. (1970), "The Tyler rationale," *School Review*, **78**, 259.

Knapp, M., and Knapp, H. (1976), *One Potato, Two Potato*, New York: Norton.

Kretzmann, Norman (ed.) (1982), *Infinity and Continuity in Ancient and Medieval Thought*, Ithaca, NY: Cornell University

Press.

Kuhn, Thomas S. (1962), *The Structure of Scientific Revolutions*, Chicago: Chicago University Press.

Langer, Susanne K. (1946), Introduction to Ernst Cassirer, *Language and Myth*, New York: Harper.

Langer, Susanne (1957), *Philosophy in a New Key*, Cambridge, Mass.: Harvard University Press.

Langer, Susanne (1982), *Mind: An Essay on Human Feeling*, vol. III, Baltimore: John Hopkins University Press.

Lashley, K. S. (1963), *Brain Mechanisms and Intelligence*, New York: Dover.

Leach, Edmund (1967), "Genesis as myth," in John Middleton (ed.), *Myth and Cosmos*, New York: Natural History Press.

Leach, Edmund (1970), *Lévi-Strauss*, London: Fontana.

Le Goff, J. (1984), *The Birth of Purgatory*, Chicago: University of Chicago Press.

Lévi-Bruhl, Lucien (1985), *How Natives Think* (Lilian A. Clare, trans.; C. Scott Littleton, Intro.), Princeton, NJ: Princeton University Press. (First published in France as *Les Fonctions mentales dans les sociétés inférieurs*, 1910.)

Lévi-Strauss, Claude (1962), *Totemism*, London: Merlin.

Lévi-Strauss, Claude (1966a), *The Savage Mind*, Chicago: University of Chicago Press.

Lévi-Strauss, Claude (1966b), "The culinary triangle," *New Society*, 22 December.

Lévi-Strauss, Claude (1960), *The Raw and the Cooked*, New York: Harper & Row.

Lévi-Strauss, Claude (1978), *Myth and Meaning*, Toronto: University of Toronto Press.

Lewis, C. S. (1982), *Of This and Other Worlds*, London:Collins.

Lloyd, G. E. R. (1966), *Polarity and Analogy: Two Types of Argumentation in Early Greek Thought*, Cambridge: Cambridge University Press.

Lloyd-Jones, Hugh (1971), *The Justice of Zeus*, Berkeley and Los Angeles: University of California Press.

Lord, Albert B. (1964), *The Singer of Tales*, Cambridge, Mass.: Harvard University Press.

Luria, A. R. (1976), *Cognitive Development: Its Cultural and Social Foundations*, Cambridge, Mass.: Harvard University Press.

Luria, A. R. (1979), *The Making of Mind*, Cambridge, Mass.: Harvard University Press.

MacIntyre, Alisdair (1981), *After Virtue*, Notre Dame, Indiana: University of Notre Dame Press.

Mackenzie, Brian D. (1977), *Behaviorism and the Limits of Scientific Method*, London: Routledge & Kegan Paul.

Malinowski, Bronislaw (1922), *Argonauts of the Western Pacific*, London: Routledge & Kegan Paul.

Malinowski, Bronislaw (1954), *Magic, Science and Religion*, New York: Anchor.

Mandler, J. M., Scribner, S., Cole, M., and DeForest, M. (1980), "Cross-cultural invariance in story recall," *Child Development*, **51**, 19–26.

Matthews, Gareth B. (1980), *Philosophy and the Young Child*, Cambridge, Mass.: Harvard University Press.

Matthews, Gareth B. (1985), *Dialogues with Children*, Cambridge, Mass.: Harvard University Press.

Maybury-Lewis, David (1969), "Science or bricolage?" *American Anthropologist*, **71** (1).

Merkel, Ray (1985), "*Visions of the way: A study of the traditional system of education of the Indians of North America*," M. A. thesis, Simon Fraser University, Burnaby, BC, Canada.

Modgil, Sohan, and Modgil, Celia (1982), *Jean Piaget: Consensus and Controversy*, New York: Praeger.

Montaigne, Michel de (1943), *Essays. Of the Education of Children*, New York: Walter J. Black.

Monroe, W. S., De Voss, J. C. and Reagan, G. W. (1930), *Educational Psychology*, New York: Doubleday, Doran & Co.

Nyberg, David, and Egan, Kieran (1981), *The Erosion of Education*, New York: Teachers College Press.

Oakeshott, Michael (1971), "Education: the engagement and its frustration," *Proceedings of the Philosophy of Education Society of Great Britain*, **5** (1), 43–76.

Ogden, C. K. (1976), *Opposition*, Bloomington: Indiana University Press.

Olson, D. R. (1977), "Oral and written language and the cognitive processes of children," *Journal of Communication*, **17** (3), 10–26.

Olson, D. R. (1986), "Learning to mean what you say: Towards a psychology of literacy," in S. de Castell, A. Luke, and K. Egan (eds), *Literacy, Society and Schooling*, New York: Cambridge University Press.

Ong, Walter J. (1958), *Ramus, Method and the Decay of Dialogue*, Cambridge, Mass.: Harvard University Press.

Ong, Walter J. (1971), *Rhetoric, Romance, and Technology*, Ithaca, NY: Cornell University Press.

Ong, Walter J. (1977), *Interfaces of the Word*, Ithaca, NY: Cornell University Press.

Ong, Walter J. (1982), *Orality and Literacy*, London and New York: Methuen.

Ong, Walter J. (1986), "Writing is a Technology that transforms thought," in G. Baumann (ed.), *The Written Word: Literacy in Transition*, Oxford: Clarendon Press.

Opie, Iona, and Opie, Peter (1959), *The Lore and Language of Schoolchildren*, Oxford: Oxford University Press.

Opie, Iona, and Opie, Peter (1969), *Children's Games in Streets and Playground*, Oxford: Oxford University Press.

Opie, Ioan, and Opie, Peter (1985), *The Singing Game*, Oxford: Oxford University Press.

Paley, Vivian Gussin (1981), *Wally's Stories*, Cambridge, Mass.: Harvard University Press.

Parry, Milman (1928), *L'Epithète traditionelle dans Homère*, Paris: Societé Éditrice Les Belles Lettres.

Parry, Milman (1971), *The Making of Homeric Verse: The Collected Papers of Milman Parry* (Adam Parry, ed.), Oxford: Clarendon Press. (This includes the previous reference in English translation.)

Patterson, Sylvia W. (1971), *Rousseau's Émile and Early Children's Literature*, Metuchen, NJ: Scarecrow Press.

Peabody, Berkley (1975), *The Winged Word*, Albany: State University of New York Press.

Permyakov, G. L. (1970), *Ot pogovorki do skazki* (*From saying to tale*), Moscow. Quoted in T. Todorov, "Structuralism and literature," in *Approaches to Poetics*, (Seymour Chatman, ed.), New York: Columbia University Press 1973.

Piaget, Jean (1951), *Play, Dreams and Imitation in Childhood*, New York: W. W. Norton.

Piaget, Jean (1962), *Comments on Vygotsky's Critical Remarks*, Cambridge, Mass.: MIT Press.

Piaget, Jean (1964), in Richard E. Ripple and Verne N. Rockcastle (eds), *Piaget Rediscovered*, Ithaca, NY: School of Education, Cornell University.

Piaget, Jean (1977), *Psychology and Epistemology*, Harmondsworth, Middlesex: Penguin.

Piaget, Jean (1978), *The Development of Thought: Equilibration of Cognitive Structures*, Oxford: Blackwell.

Pippard, Brian (1986), "Complementary copies," *Times Literary Supplement*, 25 April.

Pitcher, E. G., and Prelenger, E. (1963), *Children Tell Stories: An Analysis of Fantasy*, New York, International Universities Press.

Prince, Gerald (1973), *A Grammar of Stories*, The Hague: Mouton.

Pring, Richard (1973), "Objectives and innovation: the irrelevance of theory," *London Educational Review*, **2**, 46–54.

Putnam, Hilary (1981), *Reason, Truth and History*, Cambridge, Cambridge University Press.

Ravitch, Diane (1983), *The Troubled Crusade*, New York: Basic Books.

Rosen, Harold (1986), "The importance of story," *Language Arts*, **63** (3), 226–37.

Rosenblatt, L. M. (1976), *Literature as Exploration*, New York: Noble & Noble.

Rousseau, Jean-Jacques (1911), Émile (Barbara Foxley, trans.), London: Dent. (First published 1762).

Schwebel, Milton, and Raph, Jane (eds) (1973), *Piaget in the Classroom*, New York: Basic Books.

Scribner, Sylvia, and Cole, Michael (1981), *The Psychology of Literacy*, Cambridge, Mass.: Harvard University Press.

Seeley, L. (1906), *Elementary Pedagogics*, New York: Hinds, Noble.

Shepard, Roger (1978), "The mental image," *American Psychologist*, **33**, 123–37.

Shepard, Roger, (1988), "The imagination of the scientist," in K. Egan and D. Nadaner (eds), *Imagination and Education*, New York: Teachers College Press.

Siegel, Linda S., and Brainerd, Charles J. (eds) (1978), *Alternatives to Piaget: Critical Essays on the Theory*, New York: Academic Press.

Simon, B. (1978), *Mind and Madness in Ancient Greece*, Ithaca, NY: Cornell University Press.

Simon, Herbert (1983), *Reason in Human Affairs*, Oxford: Blackwell.

Smedslund, Jan (1979), "Between the analytic and the arbitrary: a case study of psychological research," *Scandinavian Journal of Psychology*, **20**.

Spence, Jonathan D. (1984), *The Memory Palace of Matteo Ricci*, New York: Viking Penguin.

Spice, Nicholas (1985), "An outpost of Ashod," *London Review of Books*, **27**, August.

Stein, Nancy L., and Trabasso, Tom (1981), *What's in a Story: An Approach to Comprehension and Instruction*, Technical Report No. 200, Center for the Study of Reading, University of Chicago, April.

Stenhouse, Lawrence (1975), *An Introduction to Curriculum Research and Development*, London: Heinemann.

Street, Brian V. (1984), *Literacy in Theory and Practice*, Cambridge: Cambridge University Press.

Sutton-Smith, Brian (1981), *The folkstories of Children*, Philadelphia: University of Pennsylvania Press.

Sutton-Smith, Brian (1988), "In search of the imagination," in Kieran Egan and Dan Nadaner (eds), *Imagination and Education*, New York: Teachers College Press.

Taylor, Charles (1982), "Rationality," in M. Hollis and S. Lukes (eds), *Rationality and Relativism*, Cambridge, Mass.: MIT Press.

Todorov, Tzvetan (1969), *Grammaire du Decameron*, The Hague: Mouton.

Todorov, Tzvetan (1973), "Structuralism and literature," in Seymour Chatman (ed.), *Approaches to Poetics*, New York: Columbia University Press.

Tulviste, Peter (1979), "On the origins of theoretic syllogistic reasoning in culture and child," *Quarterly Newsletter of the Laboratory of Comparative Human Cognition*, **1** (4), 73–40.

Turner, Frank M. (1981), *The Greek Heritage in Victorian Britain*, New Haven: Yale University Press.

Tyler, R. (1949), *Basic Principles of Curriculum Instructions,* Chicago: University of Chicago Press.

Vernant, Jean-Pierre (1980), *Myth and Society in Ancient Greece*, Brighton: Harvester Press; Atlantic Highlands: Humanities Press.

Vernant, Jean-Pierre (1983), *Myth and Thought Among the Greeks*, London: Routledge & Kegan Paul.

Vico, Giambattista (1970), *The New Science* (T. G. Bergin and M. H. Fisch, trans.), Ithaca, NY: Cornell University Press. (First published 1744).

Walker, R. (1988), "In search of a child's musical imagination," in Kieran Egan and Dan Nadaner (eds), *Imagination and Education*, New York: Teachers College Press.

Warner, James H. (1940), "The basis of J. J. Rousseau's contemporaneous reputation in England," *Modern Language Notes*, **LV**, 270–80.

Watson, James (1981), *The Double Helix*, London: Weidenfeld & Nicolson.

Webb, W. L. (1986), "The end of the world is nigh," *Guardian*, series on Modernism and Post-Modernism, London, 2 December.

White, Hayden V. (1973), *Metahistory*, Baltimore: Johns Hopkins University Press.

Wilson, B. R. (ed.) (1970), *Rationality*, Oxford: Blackwell.

Wilson, John (1979), *Fantasy and Common Sense in Education*, Oxford: Martin Robertson.

Wittgenstein, L. (1963), *Philosophical Investigations* (G. E. M. Anscombe, trans.), Oxford: Blackwell.

Wood, Michael (1985), *In Search of the Trojan War*, London: BBC.

Yates, Frances A. (1966), *The Art of Memory*, Chicago: University of Chicago Press.

Index